Bonavista

Bonavista

BRUCE WHIFFEN

With a Foreword by JOHN NORMAN

FLANKER PRESS LIMITED
ST. JOHN'S

Library and Archives Canada Cataloguing in Publication

Title: Bonavista / Bruce Whiffen.
Names: Whiffen, Bruce, 1957- author.
Description: Includes bibliographical references and index.
Identifiers: Canadiana (print) 2021023265X | Canadiana (ebook) 20210232706 | ISBN 9781774570203
   (softcover) | ISBN 9781774570210 (EPUB) | ISBN 9781774570234 (PDF)
Subjects: LCSH: Bonavista (N.L.)—History. | LCSH: Bonavista (N.L.)—Biography. | LCSH: Natural
   history—Newfoundland and Labrador—Bonavista.
Classification: LCC FC2199.B65 W45 2021 | DDC 971.8—dc23

PRINTED IN CANADA

This paper has been certified to meet the environmental and social standards of the Forest Stewardship Council® (FSC®) and comes from responsibly managed forests, and verified recycled sources.

Cover design by Graham Blair

FLANKER PRESS LTD.
PO BOX 2522, STATION C
ST. JOHN'S, NL
CANADA

TELEPHONE: (709) 739-4477   FAX: (709) 739-4420   TOLL-FREE: 1-866-739-4420

WWW.FLANKERPRESS.COM

9 8 7 6 5 4 3 2 1

The publisher acknowledges the financial support of the Government of Canada through the Canada Book Fund (CBF) and the Government of Newfoundland and Labrador, Department of Tourism, Culture, Industry and Innovation for our publishing activities. We acknowledge the support of the Canada Council for the Arts, which last year invested $157 million to bring the arts to Canadians throughout the country. *Nous remercions le Conseil des Arts du Canada de son soutien. L'an dernier, le Conseil a investi 157 millions de dollars pour mettre de l'art dans la vie des Canadiennes et des Canadiens de tout le pays*

To my Mother, Abbie Ellis-Whiffen

CONTENTS

". . . a hardier, healthier or better looking race of men are not to be found upon the face of the globe!" Rev. Philip Tocque (*Wandering Thoughts*), writing about the men of Bonavista.

"The woman was more than fifty per cent." Josiah Hobbs, speaking about "the role of the fisherman's wife," from Hilda Chaulk Murray (*More than 50%*).

FOREWORD

by John Norman, Mayor of Bonavista

The town of Bonavista, one of North America's oldest English settlements, has stood on the coastal edge of the North Atlantic Ocean for centuries, forever tied historically, culturally, and socio-economically to the sea, to its fisheries resources, and to its paralleled hardships. This strong connection has resulted in a built landscape and a people moulded and toughened by the salty air, strong winds, and coastal storms, as well as the many fluctuations a resource-based economy can face.

Growing up in Bonavista in the 1990s meant that you were growing up in a once prosperous and proud community that was now beginning to die. With the collapse of the cod fishery went the core reasons for communities such as Bonavista to exist. It was, since the 1600s, built by the fishery and for the fishery. Like any economy and community, it evolved and shifted over time, but its tie to the sea was unchangeable in the eyes of almost everyone. As a young boy, the Bonavista of the 1990s was crumbling; the fishery was predominantly gone, replaced only partly by shellfish. The population exodus began as the much smaller crab industry needed far fewer workers and fishermen. Homes became abandoned, stores began to downsize and close. The community of almost 5,000 quickly fell to below 4,000, and as a child you noticed that some of your friends began to move away, simply not show up to class at the elementary school one Monday morning. It is forever engraved in my mind, the actual dissolution of my hometown.

Though the cod moratorium announcement caused a shock wave through the community and province, I was luckily not directly impacted as a young boy, having parents working in other sectors; nobody in our house lost their jobs. But nonetheless, the cod closure affected us all in some way or form. How could it not affect you when your childhood home began to collapse like the cod stock itself?

Bonavista needed a new way forward, as the crab fishery would only play a supporting role in stabilizing the town, its economy, and population. Vitality was fading each year, but throughout these emptying streets, we found the most important assets Bonavista had to offer for economic diversification: our fishery had left us with a historic built landscape of provincial and even national significance! In the mid-1990s, an inventory of heritage buildings was completed by the town's newly formed Bonavista Historic Townscape Foundation. On the list were just over 1,000 buildings of heritage value. This was an inventory unlike any other on the island, outside of the city of St. John's. Bonavista never had a "Great Fire" like so many of the larger historic towns along the coast, and we also never had major development pressures causing significant demolition. The town simply grew outward over the centuries, in all directions moving away from the water's edge. As a result of these factors, buildings tied to the once prosperous cod fishery remained standing, often vacant or underutilized, buildings of over a dozen architectural styles from the last four centuries. Churches, halls, schools, homes, and outbuildings of all scales, in various neighbourhoods and in great density—this was Bonavista's big opportunity!

Starting small with select restoration works, the Townscape Foundation was put into action by the town hall to promote and encourage economic activity and diversity. For years the organization funnelled government money from all levels into projects big and small around the community, from multi-million dollar streetscapes through downtown and the harbour, to restoration of private homes through heritage grants. The organization even successfully restored and reopened Newfoundland's oldest operating theatre, the Garrick. Once more, Bonavista was active day and night, jobs were being created, and the private sector, encouraged by what was happening, began to invest.

Today, Bonavista has stabilized its population with signs of growth in the past few years, its business start-up rates are the highest in the province, vacant buildings are harder and harder to come by, and new families continue to move in each year. On this current trajectory, the town of Bonavista will be around for centuries to come, a beacon for tourism, rural economic development, research, and specialty manufacturing. The simple idea of repurposing and revitalizing existing assets, strengthening the sense of place and pride within the community, while making shrewd public and private investments, has paid off. One of Newfoundland's most historic communities remains a living, breathing, authentic coastal fishing town with a diversified economy and social fabric.

John Norman
Mayor of Bonavista

PREFACE

Bonavista was written as an effort not just to provide a history of the town, but to do so in a manner that provided insight specifically into the people who lived there and how they contributed to the town as it exists today. I wanted to write about why they came to Bonavista (there were many reasons) and how they survived. I needed to talk about their challenges, whether in terms of the tough environment in which they lived, the economic conditions of the day, or the dispiriting efforts at supporting a family in the midst of hardship. I also wanted to talk about their hopes for themselves, their families, and their communities. My focus needed to be on individuals and the lives they led.

Before writing about those who lived in Bonavista, however, it's necessary to "set the stage." The first few chapters of this book talk about the natural history of Bonavista and the surrounding area. Of necessity, we need to describe the local geography, the continental shelf, and the Labrador Current (among other components of the physical environment) in order to give the reader a sense of Bonavista's environment. We need to talk about the climatology and weather extremes, the ice age, and the fish and mammals that inhabited the region. From there, we discuss the Indigenous peoples of Newfoundland and their habitation.

As Europeans crossed the Atlantic, it's important to follow progress from the early fishery in the 1500s to ultimate settlement. As Bonavista grew into a community, we will meet the individuals who played a significant role during the early years of settlement. Rev. Henry Jones and Magistrate John Bland were just two of many individuals who helped early settlers build a community in the 1700s. With the rapid influx of people from England and Ireland in the early 1800s, and the advent of Representative Government in 1832, Bonavista residents began to play a more important role themselves in the growth of the town. Schools, business establishments, and churches all became entrenched in the fabric of Bonavista as we moved from the 1800s into the last century and today. We meet those from Bonavista or with a strong ancestral connection to Bonavista—either on the sea or through business. We'll also see how Bonavista residents played a role in supporting the war effort, helped bring

Confederation to Newfoundland, and played a leadership role in international governance of cod stocks. And finally, we'll meet a young man from another part of Newfoundland who came to Bonavista to teach and spent a lifetime serving his new home.

I have relied, for the most part, upon contemporary documents. While also relying on history books in general, I have frequently drawn from journals and diaries written by people living in Bonavista, court and colonial office records, petitions, newspaper articles of the time, and books written by individuals visiting and working at Bonavista. In many cases, I have quoted directly from them, rather than summarized the intent, not only because it preserved accuracy, but because it is more satisfying to see and read original documents than to read from a secondary source. I believe, for example, that there is a closer connection to Bonavista by reading a letter by Rev. Henry Jones in 1725, in his own words, about Bonavista, written while living in Bonavista, than a summary of his correspondence written by another hand. I hope that the reader will feel that way as well.

Having said that, I have taken some liberties when recording the written word. Surnames and place names, for example, were often recorded according to how the writer thought those names were spelled. To avoid distraction, I've adopted a single spelling in most cases. Even though "Bonavista" may have been referenced as "Bona Vista" or "Port Bonavist," I have normally kept to the accepted spelling. The same applies to "Hicks" and "Abbott" and a host of other surnames which have been spelled variously over the course of years. With respect to Canaille, however, I have retained its original spelling, "Corneil" or "Cornail," from the 1700s to recognize and preserve what I believe to have been the original pronunciation of that part of southern Bonavista. Also, I have occasionally made minor edits to phrasing or spelling of the written word for ease in reading, while ensuring that the intention of the original writer has not been changed.

Surnames were notoriously written in many different ways, for a variety of different reasons, by the early historians, ministers, magistrates, and merchants of Newfoundland. For the most part, I've taken the liberty of using the most recent spelling throughout. One exception is Skiffington. In the late 1600s and through the 1700s, "Skeffington" is used almost exclusively. "Skiffington" begins with the introduction of church records in 1786. I have also tended to use the contemporary spelling of Mifflin/Mifflen. "Mifflen" was used in the 1700s and 1800s, while "Mifflin" is commonplace at Bonavista today.

On various occasions, I've encountered petitions, letters, lists, etc. that form an important part of the story of Bonavista but which, if embedded in the story being told at the moment, would detract or slow the narration. In those cases, I have saved those documents as appendices at the end of the book. The reader is encouraged to read each appendix (particularly the letters and petitions), as they often speak not only to the realities of contemporary Bonavista, but to the heart of the author of the document as well. We learn about historical Bonavista best from those who lived it.

Any history book of a region, country, or community must face the challenge of discussing issues chronologically, while also trying to discuss specific themes (such as education or religion). It is impossible to discuss all themes in the 1600s, then all themes in the 1700s, and so on. Nor can we talk about religion from inception to present day, then education, and so on. It is necessary to write in chronological order while focusing on specific themes at each step. This necessitates some repetition—meaning that we may meet the same individuals on more than one occasion as we step forward in time through various topics. I offer my apologies to the reader for meeting some individuals on multiple occasions. Hopefully you will share my opinion that some of the more interesting inhabitants of Bonavista are worth reading about more than once.

Cape Bonavista is generally recognized as that landmark first sighted by John Cabot when he crossed the Atlantic from England in 1497. However, in the absence of conclusive proof, other sites have been proposed and debated. This book does not try to clarify the issue. Whether or not Cabot sighted Cape Bonavista and landed nearby is not critical to the story of the town of Bonavista. We write about the 500th anniversary celebrations of Cabot's landfall at Bonavista to highlight the important part played by local inhabitants within the larger goals of the province. This book, instead, is focused on the growth of the town of Bonavista itself and the important role it played not only when Newfoundland was in its infancy, but through the years and up to present day.

I have invariably spoken of "Newfoundland" to reference the island of Newfoundland, leaving "Newfoundland and Labrador" to designate the province within Canada.

PART ONE: INTRODUCTION
1 — PROLOGUE

Bernice Mouland, born and raised in Bonavista, was attending a Christmas concert at Bonavista in 1960 when she first met George Clements. George was originally from Grand Bank and, for his first teaching assignment, had chosen to work at the Salvation Army School at Bonavista. Bernice's good friend Mervie Mouland was dating Ben Snook (George's good friend from Grand Bank and also a teacher). The young gentlemen, still teenagers, escorted Bernice and Mervie back to their homes after the concert. Bernice remembered George as being very quiet—on the walk home, they hardly spoke to each other.

The following summer, Bernice and George both attended teacher training at St. John's, and Bernice began working as a teacher at the United Church School in Bonavista, on Coster Street. They were married a short while later and raised two children. Bernice left teaching and managed the Sears store. George continued his teaching profession: first at the Salvation Army School, then the "Cove School," and eventually the United Church School. During his first twelve years of teaching, he also returned to Memorial University during the summer until he completed his education degree. Later, he accepted a position as instructor at the Bonavista District Vocational School, followed by principal at the Eastern Community College. He retired in 1991. He loved his work and, in Bernice's words, "never mentioned moving somewhere else." Bonavista was home.

George began volunteering shortly after arriving in Bonavista and, according to Bernice, "he never stopped his volunteer work." And he had the medals and certificates of merit to prove it.

Meanwhile, in the mid-1990s, Newfoundland and Labrador, including Bonavista, was dealing with the aftermath of the 1992 cod moratorium. The Government of Canada had shut down the cod fishery, and much of the province was suffering the economic consequences. Tourism was being looked upon as an opportunity for diversity. History had recorded that John Cabot sighted Cape Bonavista on June 24, 1497—so the 500th anniversary of that historic transatlantic voyage was quickly approaching.

The provincial Department of Tourism, Culture and Recreation was tasked with leading the initiative. While activities were being planned throughout the province of Newfoundland and Labrador, the focus would be the arrival of the *Matthew*, John Cabot's ship, at Bonavista on that historic anniversary—June 24, 1997. In 1995, they looked to the town council of Bonavista and Mayor Don Tremblett to choose a resident to lead the local celebrations and activities. Council asked George Clements if he would do it. It was, in the words of Brent Meade, the event coordinator, a "no-brainer." Bernice told the author that "George never said no to anyone in his life. . . . He was very enthusiastic about it."

The Vista '97 Committee, which Clements led, was responsible for four full days of events, from June 23 to June 26, throughout the community. The highlight was, of course, the sailing of the *Matthew* into Bonavista Harbour at 3:00 p.m. on June 24 after its trek across the North Atlantic. Queen Elizabeth II and Prince Philip would be in attendance, accompanied by the premier of Newfoundland and Labrador, Brian Tobin, and a long list of other dignitaries. With Clements in charge, the Vista '97 Committee, with an executive team, a dozen subcommittees, and a few hundred volunteers, were responsible for pulling it off. Practically everyone was a local resident of the area. George managed the executive committee, coordinated local service groups, provided leadership to the subcommittees and volunteer groups, coordinated external engagements, and met and coordinated other events with provincial government officials. Bernice said that "sometimes, I didn't see him for days."

George was well-chosen as chairman of the Vista '97 Committee. Through years of teaching, he knew how to work toward a long-term goal— one day at a time. He knew the town well and had the respect of the community. Committee members conveyed that he could be quiet, thoughtful, and a good listener, but knew when to speak up and direct the team when it was required. He was not the same young man Bernice had met in 1960. We might even say that Bonavista had prepared him well for the responsibility for which he had been selected.

The big day, June 24, 1997, finally arrived. Bernice and George's home was full of guests. In fact, the RCMP, who were responsible for security for the Queen and Prince Philip, had recommended that George and Bernice move out of their home during the event—a recommendation which they politely declined. In the early morning, the Queen was in St. John's, and Prince Philip was in Gander. The Queen flew to Bonavista via helicopter and was accompanied by the Honourable Fred Mifflin, the Member of Parliament for the district. Upon arrival at Bonavista, they went to Bonavista Harbour to officially open the Ryan Premises. Gordon Bradley, as chair of the Bonavista Historical Society, introduced the Queen to the National Historic Site. From there, the Queen did a brief walkabout, a visit to Golden Heights Manor, and then continued on to Discovery Collegiate.

George and Bernice greeted the Queen at Discovery Collegiate at 11:00 a.m. (Prince Philip was, at that time, on his way to Bonavista from Gander.) On meeting the Queen, Bernice said, "I can't describe it. I was overwhelmed. But it was like I met a friend down the street. She put me at ease." As Brian and wife Jodean Tobin led the Queen through the line of dignitaries, George and Bernice awaited the arrival of Prince Philip. At a critical moment, George was taken aside by a phone call, just as Prince Philip arrived outside. Bernice was left to go outside to welcome the Duke of Edinburgh herself.

Left: Bernice (Mouland) Clements and Prince Philip, June 24, 1997. (Bernice Clements) Right: The Queen and George Clements, June 24, 1997. (Bernice Clements)

Bernice was the daughter of Clarence and Florence (Butler) Mouland of Mockbeggar, one of the oldest parts of Bonavista running along the western shore just north of the harbour. Her father was a Bonavista fisherman, as was his father, and his father before him. Perhaps it was appropriate that the daughter of a long line of families of the Bonavista fishery found herself welcoming the Duke of Edinburgh to Bonavista. "He was very down-to-earth, very pleasant," said Bernice, who took the Prince through the welcoming line.

Eventually, everyone gathered at the Discovery Collegiate gymnasium for the luncheon. With about 200 guests in attendance, George Clements officially welcomed Her Majesty the Queen and the Duke of Edinburgh to Bonavista.

Rev. Dr. Arthur Butt, a minister at Bonavista on two separate occasions, said the grace. George and Bernice sat between the Queen (to George's left) and Prince Philip. Bernice said she felt that she would be "too nervous to eat," while having been told by Mary Francis, the aide to the Queen, that she, the Queen, might not eat at all. In fact, according to Bernice, the Queen "cleaned her plate!" Meanwhile, Prince Philip and Bernice chatted about everything from whales to blueberries.

After lunch, the Queen and Prince Philip visited the war memorial on Church Street, where she laid a wreath and met local veterans, and from there, at 3:00 p.m., everyone went to Bonavista Harbour for the arrival of the *Matthew*. George and Bernice took their seats at the Royal Box—Bernice was sitting directly behind the Queen.

It was intensely cold on June 24, 1997, with a brisk north wind running off the Labrador Current. The temperature hovered around 1°C. But the Queen had a blanket and an electric heater. Bernice said it took her own feet two hours to thaw out. The ceremony opened with "God Save the Queen" and "O Canada." The arrival of the *Matthew* into Bonavista Harbour was followed by ceremonies, music, and, of course, speeches. The event closed with the "Ode to Newfoundland."

The celebrations did not finish until June 26, but for George and Bernice, the pressure event was over. Bernice said, "It was very draining . . . it was all on his shoulders."

Among the recognition George received for his work with respect to the Vista '97 celebrations, two were especially appreciated.

Mary Francis's letter:

> The Queen and the Duke of Edinburgh have asked me to write with a double "Thank You," first for the delicious lunch which you hosted at Discovery Collegiate today and secondly for your personal contribution to the Matthew Landfall Re-enactment which followed. This has been an historic day for Bonavista. The guests you had gathered at lunch, bringing together national leaders and so many local volunteers, were testament to the enormous amount of work which has gone into the Vista '97 celebrations. Her Majesty and His Royal Highness were struck by the atmosphere of warmth and co-operation which you had engendered.

The Queen and Duke of Edinburgh send their congratulations and best wishes to everyone that has played a part in Vista '97, in this 500th anniversary year of John Cabot's Landing in Newfoundland.

Yours truly,
Mary Francis.

Thank you from Honourable Fred Mifflin, Minister of Veterans Affairs:

As a Member of Parliament, I convey to you my congratulations and heartfelt thanks on your personal contribution to the Cabot 500 Celebrations. The success of the spectacular landfall and re-enactment ceremonies that followed can be directly attributed to your dedication and leadership. On behalf of your community, your province and your country, I thank you for the awesome sight that will be etched forever in the memories of those who bore witness.

Honourable Fred Mifflin.

The Sovereign's Medal for Volunteers from the Governor General of Canada is awarded to Canadians who have made a significant and continual contribution to their community. On September 1, 2020, the Sovereign's Medal was awarded to George Clements at Bonavista by the lieutenant-governor for Newfoundland and Labrador, Judy Foote.

2 — NATURAL HISTORY

To tell the history of Bonavista, we first need to understand the physical environment in which the people of Bonavista lived. From that environment, we can understand the opportunities afforded early settlers, and the challenges they were forced to confront. The continental shelf and the abundance of cod, the Labrador Current, ice floes, harsh shorelines and harsh winter storms, and even hurricanes all played a role in defining life in Bonavista. This chapter will also highlight why Bonavista is a place of beauty, where whales and icebergs, fossils and the Dungeon, all find a home.

i. Geology

As scientists have discovered over the past several years, the seven continents that presently share the surface of the earth with our oceans are not static, silent, and stagnant land masses. Instead, they are forever in motion, crashing into each other, moving farther apart, rifting over and sinking beneath each other, not unlike pans of ice sitting atop the Labrador Current and pushing into the northeast coast of Newfoundland. We think of these continents as frozen in time only because our own experiences are a blink of an eye in geological time.

Over 1 billion years ago, the surface of the earth was comprised of a single supercontinent, called Rodinia: a consequence of the merger of separate land masses throughout the globe. About 300 million years later, Rodinia slowly split into two continents, called Laurasia and Gondwana, separated by the Iapetus Ocean. A micro-continent, called Avalonia (named after the Avalon Peninsula of Newfoundland, and including, as we shall see, the Bonavista Peninsula), broke away from Gondwana. At that time, Avalonia was along latitude 60 degrees south, and therefore closer to the South Pole than Australia or where the southern tip of South America is today.

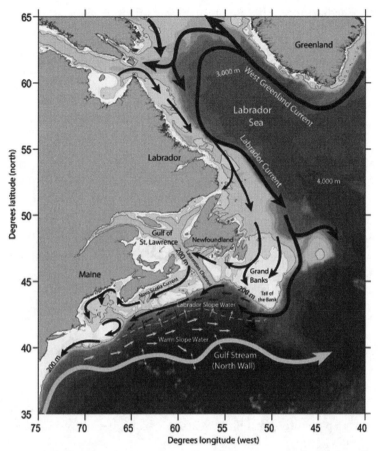

Continental shelf, Labrador Current, and Gulf Stream around Newfoundland. From "Water Masses and Nutrient Sources . . . ", *Journal of Marine Research* 73(3), 2015/05/01, Townsend et al.

Around 400 million years ago, the continents throughout the globe reconnected into a single supercontinent, called Pangea, with Avalonia near its centre. Pangea divided into its components once again, eventually leading to the seven continents we know today. Avalonia, during the separation of Pangea, itself split in two, with each half attaching itself to a larger continent. Eastern Avalonia connected with today's Europe. England, Wales, southern Ireland, parts of Belgium, northern France, southern Spain, and even parts of northwest Africa are all part of what was once Eastern Avalonia. Western Avalonia connected with eastern North America and eventually helped to define parts of Nova Scotia, New Brunswick, and the New England states, as well as the entire Avalon, Burin, and Bonavista Peninsulas of Newfoundland.

The northern tip of the Bonavista Peninsula today hosts the community of Bonavista, the nearby Cape, and local geological formations such as the Dungeon and the "Spillars." Eons ago, it found itself at the centre of Avalonia, which was itself at the centre of Pangea, Earth's single supercontinent. For a brief period of geological time, then, one could say that Bonavista was the centre of the known universe!

As the new continents of North America and Europe slowly drifted away from each other, the valley separating these great continents slowly filled with salt water from the ocean to the south, to eventually form the North Atlantic Ocean. As the continent of North America continued its slow drift westward away from Europe, its trailing edge, closer to Europe and at a slightly lower elevation, became covered with the waters of the North Atlantic and formed the continental shelf, including that part of the shelf east of Newfoundland called the Grand Banks. The porous and fractured rock formations embedded within the Grand Banks led to the hydrocarbon reservoirs being recovered today.

ii. First Life

The development of life on earth began less than 4 billion years ago when conditions were conducive to the formation of single-cell organisms and bacteria. These building blocks to future life forms developed initially in the ocean and, within 1 billion years or so, slowly moved onto land. Life evolved from simple organisms to plant life. One billion years ago, plants became established on the surface of the earth.

The first complex multicellular organisms started in the ocean during what is called the Ediacaran Period (from 635 to 541 million years ago). These organisms lived at the bottom of the ocean. Although fossils from this period have been discovered worldwide, the first were discovered in 1868 by Alexander Murray on the Avalon Peninsula. A century later, in 1968, S. B. Misra discovered the oldest large and complex organisms in Earth's history, at Mistaken Point, near Cape Race. Four decades later, in 2009, a team of researchers from Memorial University of Newfoundland, the University of Cambridge, and the University of Oxford discovered fossils at Port Union, a few miles south of Bonavista, dating from 560 million years ago, and therefore, perhaps, the oldest complex organisms yet discovered. There were a variety of life forms living on the bottom of the seabed, preserved in fossil form perhaps during an avalanche of mud and silt.

Embedded in the Ediacaran Period is the Avalon Explosion (named after the Avalon Peninsula) of about 575 million years ago. During this period, conditions were more conducive to growth and diversity, though most life forms succumbed to the later Cambrian Period. Nonetheless, Bonavista and environs, at a time when its home, the micro-continent Avalonia was forming off the shores of Gondwana, was host to the development of the first complex organisms on Earth.

The fossils that formed when Avalonia was a single, connected micro-continent remained with this micro-continent as it separated into its component parts through the ages. Hence the fossils that may be found near Bonavista, or at Mistaken Point on the Avalon Peninsula, also occur in North Africa, while the fossils on the west coast of Newfoundland, which originated at a time when this area was thousands of miles distant from eastern Newfoundland, are distinctly different.

The Dungeon, just outside Bonavista. (From DiscoveryGeopark.com)

The unique nature of the geological formations around Bonavista, as well as the historic significance of the fossils, were formally recognized by the United Nations Educational Scientific and Cultural Organization (UNESCO) in July 2020. At an earlier UNESCO meeting in Paris, it was agreed that the Bonavista Discovery Geopark would join about 150 other Geoparks around the world. According to UNESCO, a Geopark is a "single, unified geographic (area) where sites and landscapes of international geological significance are managed with a holistic concept of protection, education and sustainable development

... (thereby) raising awareness of the importance of the area's geological heritage in history and society today." The Discovery Geopark contains ten specific sites scattered throughout the northern half of the Bonavista Peninsula. They include unique geological formations (the Dungeon, Sea Arch, and the Devil's Footprints), the impacts of tsunamis from centuries ago (Long Beach and the Lisbon earthquake), the unique adaptation of local inhabitants to the local environment (root cellars), and, in honour of the Beothuk language, "Haootia," the chosen name for one of the oldest complex animal fossils in the world.

iii. Ocean Currents

Two-thirds of the surface of the earth are, in fact, oceans, and embedded within these oceans are the currents that define everything from life within the ocean to meteorological conditions over land. The two currents that have impacted Newfoundland through the millennia are the Gulf Stream to the south and the Labrador Current farther north.

We might say that the Gulf Stream has its origin as it passes from the Gulf of Mexico, south of Florida, and heads northward along the eastern seaboard of the United States, then turning eastward and tracking south of Newfoundland and the Grand Banks, and then continuing northeastward as the North Atlantic Drift. Meanwhile, the Labrador Current originates from cold arctic waters in the north and passes southward just east of Labrador and along the northeast coast of Newfoundland before turning westward along the south coast of the island. The Labrador Current carries icebergs from Greenland and pack ice from the Arctic Ocean along the northeast coast of Newfoundland, both of which are routinely seen in springtime off the coast of Bonavista.

The Gulf Stream and the Labrador Current provide the rich nutrient environment that sustain life, and the cod fishery, around Newfoundland. As noted by Dr. George Rose (*Cod: An Ecological History of the North Atlantic Fisheries*, see References), "The exchange of cooled Arctic water for warmer Gulf Stream waters is the key to the ample productivity of the North Atlantic. The exchange makes the northern waters warmer overall, but even more importantly, results in nutrient enrichment through a natural fertilizer pump into the sterile surface Arctic waters." Evolutionary processes led to the appearance of cod, and related species, into the Grand Banks and surrounding continental shelf regions from 5 to 10 million years ago. Over time, the ocean off the coast of Newfoundland grew abundant in a variety of species of fish, birds, crustaceans, and mammals. Today, for example, schools of capelin (or caplin), each of which is no longer than a few inches, spawn along the beaches of Bonavista in season, chased by whales weighing several tons. Lobster and crab reside at the bottom of the oceans—puffins, seagulls, and a host of other birds fly overhead and inhabit the rocky shoreline. But it was the abundance of codfish that provided the motivation for the early fishery at Bonavista and, ultimately, to permanent settlement.

iv. The Ice Age

A brief 2.6 million years ago saw the beginning of the last ice age, more formally known as the Quaternary Glaciation, during which the Arctic ice cap, encompassing the North Pole, expanded deep into more southern latitudes. During the Last Glacial Period (from about 100,000 to 10,000 years ago), the glacial extent encompassed all of Canada, including Labrador, the island of Newfoundland, and extending into the Grand Banks. It is difficult to image this gigantic glacial sheet. At its maximum, it was over 10,000 feet thick, then tapered toward the margins. By comparison, Elliston Ridge (near Bonavista) is about 460 feet above sea level at its peak, Cabot Tower is 472 feet above sea level, and Gros Morne Mountain is 2,648 feet. Life throughout Newfoundland, including Bonavista, was laid bare. Then, 12,000 years ago, rapid warming resulted in a retreat of the ice sheet, and the island of Newfoundland was uncovered once again, though laid bare of life. This began the Holocene glacial retreat and the Holocene Period, and a rebirth of life in Canada, to Newfoundland, and into Bonavista.

More recent changes in climatic conditions have been relatively minor in comparison to the last ice age. One thousand years ago, temperatures were somewhat milder than today, with gradual cooling thereafter leading to the "Little Ice Age" from the 1500s to the mid-1800s. In Newfoundland, cold and warm periods have alternated through early fishing by Europeans in the 1500s through to the present day.

v. Climate

Meteorological conditions in Newfoundland during the winter season are among the most severe of any settled region on earth, with good reason. During the winter, North America is often covered with an extensive area of very cold, dry air (often referred to as the Polar Vortex) extending as far east as the eastern seaboard of the US through Quebec and into Labrador. Meanwhile, temperatures over the open ocean in the western area of the North Atlantic are quite warm (relatively speaking) and peak with the passage of the Gulf Stream. This very strong gradient between very cold arctic air over North America, and relatively warm air over the Gulf Stream and surrounding waters, is very unstable and gives rise to intense winter storms. These storms typically form along the eastern seaboard and then intensify rapidly as they approach New-foundland before continuing northeastward toward Iceland. Hurricane-force winds, high waves, heavy snowfall, and occasionally prolonged periods of freezing rain, accompany these storms. As we shall see, coastal infrastructure (flakes, boats, homes) can be easy fodder for some of these storms. The *Ocean Ranger* disaster, the Newfoundland Sealing Disaster, and, as we will see, the disaster of the SS *Greenland*, were all precipitated by these types of storms.

Icebergs off shore from Mockbeggar. (Herman Callahan via Ross Abbott)

Although hurricanes are typically associated with southern climates, they occasionally invade eastern Canada. Newfoundland, lying farthest seaward, is most vulnerable. Under normal circumstances, these late summer, early fall storms will dissipate as they pass over the colder waters around Newfound-land. Occasionally, however, they are able to draw upon energy within the up-per atmosphere and redevelop as a post-tropical storm. Hurricane Igor struck

Newfoundland in 2010 with widespread damage. We shall see the impacts of other tropical storms later.

A discussion of weather conditions in Newfoundland would not be complete without a recognition of its fog. We've already discussed the warm waters of the Gulf Stream south of Newfoundland and the Labrador Current, which passes northeast, and east of Newfoundland, before turning westward along the south coast of the island. Air over the Gulf Stream and waters farther south are naturally very warm and moisture-laden. As this air moves northward and passes over the Labrador Current, it cools, leading to condensation of the moisture in the air to form small, suspended water droplets. These water droplets are fog, and as they severely restrict visibility, they have had a serious, even devastating impact on those living within the marine environment.

Notes

Referenced books by Dr. Martha Hickman Hild and Dr. George A. Rose are especially insightful in providing a general description of the geology and natural environment of Newfoundland.

UNESCO Geopark:
http://www.unesco.org/new/en/natural-sciences/environment/earth-sciences/unesco-global-geoparks/frequently-asked-questions/what-is-a-unesco-global-geopark/

Discovery Geopark:
https://discoverygeopark.com/

PART TWO: FIRST VISITATION AND EARLY SETTLEMENT
3 — INDIGENOUS PEOPLES

Habitation of the Americas is generally believed to have begun after the end of the last ice age 10,000 years ago as people crossed the Bering Strait into Alaska and southward into Canada. As the most easterly point of North America, separated by the Gulf of St. Lawrence, the island of Newfoundland was one of the last areas to be inhabited. The early inhabitants are known as the Maritime Archaic Indians. The time of initial habitation in Newfoundland is unknown, but 4,000 years ago, they were well-established along the coast of the island. Although they were apparently well-adapted to life along the coast, they seem to have disappeared suddenly about 3,000 years ago. Around that same time, in geological terms, the early and late Palaeo-Eskimos (the latter group usually referred to as Dorset) established themselves along coastal Labrador and in Newfoundland.

One thousand years ago, the early Beothuk, known as the Little Passage people (named after a site at Little Passage on the south coast), lived along Newfoundland's coastline. They were the ancestors of those Beothuk who witnessed the arrival of the first Europeans.

When Cabot first landed in Newfoundland, and as others first fished from its shores, the hunter-gatherer Beothuk numbered about 1,000 souls, scattered throughout the island. They visited the coastlines of Newfoundland during the spring and summer seasons in search of fish, seals, sea mammals, and birds, then moved inland during the fall and winter to hunt and trap caribou and other mammals. They lived in tents in summer and semi-subterranean houses in winter.

John Day, a Bristol merchant, wrote in a letter a few months after John Cabot's return to Bristol that, when Cabot and his crew went ashore, they raised a cross and banner of England, claiming the land for King Henry VII. Later, in Day's words, "they found a trail that went inland, they saw a site where a fire had been made, they saw manure of animals which they thought to be farm animals, and they saw a stick half-a-yard long pierced at both ends, carved and painted with brazil, and by such signs they believe the land to be inhabited." Cabot and his men claimed this land for the King of England in the midst of an established habitation.

Less than 100 years later, Sir Richard Whitbourne made several trips to Newfoundland. He indicated that Trinity, Trinity Bay, was, in 1579, the most northerly fished harbour in the land "where our nation practises fishing," and indicated that "the savage people of that country do there inhabit; many of them secretly every year come into Trinity Bay and Harbour, in the night time, purposely to steal sails, lines, hatches, hooks, knives and the like . . ." During the 1500s, the English, French, Spanish, and Portuguese all fished along the coastline of eastern Newfoundland and on the Grand Banks. As Whitbourne noted that the English did not fish farther north than Trinity, perhaps other nations were fishing at Bonavista and encountering those same peoples noted by Cabot.

As late as 1680, the mayor of Poole, southern England, reported that "The Indians having been so bold this last year as to come into our harbour (at Bonavista) and do mischief." That the mayor of Poole referred to Bonavista as "our harbour" reflected the extent of activity between the two communities in later years.

The connection between the settlers at Bonavista and the Indigenous Beothuk was occasionally productive. George Cartwright, in 1770 (as related in Fay's *Life and Labour in Newfoundland*), wrote that:

> Formerly, a very beneficial barter was carried on in the neighbourhood of Bonavista, by some of the inhabitants of the harbour. They used to lay a variety of goods at a certain place, to which the Indians resorted, who took what they were in want of, and left furs in return. Once day, a villain hid himself near the deposits, and shot an Indian woman dead, as she was furnishing herself with what pleased her best. Since that time, they have always been hostile to Europeans. I fear that the race will be totally extinct in a few years.

Magistrate John Bland is discussed in greater detail in Chapter 13. His letters to the governor of Newfoundland, written during his tenure of over twenty years while in Bonavista in the late 1700s and early 1800s, indicate that a Beothuk presence at or near Bonavista had disappeared. What Bland knew of the Beothuk came from those in Bonavista who were engaged in the salmon and fur trade farther west, either deeper into Bonavista Bay or west of Greenspond toward Gander Bay. He wrote that "the Indians of this Island have a singular veneration for the Cross, and the furriers, it is said, by erecting a cruciform figure upon their winter houses have saved them from being destroyed during their absence in the summer." Of one Beothuk in particular he wrote that "this savage, the first remembered to have been in our possession, was taken when a boy, and became uncommonly expert in all the branches of the Newfoundland business. An old man in this bay who knew June (the name given by the locals to the boy) told me that he frequently made visits to his parents in the heart of the country." We don't know for certain, but when Bland referred to "this bay," he was likely referring to "Bonavista Bay" generally. Bland also recounted that "in the summer season, the Indians frequent the sea coasts, to provide stock for the winter . . . they have been known to adventure as far as the Funk Islands."

While Bland, from his station in Bonavista, knew something of the Beothuk farther into Bonavista Bay and west of Greenspond, he was quick to relate that knowledge of them generally was sparse. "I cannot help holding an opinion," Bland wrote, "that we know almost as little of the Newfoundland Indian as we do of the inhabitants of the interior of Africa."

While Bland was able to provide general information about the Beothuk to the governor of Newfoundland, it was his broader sense of justice, injustice, and the future of the Beothuk that was most striking. He wrote that "they have been progressively driven from south to north and though their removal has been produced by a slow and silent operation, it has nevertheless had all the effect of a violent expulsion." "It ought to be remembered that these savages have a natural right to this Island, and every invasion of a natural right is a violation of the principle of justice."

Bland's most prophetic commentary came in a letter to the governor's office dated September 1, 1797. "In proportion as their means of procuring subsistence became narrowed, their population must necessarily have decreased and before the lapse of another century, the English nation, like the Spanish, may have affixed to its character the indelible reproach of having exterminated a whole race of people!" The last Beothuk, Shanawdithit, died of tuberculosis in St. John's in 1829.

Notes

Information on pre-European settlement in Newfoundland is widely available. A good general source is: https://www.heritage.nf.ca/browser/theme/520

Reference by the mayor of Poole is found on:
http://ngb.chebucto.org/Articles/bonavista-1497-1700-bon.shtml

Bland's quotes are taken from letters found in the D'Alberti Papers.

John Day's Letter: www.heritage.nf.ca/articles/exploration/john-day.php

4 — THE 1500s

In the absence of definitive proof, Cape Bonavista is generally accepted as that landmark first sighted by John Cabot upon crossing the North Atlantic. And although Mason's map, which denotes Cape Bonavista as land first visited by John Cabot, has been used as evidence to that end, historians may never resolve the question with certainty. In any event, John Cabot did not, of course, actually "discover" Newfoundland. As we've seen from Chapter 3, Newfoundland was inhabited by the Beothuk and others long before Cabot, and long before those Europeans who followed Cabot in search of fish.

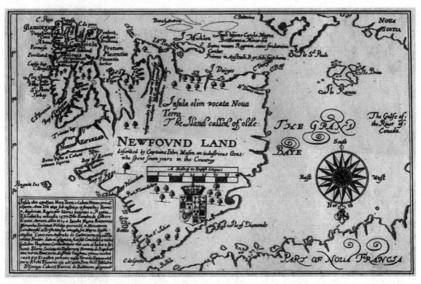

John Mason map of Newfoundland, 1617. Unlike convention, north is at the bottom, south at the top. At the tip of the Bonavista Peninsula is written "Bona Vista a Caboto primum reperta" (first seen by Cabot). Centre for Newfoundland Studies, QEII Library, Memorial University.

When Cabot returned to England, reports circulated on the abundance of cod in Newfoundland. Raimondo de Soncino was ambassador in London

17

for the Duke of Milan. In a letter to the Duke written a few short months after Cabot and his crew returned to Bristol, he wrote:

> The said Master Zoanne, being a foreigner and a poor man, would not be believed if the crew, who are nearly all English and from Bristol, did not testify that what he says is true. This Master Zoanne has a drawing of the world on a map and also on a solid globe, which he has made, and shows the point he reached . . . and they affirm that the sea is covered with fish which are caught not merely with nets but with baskets, a stone being attached to make the basket sink in the water, and this I heard the said Master Zoanne relate. And said Englishmen, his companions, say that they will fetch so many fish that this kingdom will have no more need of Iceland, from which country there comes a very great store of fish which are called stock-fish.

Very little is known of the early years following Cabot's sighting of Cape Bonavista. It is generally believed that fishermen from England, France, Spain, and Portugal crossed the North Atlantic each year and fished on the Grand Banks or established a seasonal base along the eastern coastline of Newfoundland. At the shoreline facilities they built wharves, stages, flakes, and temporary living facilities while fishing near shore in small boats that had been transported across the Atlantic. They arrived in the spring and returned to Europe in the fall. Those who participated were born, lived, and died in Europe and the British Isles. They could not, in fairness, be called the early settlers of Newfoundland since they visited these shores for brief periods of time simply to earn a living. This was business, albeit conducted from afar, but business nonetheless.

This fishery became known as the migratory fishery. We can't be certain to what extent the various nations of Europe participated in the migratory fishery over eastern Newfoundland in the 1500s. Handcock has suggested that in the early years, nations may have claimed various harbours for their own. English Harbour, near Bonavista, for example, may have identified a common area for English fishermen. This, in fact, is supported by Sir Richard Whitbourne, who indicated in 1579 that Trinity "standeth northmost of any harbour in the land where our nation practiseth fishing," thus implying that any fishing at Bonavista would have been conducted by other nations.

In the 1600s, the English began to assert dominance at Newfoundland, including Bonavista. Whereas in 1579, Whitbourne indicated that the English did not fish farther north than Trinity, in the second half of his Discourse (written around 1620) he indicates otherwise.

"Cape Bonavista is the headland on the north side of the entrance to Trinity Bay, and there is a reasonably good harbour, where ships do yearly vie to fish, called the harbour of Bonavista, and divers (various) small islands are near thereunto; where yearly breed great abundance of divers forts of sea fowl, of which birds and their eggs, men may take so many of them as they lift."

The Western Charter of 1634 and King William's Act (1699) formed the framework for English law in Newfoundland during the 1600s and early 1700s (see Bannister in Notes). Newfoundland would not formally become a British colony until the early 1800s. Before that time, Newfoundland was seen as a seasonal fishing station to be used as a base for commercial enterprises by the West Country merchants in England. To help maintain law and order at each location along the coastline of Newfoundland, such as at Bonavista, the first master of an English ship to arrive at a shore base after March 25 of a given year was given the title of fishing admiral for that location and was responsible, and even given authority, for maintaining law and order for the year. The fishing admiral also had choice of the best of the various Ship's Rooms (such as wharves, stageheads, flakes) erected along the coastline. The second and third masters to arrive were respectively called the vice and rear admirals and chose their Ship's Rooms accordingly. The Ship's Rooms evolved over the years, as we will see in Chapters 5 and 11.

While the local fishing admirals governed the fishing sites during the summer season, the Royal Navy patrolled the coastline as well. The naval commanders acted as an appeal judge if necessary with respect to decisions of the fishing admirals. Although Newfoundland's coastline slowly became inhabited during the winter season during these early years, there was no provision for law, as the masters of the fishing vessels and the Royal Navy had returned to England in the fall.

The migratory fishery, then, continued in strength among the English from the beginning of the 1600s, with a well-established system for catching and processing fish. Each ship that sailed from England in the spring established its presence in a local harbour, with all of the required infrastructure as necessary to secure its produce for the return home to England in the fall.

The Spanish and Portuguese, meanwhile, abandoned the migratory fishery in Newfoundland through the 1500s and early 1600s. The French continued to participate, leading to hostilities within Newfoundland and specific confrontations at Bonavista.

Notes

A more detailed account of the early fishery in Newfoundland can be found at:
https://www.heritage.nf.ca/articles/exploration/16th-century-fishery.php

Laws pertaining to Newfoundland, the fishery, and settlement from the 1600s to early 1800s may be found in (Bannister):
https://www.heritage.nl.ca/articles/politics/formal-law.php
https://www.heritage.nf.ca/lawfoundation/articles/primary.html

The Soncino letter:
www.heritage.nf.ca/articles/exploration/soncino-letters.php

5 — EARLY SETTLEMENT

In the early 1500s, Cape Bonavista was, from the perspective of the early explorers, an uninhabited outpost whose offshore fishing grounds were teeming with codfish. By the end of that century, fishermen from Europe were using the shoreline as a staging ground. They arrived in the spring from across the Atlantic and returned home in the fall. In the 1600s, plantations, or Ship's Rooms, were being firmly established both at the harbour at Bonavista and in an area known today as Bayley's Cove. These plantations were the processing facilities by which fish was brought ashore, processed, salted, and prepared for the return to Europe in the fall.

The Codfish Map, as it is sometimes known, from Herman Moll's *The World Described*, 1715. It provides a detailed depiction of salt-fish processing in Newfoundland in the 1600s and 1700s.

In the 1670s, Admiral Sir John Berry, a naval officer of the British Royal Navy, was the captain of the fleet sent to Newfoundland each summer season to police and protect the coastline. In 1675, and again in 1677, he conducted a census of inhabitants in Newfoundland (planters, their families, and servants) as well as their property. Thirty harbours were tabulated. "Port Bonavista" was one of them.

These were not "residents" in the traditional sense, since there was a high degree of mobility at that time. Some planter families and their servants returned to England after the fishing season ended in the fall and returned again in the spring. Others moved farther inland, or north, for furs and seals, in winter, while some remained in the community to protect infrastructure, perform repairs, and to prepare for the next season. Some planters moved from one harbour to the next or abandoned the fishing industry entirely. The census was a snapshot for the time at which the naval officer visited the shoreline. These names were taken from handwritten accounts from the spoken word—spelling variations were common.

Meanwhile, officially, Newfoundland was ruled by the Western Charter and the fishing admirals, with overarching authority by the Royal Navy (see Chapter 4). As noted in *A Short History of Newfoundland and Labrador* (see References), Newfoundland was "a naval state, a colony administered by the Royal Navy . . . the English Shore remained an anomaly: a civil society essentially without local government."

1675: Port Bonavista

Planter	Wife	Sons	Daughters	Men	Boats	Stages
Richard Wallis	1	1	1	2	1	1
John Curtis				2	1	
Richard Phippard				2	1	
Thomas Crew				11	2	1
Thomas Warrey	1		2	1	1	1
James Shambler				28	5	1

Planter	Wife	Sons	Daughters	Men	Boats	Stages
Thomas Newell				5	1	1
Robert Newman				10	2	1
William Tilley	1	7	2	5	2	1
William Newman	1		1	5	1	
Thomas Wiry	1			5	1	

Population: 106 (Planters and family = 30; Servants = 76)

1677: Port Bonavista

Planter	Wife	Sons	Daughters	Servants
Thomas Newell	1	3		15
James Shambler	1	1	1	22
Thomas Warrey	1	1	1	1
Richard Wallis	1	1	2	1
Richard Phippard	1	1		1
Thomas Wiry	1			2
John Kates	1	1	1	3
John Curtis	1			3
Thomas Crew	1	2		11
William Newman	1		1	1
Robert Newman				16

Planter	Wife	Sons	Daughters	Servants
William Tilley	1	6	2	10
Joseph Vickery				2
George Brent	1	2	3	2
Barn. Gantlett				4
George Talbott	1	3	2	3

Population: 160 (Planters and family = 63; Servants = 97)

Also included in the 1677 census for "Port Bonavista" were 17 houses (Shambler owned two), 19 storerooms and lodgings, 13 gardens, 18 stages (Shambler owned three), and 26 flakes. There were also 8 head of cattle, 28 sheep, and 51 hogs—mostly owned by Thomas Newell.

The 1675 and 1677 census numbers provide a glimpse into the transition that was occurring in Bonavista over the years. On the one hand, we can see the transitory nature of the migratory fishery; on the other hand, we see the beginning of a stable and self-sustaining community.

The Western Charter and King William's Act established the supremacy of the seasonal cod fishery by the West Country merchants. Nonetheless, Bannister (see Notes) indicated that its provisions "did not correspond to the island's actual economic development" and, in fact, that "Keith Matthews, a noted Newfoundland historian, argued that it was generally ignored in practice." Bonavista was in the process of establishing itself as a "community." The population (though highly variable), of something exceeding 100 individuals, tells us that Bonavista was the second-most populated site in Newfoundland (after St. John's). Consistency in habitation is indicated in that all eleven surnames recorded for 1675 are repeated in 1677. There are four families (i.e., husband, wife, and at least one child) present in 1675, and eleven families in 1677. Despite the recognition that, in some cases, these families would have returned to England in the fall, the presence of the Wallis, Warrey, Tilley, and Newman families spanning a three-year period indicates that some semblance of stability and continuity, even settlement, had begun. The presence of homes, lodgings, gardens, and livestock further support the notion that Bonavista had firmly transitioned from a point of land for the seasonal harvesting of codfish to a home for at least some of the planters. Head, in *Eighteenth Century New-*

foundland, further notes that there was, by contemporary reports, "an opening wilde road," that the harbour was "verry ffowlle ground," being made "onely by ledge of rocks called the Swerges." Perhaps "the Swerges" morphed into Squarry Island and Squarry Head of today.

The census numbers report fourteen sons and daughters in 1675, and thirty-four sons and daughters in 1677. Although this does not necessarily indicate the number of children (sons and daughters may have been young men and women supporting their parents), the presence of wives would suggest that at least some may have been at a very young age.

The Wallis family saw an addition of one daughter to its family unit between 1675 to 1677. If Mrs. Wallis had given birth to her daughter in Bonavista, it would not have been Bonavista's first newborn baby. George Davis, a merchant, wrote to Captain James Cook on March 14, 1764, stating that ". . . Mrs. Tizzard was born in Bonavista whose uncle Mr. John Walcome was the first manchild born there who was 80 years old when he died and has been dead upwards of 30 years . . ." (Appendix 1). This would place young Walcome's birth around 1654, which, in and of itself, would indicate a level of stability at Bonavista well before that first 1675 census. The surname "Walcome" was replaced with "Walkam" through the 1700s, but the early start to the surname at Bonavista did not lead to longevity. The last marriage or birth recorded in the parish records seems to be the marriage of James Walkam and Elizabeth Short in 1794. With the exception of "Walkham's Bridge" and "Walkham's Hill" at the centre of town, the name has since disappeared.

Although the family unit, and therefore settlement, was becoming established in Bonavista in the 1600s, the transitory nature of the community is clearly evident. A population change from 107 to 160 over a three-year period, including a doubling in the population of planters and their families, highlights the extent to which the fishing industry varied on a yearly basis, and perhaps reflects the extent to which planters moved from one community to another along the coastline. George Talbott and wife, for example, were listed as inhabitants of English Harbour in 1675, and in Bonavista two years later. The presence of servants (mostly boys or young men from southern England hired on a yearly basis to support the seasonal fishery) also contributed to the transient nature of Bonavista at that time. Variation in numbers between 1675 and 1677 might have also been a consequence of the time of year during which the numbers were taken, since we know that many inhabitants moved inland and northward in the fall.

Captain James Story, reporting back to the English Lords of Trade and

Plantations, wrote of conditions in Newfoundland in 1681. He called it "An account of the fishing ships, sack ships, planters and boat keepers from Trepassey to Bonavista, and from thence to Fair Island, the northward part of the island." St. John's and Bonavista were easily the largest sites. St. John's numbered 18 ships and 29 planters (plus 21 sack ships . . . likely for trade between fishermen, cod and wine and between Newfoundland, Europe and England . . . and 12 boat keepers), while Bonavista counted 17 ships and 32 planters. Other communities that would grow over the next century, such as Trinity (included with five other communities with a total of sixteen planters) and Harbour Grace (five ships, five planters), were in their relative infancy.

Story's reference to selling women from Ireland (presumably) when they arrived in Newfoundland is noteworthy. We need to be careful that we don't automatically construct an image of female slaves being captured and brought against their will to Newfoundland. Nor should we naively presume that there was something adventurous or romantic about this migration. Striking comments can also be found 100 years later in the Lester diaries about southern England. Isaac Lester wrote, in 1769 while in southern England, near Poole, that he "met with three poor young fellows on the road and ordered them to call here—when I came home shipped them to go on the *Two Sisters*." We perhaps should assume that they received the approval of the parents of the "three poor young fellows," but the brevity and indifference of the entry is remarkable. As late as 1829, Thomas Gaylor's diary at Bonavista records (January 1, 1829) that "several people on shore from their schooner. Some stole a boy and others got very drunk and remained on shore all night."

Captain Story went on to describe the activities after the fishing season had ended in the fall and the ships had returned to England with their now-salted catch. "The fur trade is further north, towards Bonavista (in fact, it was in Bonavista Bay, toward the Gander River, for example, or around Gander Bay). The planters go a furring about the middle of September and take no provisions with them but bread and salt, finding beavers, otters and seals enough to feed on. They carry guns and kill also a great deal of venison, which they salt down for the winter. They return about 1st May."

The next census, of sorts, conducted in Newfoundland was in 1703. Twenty-seven communities were listed. The largest was St. John's, with a population of 300, followed by Bonavista (including Bayley's Cove and Green Island), with 266. The third-largest was Old Perlican, with 108.

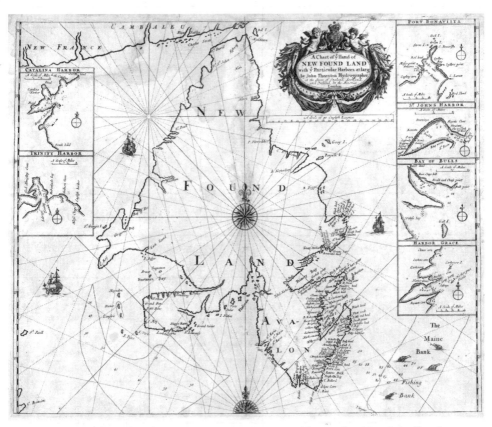

Created by John Thorton. Date: 1698–1706. (Centre for Newfoundland Studies, Memorial University, No. 269)

The next detailed census for Bonavista was completed in 1708.

Town	Boat Keepers	Wives	Children	Servants
Bonavista	13	8	17	80
Green Island	8	2	7	60
Bayley's Cove	5	2	5	32

Town	Inhabitants	Wife	Children	Servants	Boats	Skiffs
Bonavista	John Wakeham	1	4	6	1	1
	Stephen Shepherd			13	2	1
	Benjamin Stackalls		1	6	1	1
	Stephen Gasson	1		5	1	1
	William King	1		5	1	
	William Roberts			6	1	1
	Thomas Andrew	1	5	5	1	1
	William Knight	1	3	9	2	1
	John Ayres	1		5	1	1
	George Travis			5	1	1
	Robert Watts	1	3	4	1	1
	James Newell	1	1	5	1	1
	George Skeffington			6	1	1

Population: 118

Town	Inhabitants	Wife	Children	Servants	Boats	Skiffs
Green Island	Thomas Newell, Sr.	1	3	12	2	1
	Thomas Newell, Jr.	1	4	12	2	1

Town	Inhabitants	Wife	Children	Servants	Boats	Skiffs
	Samuel Shambler			6	1	1
	Edward Trock			6	1	1
	John King			6	1	1
	John Korloy			6	1	1
	Richard Tilleys			6	1	1
	William Landers			6	1	1

Population: 77

Town	Inhabitants	Wife	Children	Servants	Boats	Skiffs
Bayley's Cove	Barnaby Gantlett	1	4	10	2	1
	William Norton			10	2	1
	Richard Howard			5	1	1
	George Brint			5	1	1
	Francis Ross	1	1	2	1	

Population: 44
Total Population: 239 (Planters and family = 67; Servants = 172)

As with comparing the census for 1675 with 1677, a similar comparison between the names listed for those censuses with the census for 1708 illustrates some consistency in habitation over time, while also showing that there was considerable turnover. Of the sixteen surnames listed in the censuses for 1675 and 1677, only four (Shambler, Newell, Brent/Brint, and Gantlett) are repeated in 1708. Of note is the presence of "John Wakeham," which might be that same John "Walcome" born in 1654 at Bonavista.

The 1711 census gave general population numbers, which, although not useful in terms of capturing the names of the planters, was at least useful in seeing Bonavista's size relative to the rest of Newfoundland and in watching the growth in population.

1711 Census

Bonavista and adjacent places	290
Dildoe Island and adjacent places	205
Fox Island and adjacent places	185
Carbonear Island and adjacent places	130
Harbour Grace Island and adjacent places	150
Little Belle Island and adjacent places	50
Fort William of St. John's and adjacent places	349
Gull Island and adjacent places	200
Ferryland and adjacent places	366
Total	1925

In 1715, the total population for Bonavista, Bayley's Cove, and Green Island was 474 (including 32 women and 70 children), second in total population to St. John's, with 1210. In 1722, it was noted that there were 40 "masters," 300 "menservants," 30 "mistresses," 10 "women servants," and 50 children at Bonavista. The total population, then, was 430 (though it would appear some rounding may have happened). The record keeper noted that 400 of these 430 "had remained in the country last year," or, presumably, had stayed on the island of Newfoundland through the winter season.

The transitory nature of the inhabitants of Bonavista in the late 1600s and through the 1700s is evident from an entry by Captain Ogle of the British Navy in 1719. He writes:

The furring trade the last year proved of very great advantage to the inhabitants of Bonavista, many persons having taken to the value of £40 sterling per man for the winters' season, all the furs so taken is sent to Great Britain by the Poole and Livington ships using that trade, the seal fishery to the northward is likewise to very great advantage and greatly encouraged by the said Mr. Keen who yearly purchases all of that commodity. Recommends Christopher Sheppard as a good person to help police Bonavista during the winter season.

The notes taken by the captains of the Royal Navy are telling on a couple of levels. First of all, the 1722 entry that 400 of the 430 inhabitants in Bonavista remained "in the country last year" highlights that there was now a high level of stability among most of the residents of the town. They called Bonavista their "home." Meanwhile, the 1719 entry illustrates that "winter housing" was an inherent component of the livelihood. When the fishing season ended in the fall, many residents moved inland and north. We'll discuss this in greater detail in Chapter 17 as it forms an important part of life in early Bonavista. In fact, in 1722, it was noted that in Bonavista, and elsewhere, many planters "are obliged to take down their stages to preserve them from being carried away by the sea and ice in the winter season; they build and repair their stages, flakes, etc., with wood fetched out of the woods and not otherwise."

In summary, then, we should note that Bonavista was clearly in the forefront of settlement in Newfoundland in the 1600s and 1700s. St. John's was invariably the most heavily populated community, and would be chosen as the home of Newfoundland's governor in 1729, while Bonavista was always among the top few settlements, and frequently second only to St. John's.

Notes

The Colonial Office CO194 Series (Board of Trade & Secretary of State) contains the original records upon which most of the information above can be found. Dr. Gordon Handcock's *Origins of English Settlement in Newfoundland* was used as the overarching guide on settlement in Newfoundland.

The 1675 census:
http://heritage.canadiana.ca/view/oocihm.lac_reel_c1446/742?r=0&s=4

Captain George Story's account is from the Calendar of State Papers, Colonial Series, America and West Indies, 1681.

With respect to Captain Story's indication of Irish females sold as servants, see additional reading:
https://psmag.com/social-justice/the-irish-were-not-slaves
https://www.heritage.nf.ca/articles/society/irish-newfoundland.php
https://en.wikipedia.org/wiki/Irish_indentured_servants

The 1722 reference to taking down stages is taken from the Calendar of State Papers, Colonial Series. America and the West Indies, Vol. 33. 1722-23.

George Davis's letter to Captain James Cook (Appendix 1) is related in *Life and Labour in Newfoundland* by C. R. Fay (page 74). Reference may also be found here: http://ngb.chebucto.org/Articles/bonavista-1497-1700-bon.shtml

Captain Ogle's entry is taken from CO194, vol. 5.

Early settlement in Newfoundland is also discussed within the context of the Western Charter and King William's Act in (Bannister):
https://www.heritage.nf.ca/lawfoundation/articles/primary.html
Bannister writes ". . . it is hoped that readers will be better able to make independent evaluations of important issues, such as whether settlement was actually illegal, or whether statute law significantly limited property rights."

Bannister, in https://www.heritage.nl.ca/articles/politics/formal-law.php, wrote in part that "The 1699 Act has been universally decried as an unmitigated disaster." Its provisions did not correspond to the island's actual economic development—the increasingly complex cod fishery encompassed migratory and resident operations, West Country merchants, and year-round settlers—and Keith Matthews, a noted Newfoundland historian, argued that it was generally ignored in practice.

Further reading on the migratory fishery and early settlement: *A Short History of Newfoundland and Labrador*, Newfoundland Historical Society. Boulder Publications. 2008.

6 — QUAKERS

Anyone born and raised in Newfoundland who wanted to read about the early history of religion in Newfoundland would expect to see a discussion of early Protestant and Catholic residents and churches in the area. A Quaker presence, however, is something we wouldn't expect. It's rarely discussed in the history books, and it's not part of today's religious community. But it was a significant component of early settlement at Bonavista.

In the first census of Bonavista in 1675, James Shambler, with 28 men, 5 boats, and a stage, was easily the most prominent plantation owner in Bonavista at that time (the closest to Shambler was Thomas Crew with 11 men and 2 boats). He was present again in the 1677 census, this time with his wife, a son, and daughter. James Shambler was a Quaker, one of many in early Bonavista.

Quakers, or the "Religious Society of Friends," were a Christian group that began in England in the 1640s. They believed in a personal relationship with God and rejected the authority of church and state. They refused to pay "tithes" to the state church, would not take oaths in court, refused military service and combat, and even declined to doff their hats to those in power. They did not believe in corporal punishment.

The Shambler success at Bonavista continued into the early 1700s, where we find Samuel Shambler (perhaps James's son from 1677) in the 1708 census. In that same census is George Skeffington, that same gentleman noted in Chapter 7 on Queen Anne's War. Skeffington first appears in a meeting of Quakers in Philadelphia in present-day USA, where he is listed as "George Skeffington late of Newfoundland." Skeffington and Shambler were descendants from Ringwood, a small town close to Poole, in southern England.

In the early 1700s, Skeffington was engaged in the salmon fishery northwest of Bonavista toward Greenspond and westward to Gander Bay. This involved taking his men in the fall of the year (after the summer fishery was completed) to "clear lands of the wood, and the rivers or brooks of rocks and stones and other obstructions, build houses, stages, flatts, works and other conveniences for catching and curing salmon in said brooks or rivers." William Keen, Samuel Shambler, William Knight, all plantation owners at Bonavista, as well as an Isaac Bonovrier, were engaged in a business arrangement with Skeffington. Skeffington's salmon fishery extended at times from Gambo River in Bonavista Bay to Dog River west of Gander Bay. The plantations, or Fishing Rooms (Appendix 2), of Keen, Skeffington, and Shambler were all located next to each other near the site of the present-day Ryan Premises.

We know Skeffington as a Quaker not only from the documents of record but from his own writing, where, as in Quaker practice, he referred to his fellow plantation owner as "Friend Keen" and signed his name as "Thy real friend George Skeffington." As church records were not kept in the early 1700s, we don't know what became of Skeffington. His name does not appear in the 1742 and 1752 petitions (Appendices 3 and 4), but this may be more a consequence of his beliefs with respect to church and state. The will of a Joseph Skeffington "of Bonavista, in the Island of Newfoundland" is registered on January 31, 1789. The Skiffington name (with a new spelling) was common when Anglican church records commenced in 1786, including the baptism of a George Skiffington in 1805.

A Quaker presence continued in the area through the 1700s and early 1800s, though it is difficult to establish documentation, as the Quaker faith did not adhere to the procedures, hierarchy, and missionary presence of the contemporary churches. Handcock and Rollmann indicate that the Taverner, Jeffrey, White, Vallis, and Rolles families of Trinity, with influence and agents (such as Samson Mifflen) in Bonavista, had strong Quaker backgrounds. In time, with the introduction of Church of England, Methodist, and Catholic missionaries, ministers, and priests, the Quaker presence slowly died.

Notes

Further details on George Skeffington can be found from Hans Rollmann's "Thy Real Friend George Skeffington: Quaker and Salmon Fishing Pioneer in Eighteenth Century Newfoundland." Memorial University of Newfoundland. https://journals.sas.ac.uk/fhs/article/view/3508/3459. Retrieved March 24, 2020.

The description of Skeffington's salmon fishery is taken from CO194, vol. 7.

Joseph's Skeffington's will can be retrieved from the National Archives, UK: http://discovery.nationalarchives.gov.uk/

Further reading on Quakers Samuel White, Samson Mifflen, John Rolles, and Samuel Vallis, all of whom had a Bonavista connection either directly or through their descendants, is found in *Mansions and Merchants of Poole and Dorset*.

7 — QUEEN ANNE'S WAR

As North America, including Newfoundland, grew in importance over the 1600s and 1700s, England and France engaged in various conflicts for domination in the New World. Bonavista, for the most part, was spared any direct involvement. However, Queen Anne's War (1701–1713) saw a direct attack on Bonavista.

The author's account, below, of the confrontation between the French and English at Bonavista is based upon early information provided by Charlevoix, Penhallow, and Prowse in addition to the Colonial Records. As might be expected, given that this information was perhaps second- or third-hand, and that accounts provided by either side of the battle might not be fully unbiased, the contemporary accounts differ at times in detail. With additions and editing, this narrative has been earlier related in Whiffen's *Prime Berth*.

Under the command of Jean Leger de la Grange, about 140 Frenchmen and Indians, in two vessels, the *Joybert* and the *Philipeau*, equipped with canoes and having departed from Placentia, quietly approached Bonavista Harbour after sunset on August 17, 1704. At least four English vessels were anchored just outside the harbour. The 250-ton galley *Pembroke* of London with 44 men and 20 guns, under the command of John Noll, was laden with dry fish. Captain Auten led the *Society* of Poole: 140 tons, 14 guns, and 24 men. The *William*, also with 14 guns and 24 men, carried 30 tons of lamp oil. A fourth vessel was commanded by Captain Michael Gill of Charleston, Massachusetts.

The French quickly and quietly overtook the *Pembroke*, the *Society*, and the *William* and took the officers and seamen captive. Captain Gill, finally alert to the attack, turned his vessel upon the invaders. The ensuing battle between the French and Gill lasted through the night. When Grange realized that guns and cannon fire would not be successful in defeating Gill, he ordered his men to set fire to the *Society* and sent it adrift toward Gill's vessel. Contrary winds, however, directed the burning ship harmlessly aground. Later, Grange directed his men to set the *William* ablaze. With its cargo of oil, the *William* was reportedly an inferno as it bore down upon Gill's ship. According to Penhallow, the *William* would have devoured Gill and his men, but "the buoy-rope of the anchor got between the rudder and the stern" and the *William* never reached its target.

Meanwhile, the inhabitants of Bonavista had fled their homes in anticipation of a French victory. Taking advantage of this retreat, some of Grange's men landed at Green Island and destroyed its fortifications. Gill's persistent defence ultimately inspired new hope in the settlers, and they returned to assist. This new development precipitated a retreat by Grange, who released his captives after having reached a comfortable distance from shore. According to the captives, it had been Grange's intent to burn the entire town to the ground.

The episode was not a total loss for Grange. He at least had destroyed two ships and had been able to seize the *Pembroke* and its 2,500 quintals of dry cod. Grange, his men, and their newly acquired vessel returned to Quebec, where the fish was sold and, according to Doyle, the profits split among the sailors. When the French were returning the *Pembroke* to Europe, and its new home in France, it was recaptured by the English.

Remnants of the *William* were uncovered in 1950 when dredging operations were being conducted around Walkham's Bridge. Sections have been preserved in the Bonavista Museum.

Captain Michael Gill was born in Dover, England, in 1673, a son of William and Elizabeth (Stone). When only twenty, he sailed across the Atlantic, master of his own vessel, and initiated a business in Charleston, Massachusetts. He quickly established a thriving fish trading exchange between New England, Bonavista and Trinity Bays, the West Indies, and Europe. In 1696, he married Relief Dowse—they raised ten children. Captain Michael Gill died in Charleston in 1720.

Shortly after Captain Gill's death, three of his sons, Michael, Jr., Nicholas, and James, moved to St. John's. They continued their father's success and established a very prosperous business at St. John's. Michael, Jr. was appointed a justice of the peace in 1733 and served in later years as a judge of the Vice Admiralty Court. In 1757, he formed a militia for St. John's in response to the inception of the Seven Years' War. He died in St. John's on March 8, 1772. Nicholas was, for a time, chief magistrate of St. John's.

Thomas's journal of 1794 records the epitaph for Michael Gill, Jr.

Here lies the remains of Michael Gill, Esq., Judge of the Admiralty of this Island and for a number of years justice of the peace. He was an indulgent Father and a tender Husband. This tomb is inscribed to his memory by his disconsolate widow and son. He was born in Charlestown in America in 1699 and died at St. John's, Nfld. 8th March, 1772.

Gill's antagonist in this battle was Jean de la Grange. An unlikely combatant, perhaps, Grange was a French surgeon and merchant who, in 1696, became commandant of the *Wesp*, then under the jurisdiction of Pierre Le Moyne d'Iberville. Subsequent to the Bonavista attack, Grange was appointed a captain in the King's Navy. He eventually returned to his profession, as chief surgeon at Louisburg, on Cape Breton Island.

One of the businessmen at Bonavista at that time was William Keen, who had come to Newfoundland in 1704 as an agent for New England merchants established at St. John's. Keen established his own business in 1713 and quickly became one of the most successful merchants on the island. He was appointed justice of the peace for St. John's in 1729 and was the first judge to be appointed to the Vice Admiralty Court established in 1744. Both of William Keen's sons, William, Jr. and Benjamin, served as magistrates in Bonavista. The Keen properties, as we'll see, were sold to James Ryan in 1869 and ultimately became a National Historic Site.

In 1754, Newfoundland was shocked by the news of Keen's murder at his home in St. John's. Eight Irish men and an Irish woman slipped into his home at night and took his life—partly as revenge for the punishment of an acquaintance and partly for money. On October 7, 1754, the day before the trial, Governor Bonfoy ordered the sheriff to erect gallows "at the end of Mr. Keen's wharf, for the execution of sundry persons now in custody for murder of the late Wm Keen, Esq." On October 8, the day of the trial, he further ordered the construction of a gibbet "capable of containing two men in chains." Two days later, after the trial in which all were found guilty, two men were hanged at the end of Keen's wharf, and the following day, a man and his wife were hanged. The remaining men, though initially retained, were ultimately deported.

Through the winter of 1704–05, the French, led by Jacques Testand de Montigny, attacked the Avalon Peninsula. Montigny had served as a lieutenant for d'Iberville during his attacks on Newfoundland in 1696–97. From January 1705 till spring, Montigny attacked and pillaged nearly every settlement, including St. John's. Homes, stages, and flakes were destroyed, and people killed. In April, they reached Bonavista. George Skeffington, a resident merchant and Quaker who had been charged with protecting the town, was no match for the French soldiers.

We have already met George Skiffington in Chapter 6. He had come to Bonavista sometime in the 1690s and originally worked as a ship chandler (providing supplies to ships) and cooper (making barrels, casks, etc.) but, according to Rollmann, worked at Bonavista as an agent for the London merchant house of James Campbell. In the early 1700s, he also began a salmon fishery, which gradually grew throughout Bonavista Bay and by the 1720s extended to the Gander River in Notre Dame Bay. At various times he worked in partnership with both William Keen and Samuel Shambler.

Lt. Moody, stationed at St. John's, reported the 1705 attack.

> The French surprised Bonavista but about 80 or 90 of the inhabitants got on Green Island where they fortified themselves and might have made good their defence but their courage failing and unwarily admitting the enemy to come among them, they heaved their guns (being nine in number) over the cliffs into the sea and afterwards the inhabitants capitulated and ransomed their homes for £450 payable to Montigny.

A French account of events at Bonavista (by an unknown author recorded by Prowse) differs in some details with that of Moody's.

> ... [Montigny] continued his course to Bonavista, where he found the inhabitants entrenched on the island. He attacked them and, without much resistance, they surrendered to about 50 men. The commander of the English, who was a merchant, asked to ransom himself for £4000 sterling. [Montigny promised] the people that they should be further molested by the French and that they might pursue their fishery in peace. . . . After that another Canadian went to Bonavista and seized more prisoners, who also had to offer round sums to secure their ransom.

According to Doyle, Skiffington was taken prisoner to Placentia, and from there to France. He eventually found his way back to England, and was in Bonavista in time for the 1708 census. In a letter by Skeffington's employer, James Campbell, in London, to a "Sir Charles Hedges," Campbell described that the French killed "nine men, a boy and a girl at Bonavista" and carried away "some of the people from thence to Placentia as hostages for a ransom . . . amongst these is my 'Factor' at Bonavista (George Skeffington)." The Nimshi Crewe Collection states that the ransom papers were lost when "Old Oakley cottage" near the Bonavista courthouse burned to the ground around 1900.

Colin Campbell (James's brother), in a detailed "oath" on damages (July 27, 1709), recorded that "the French and Indians had twice in that year invaded that settlement (Bonavista) and that the first time after several abuses committed they ransomed the harbour for £400 or £500 sterling which George Skeffington paid them in plate gold rings and bills with which they departed at that time. But contrary to their faith immediately returned and burnt, plundered and destroyed the harbour and amongst the rest of the effects belonging to the said Mr. James Campbell and withal murdered many of the inhabitants and carried the said Skeffington prisoner to Placentia and sent him from thence to France."

Through the remainder of Queen Anne's War, other battles were intermittently fought on the Avalon Peninsula, but Bonavista was spared.

Queen Anne's War ended with the Treaty of Utrecht in 1713. Its most significant article with respect to Newfoundland was that the island was given to Great Britain, who consequently had exclusive right to settlement. France was granted the right to fish from Cape Bonavista northwestward to the Great Northern Peninsula and southward along the west coast to Point Riche—the so-called French Shore. Since the town of Bonavista lies a few miles south of Cape Bonavista, it was in fact located on the French Shore. The conflicts and confusion that arose at this, the easternmost point of the French Shore at Bonavista, will be revisited in Chapter 10.

Although it is clear that Bonavista was fortified to some degree during the late 1600s, and that these fortifications were presumably destroyed during Grange's attack in 1704, details are sparse. Contemporary English records contain little information. Penhallow tells us that the "Fort . . . was . . . laid in ashes" by Grange's attack. The French accounts provide a more impressive description of Bonavista's defence. Charlevoix, for example, states that there were "six hundred English at Fort Bonavista." With respect to conditions subsequent to Grange's destruction of the fortifications, Lt. Moody recounts only that the inhabitants "fortified themselves" on Green Island and refers to their nine guns. Both the French and English versions of the 1705 battle note the presence of between 50 and 90 "inhabitants" on Green Island during their attempted defence—though it is unclear if this was also the site of the fort.

Notes

As noted, the account of the battles at Bonavista were based upon Charlevoix, Penhallow, Prowse, and the Colonial Office Papers, with additional information from Doyle, Rollmann (see Notes at end of Chapter 6), and Thomas.

The *Dictionary of Canadian Biography* and the *Dictionary of Newfoundland and Labrador Biography* are useful for milestone information about many of the referenced individuals. Additional information on Gill, Keen, and Skeffington were obtained through the Colonial Office Papers.

Information on the attack on Keen in St. John's:
https://www.heritage.nf.ca/articles/exploration/keen-capture-st-johns.php
http://www.biographi.ca/en/bio/keen_william_3E.html
CO194, vol. 13, p. 153-170.

The letter by James Campbell is found in the Calendar of State Papers, Colonial Series, America and the West Indies, Vol. 22. 1704-05.

Colin Campbell's letter is found in CO194, vol. 4, page 467.

The details of Keen's murder and trial are contained in the *Letter Books of the Colonial Secretary's Office, 1752-59, Volumes S1 & S2.* Summary comments are contained in the Nimshi Crewe Collection, Box 7, File 174.

8 — THE WHIPPING POST

Through naval governance by the seasonal fishing admirals and the captains of the Royal Navy, and continuing with naval governance by the governor of Newfoundland commencing in 1729, corporal punishment was recognized as a common means of instilling adherence to local authority. It would not be surprising, then, to find whipping posts and stocks in local communities, prominently displayed for everyone to see.

The year 1729 saw the introduction of the first naval governor for Newfoundland, stationed in St. John's. Newfoundland's first governor was Captain Henry Osborne. Justices of the peace and constables were appointed at the local level by the governor to ensure peace and security within the community. As magistrates at Bonavista, he appointed Reverend Henry Jones, Mr. John Clarke, and Mr. John Henning. Constables were Mr. John Sheppard and Mr. John Tilley in the town of Bonavista, and Mr. Stephen Burton at Bayley's Cove. The formal structure for the administration of justice may have changed, but the option for corporal punishment remained.

Shortly after Reverend Jones and Henning were appointed as JPs in Bonavista, they initiated correspondence with the governor on their responsibilities. Jones had been trained as an ordained minister, of course, not as a magistrate. They noted that they were not "learned in the law" and were therefore inadequately prepared for administering cases, seizing debts, and for court and jail charges. On a number of levels, the simultaneous responsibilities of pastoral care and imposing law and order is not a good idea, and within a few years (perhaps following the departure of Jones from Bonavista in 1742), William Keen, one of the dominant merchants in Bonavista and owner of Keen's Room, was appointed justice. Keen was the son of that same William Keen who had been resident in Bonavista during the French attacks on Bonavista during Queen Anne's War (Chapter 7) and who later moved to St. John's. William, Sr., in fact, was appointed justice of the peace for St. John's by Governor Osborne in 1729.

Documentation of the use of corporal punishment prior to 1729 is practically non-existent. Under the rule of the governor, however, and with the appointment of justices of the peace, court proceedings, and the administration of justice, documentation became more structured and standardized. Bonavista saw its first, and only, record of corporal punishment in 1748.

Before relating the story as recorded in the court records, it is important to recreate societal structure at that time. We will see in Chapter 12 that Rev. Jones saw the inhabitants of Bonavista as comprising two classes: the "masters" (as he called them) and the servants. Masters were the owners of the various Ship's Rooms, or, as they were later called, Fishing Rooms, located along the coastline of Bonavista Harbour and in Bayley's Cove. Bland's Register of Fishing Rooms, 1805, in Chapter 11, will identify them for that time. The servants, meanwhile, comprised those young men who worked for a few seasons at Bonavista (and perhaps stayed for a winter or two) as well as those families who had established a permanent residence.

In the court records below, George Walkam is referred to as "Master George Walkam" with that same specific intent used by Rev. Jones. Walkam owned the plantation next to Walkam's Brook, over which crosses Walkam's Bridge in present-day Bonavista. That plantation, known as Walkam's Room, ran from Walkam's Bridge westward toward the ocean. The whipping post was on George Walkam's property.

Magistrate Keen, on the other hand, owned Keen's Room farther south along the shoreline toward present-day Canaille. Keen's Room eventually became a National Historic Site—the Ryan Premises.

The names of Vincent, Batt, Dike, Cotterall, English, and Hobbs in the following story are not found in the petitions of 1742 or 1752 (Appendices 3 and 4), nor do those names occur elsewhere in the contemporary records. It is likely that they were seasonal workers (Jones might have referred to them as servants) employed by Walkam, Keen, and perhaps others. George Walkam's name, however, occurs on both petitions and reflects his stature in the community.

In December 1748, John Vincent promised a friend, Joseph Batt, the use of his pipe. When Batt visited Vincent on December 20 to borrow the pipe, Batt stole a pair of women's shoes and buckles. Vincent did not realize that the shoes and buckles were missing until later and didn't, at first, connect Batt's visit with their disappearance. Over a month later, Vincent saw Elizabeth Dike wearing the shoes that had been removed from his home and, a few days later, noticed that John Cotterall was wearing his buckles. When Vincent confronted Elizabeth Dike about the shoes, she told Vincent that Joseph Batt had told her that he had bought the shoes, and that he had sold the buckles to Cotterall.

Vincent took his case to Magistrate Keen. On hearing the evidence of Batt, Dike, Cotterall, and Vincent, as well as that of James English and Joseph Hobbs (who were present at Vincent's house when Batt came to borrow the pipe), Keen brought down his verdict: "15 stipes on the bare back by the hands of the Beadle at the Publick Whipping Post." The whipping post at Bonavista was, as noted earlier, on George Walkam's land, near Walkam's Brook leading to what was then called Burton's Pond (now Harbour Pond). It was therefore in a prominent location and a constant reminder of the consequences of disobeying the law. After sentence had been handed down by Keen, Batt was taken to the whipping post, stripped to the waist, and secured to the beams. However, a few moments before punishment was to be given, Master George Walkam (as he was referenced in the court records to denote plantation ownership) demanded that another hearing be granted. Immediately, James Walker, John Parker, and John Cotterall untied Batt and led him quickly away from the site.

Keen would not be overruled, however, and upon enlisting the support of his constable, he recovered Batt and had the sentence carried out. George Walkam was quoted as saying to the mob, "Now, gentlemen, if you would all be of my mind, we would take the plaintiff and serve him the same way." Walkam's accomplices agreed, and John Cotterall and Joseph Batt seized Vincent and began to batter him. Keen's report states that if he, Keen, had not intervened on Vincent's behalf, Vincent probably would have died. A few days later, George Walkam and others gathered at "Cook's Room," owned by Mr. Joseph White and a short distance from Keen's Room, and from there proceeded to William

Stocks in front of the courthouse in Bonavista. (Glenn Mitchell)

Keen's premises, where they used hatchets to destroy his flake. On February 14, that same group gathered around the whipping post and tore it down. It is unknown if the whipping post was replaced, but there are no further references to the use of either a whipping post, or the blocks, in the records. We can only conjecture on whether competition, or even hostility, may have existed between Keen and Walkam to precipitate the confrontations. But there is another possibility. We talked about the Quaker presence at Bonavista, in Chapter 6, and that the Quakers did not believe in corporal punishment. Joseph White was a well-known Quaker, and it was at his Fishing Room that George Walkam and his men gathered on February 14. Aggression by Walkam and the threat of punishment against Vincent would appear to be inconsistent with the conduct of Quakers. Magistrate Bland, in 1802, noted that criminals occasionally went unpunished as a consequence of the lack of a jail, suggesting that stocks and whipping posts were no longer in use. The actions of Walkam and others may have ended corporal punishment at Bonavista for good.

Notes

Correspondence and governor's appointments are found in the Colonial Office 194 Series.

The details of the trial are found in the Colonial Secretary's Letterbooks, GN2/1/A, Vol. 1.

Cook's Room is likely White's Room in Bland's Register of Fishing Rooms (Appendix 2).

9 — CAPTAIN GEORGE RIDER

As a counterpoint to the mercy shown by George Walkam in eighteenth-century Bonavista, we should introduce Captain George Rider. Rider worked for the Lesters in Trinity and, for a time, ran his own enterprise from Bonavista with a "Thomas Thompson" as his agent. Perhaps his first appearance in the court records occurs in 1755, in Trinity, when a Sarah Legge demanded support from Captain Rider for her baby daughter, Martha, who, Legge claimed, was his child. The court's decision is unclear.

The St. John's court, October 3, 1774, records the following: "George Rider, merchant, late of Poole in the county of Dorset, Merchant, not having God before his eyes but being moved and seduced by the instigation of the Devil, on the first day of January (1774) with force and arms near his house in Bonavista in the Island of Newfoundland in upon one Michael Kennedy, a native of the Kingdom of Ireland . . . standing near the door not having any weapon then drawn, nor the aforesaid Michael Kennedy having first struck on the aforesaid George Rider or feloniously did make an assault, and that the aforesaid George Rider with a certain gun of the value of ten shillings which he, the said George Rider, in hands then there had hold, loaded with lead, shot the said Michael Kennedy under the ear of him, the said Michael Kennedy, the aforesaid Michael Kennedy three mortal wounds . . . Michael Kennedy then thereon instantly died . . ."

Two days later, on October 5, the court entry reads as follows:

". . . the court adjourned till tomorrow morning 10 o'clock, after discharging George Rider (upon) paying his fine(?)."

And two days after that, on October 7, in a curious and perhaps telling move, Governor Shuldham appointed George Rider as naval officer for Bonavista. In 1776, Shuldham's replacement, Governor Montagu, ordered William Keen and George Rider to answer for the charges against them for the "improper transaction" relative to one James Barnes of Greenspond, "to refund the exorbitant fee" and warning them "against like behaviour in the future." A year later, August 9, 1777, Governor Montagu appointed George Rider justice of the peace in Bonavista. A short while after that, twelve individuals of Bonavista sent a petition to Keen to present to Governor Montagu claiming that since becoming justice of the peace, Rider punished and mistreated them "severely and corporally," especially when drunk, and that he "generally abuses his power and authority." In the petition, they further accuse him of "premeditated and wilful murder" (presumably referencing the Michael Kennedy murder) and that they, the petitioners, fear it will only get worse. The full petition, and the governor's letter back to Rider, is found in Appendix 5.

Little is known about George Rider thereafter. The surname Ryder and Rider appears from time to time thereafter in Bonavista, though there is no clarity on whether those individuals were related to George Rider, or even, in fact, if Rider had a family.

Notes

Captain Rider's trial for murder is located in CO 194, vol. 32, pages 19-25.

The petition of 1777 (Appendix 5) can be found at The Rooms Archives, St. John's, GN2/1/A, Box 3.

10 — FRENCH PRESENCE

The hostility between the French and English during Queen Anne's War in North America, and which we saw in part at Bonavista, ended in 1713 with the Treaty of Utrecht. One component of this treaty was the French Shore, which extended from Cape Bonavista along the coastline to Point Riche on the Northern Peninsula. On the French Shore, the French were not permitted to settle permanently but were given the right to prosecute a seasonal fishery. Although the harbour and town of Bonavista were actually south of Cape Bonavista, and therefore part of the coastline on which the French were permitted to fish, the French for the most part confined fishing activities farther north and west, toward Cape St. John. Correspondence by Rev. Jones and Mr. Peasely at Bonavista, and the Colonial Records, do not indicate any French presence at Bonavista through the first half of the 1700s. George Davis's letter to Captain James Cook in 1764 (Appendix 1) further states that "(Mr. Tizzard) has known that part of Newfoundland (around Fogo) for 40 years, and that he never knew a French boat or ship to the southward of Cape John—which is 14 leagues NNW from Twillingate . . . Bonavista was settled as early as any part of the land and never any Frenchman yet fished there."

The year 1756 saw the beginning of the Seven Years' War. At that time, French fishing paused in Newfoundland and did not restart until the end of the war in 1763. With the war's end, the new Treaty of Paris re-established the same French Shore. After 1763, the French began to assert their right to fish along the French Shore near Bonavista. The arrival of French ships was new to the merchants and fishermen of Bonavista, who were strongly opposed to their presence.

In 1764, orders from England were sent to the "Governor of Newfoundland and the commanders of the British supervising ships" that there would be no interference by fishermen along the French Shore from "Cape Bonavista to Point Riche" as they were obligated to "conform to the treaty." There would be "no obstruction" by the fishermen and merchants, and the "admirals in charge of the harbours shall protect and allow the French to build huts and stages (while) the French shall not, in turn interfere with English fishing."

Conflicts arose at Bonavista, however, as the merchants and fishermen were not willing to allow interference with their operations. Finally, in 1770, the French ambassador to England submitted a "Memorial on the subject of the Fishery of Newfoundland during the season of 1769," in which he wrote that the French "have suffered injustices, contrary to their treaty rights." Specifically, they were being denied the use of "Bonavista Cove." In response, England wrote to Newfoundland's Governor Byron that "The King's orders are to observe strictly and fairly the treaty rights of France in dealing with French fishermen between Cape Bonavista and Point Riche."

Two years later, on July 4, 1772, Benjamin Lester, a merchant at nearby Trinity, in Trinity Bay, wrote to Governor Shuldham in St. John's that "eighteen boats from two French vessels fished in the harbour of Port Bonavista and landed to cure their fish and build a landing stage. . . . The English fishermen recently combined to throw part of their catch into the sea." Captain James Hawker, at Trinity, also sent a letter to Shuldham, saying that the French have tried to build stages and cure fish in "Port Bonavista" and that they have been several times driven off—sometimes even coming to blows. In Governor Shuldham's letter to England, he noted that he instructed Captain Hawker, who was responsible for patrolling the region, "to proceed forthwith (to Bonavista) to settle the affair in the most amicable manner he can until His Majesty's pleasure is known." Governor Shuldham went on to say that he believed that "the French have no claim or title to fish at, or resort to Port Bonavista, as it lies south from the Cape of that name, which by treaty is their boundary." In other words, in Shuldham's opinion, the French Shore was "north of Cape Bonavista," and since the harbour and town of Bonavista were "south of Cape Bonavista," the French had no rights. Shuldham, therefore, wrote that he was "inclined to continue in this belief from an order I see in the records of 1767 from Commodore Palliser directed to the Justice and Fishing Admirals at the Harbour of Bonavista, authorizing them for the above reason not to permit the French to resort to or fish at that Port."

Captain Hawker's letter was revealing in that he described the event itself. "Soon after my arrival here, I was told of the French having attempted this spring to build stages and cure their fish at the Port Harbour of Bonavista. Mr. Lester, who was there at the time as well as several other English people having fisheries at that place, obliged them to go away with all their boats from which was attended with a great deal of altercation on both sides, and I am afraid not without some blows and, as I expect, shall have some complaint from the French." "The right of the French curing and fishing at Port Bonavista has been long disputed . . . they have often attempted it, and as often been drove off by the English." Captain Hawker went on to explain that the harbour of Bonavista was "two leagues southwest of Cape Bonavista" and stated that he "must beg to know whether I am to suffer the French to take and cure fish at the Port or Harbour of Bonavista." Hawker closes his letter with a glimpse into Bonavista's history:

> "I am told by Mr. Lester that he has now at one of his Rooms at Port Bonavista an Order from Mr. Palliser (a former governor of Newfoundland) not to suffer the French to fish there, and strictly forbidding him giving them any assistance, or suffering them to harbour there. Mr. Lester is one of the principal men trading in the country, has sixteen ships of his own in the trade besides many coasting vessels, and comes every year to this country from England."

In Lester's own letter, he wrote to Governor Shuldham that he was in Bonavista on June 11, 1772, and that the French had eighteen boats fishing in the harbour belonging to two vessels of France and that they were using "one of the inhabitants stages at Bonavista" to process their catch. The French, according to Lester, were also building a stage and lodge for their men. Lester met with the "principal merchants and masters of fishing ships, and it was our opinion that they should not land any more fish." Lester instructed the French "officer" that they had no right at Bonavista, as it was "southward of Cape Bonavista." "We gave them till the 13th to move, but to the contrary they brought more fish." "We then insisted on their moving it (their buildings) immediately, or we would heave it into the sea, which they dared us to do, they having 6 or 7 quintals on the land, which we hove into the sea, hauled down their tilt and what part of a stage they had built and sent that afloat also, and that evening or about midnight they quitted the place and went to their ships." "This we did in consequence of His Excellency Hugh Palliser's Esq. Order and the Words of the Treaty." The French leaders of the failed effort at Bonavista were Le Marie of Granville and Thomas le Tournour of Havre de Grace. Both communities (Granville and Havre de Grace) lie along the northeast coast of France.

As noted earlier, Governor Shuldham sent all correspondence to England seeking clarity on French rights at Bonavista. Two months later, on September 2, the Earl of Dartmouth made it clear. "(Your letters have been) received and laid before the King and it being the unanimous opinion of all His Majesty's confidential servants that the subjects of France have an indisputable right to a concurrent fishery in the harbour of Bonavista. It is His Majesty's pleasure that you do not dispute that point, and that the subjects of France be permitted to carry on a concurrent fishery in that harbour . . ." This was certainly not the response that either Governor Shuldham or Benjamin Lester wanted to hear.

Over the ensuing months, correspondence between English officials in England, and French officials at Versailles, France, came to quick agreement that the French had, indeed, a right to fish at the harbour in Bonavista. In one letter, Rochford, in England, to Blaquiere, in France, summarized that the English were at fault in opposing French fishing in the Bay of Bonavista and that "French rights begin at Cape Bonavista and follow the coast northwards round to Point Riche." Further, Rochford indicated that he had instructed Lord Dartmouth to write Governor Shuldham, ordering compensation to the French fishermen for their loss. The wording ". . . and follow the coast northwards round to Point Riche" is, of course, unfortunate. From Cape Bonavista, the coast actually runs southward, along the west side of the Bonavista Peninsula, before turning northward and westward.

On February 15, 1775, Governor Shuldham had finished his assessment of the damages claimed by the French, which, accounting for damage to nets and loss of fish, came to 43,460 livres. London believed that the interpretation was open to some discussion but agreed to pay the entire amount.

Upon completion of his duties, Governor Shuldham was relieved of his duties, and the new governor, Robert Duff, was sent to Newfoundland. At the same time, an Act of Parliament was passed in England clarifying the rules as they pertained to Newfoundland. When Governor Duff arrived in St. John's, he "caused the principal inhabitants of this town to be assembled, my commission to be solemnly and publicly read to them, and took upon me the Government of this island its dependencies accordingly." Governor Duff also clarified the new rules, including "a proclamation forbidding all persons from offering or allowing any obstruction or interruption to the subjects of France, in the enjoyment of a concurrent fishery between Cape Bonavista and Point Riche," and "a proclamation for preventing any exclusive possession of land to the northward of Cape Bonavista and Point Riche." Once again, the words "northward of Cape Bonavista" appears in the formal proclamation.

In any event, clarification on the Treaty of Paris did not appear to have resulted in a resurgence of French fishermen at Bonavista. There are no references to a French presence thereafter, and, with the Treaty of Versailles in 1783, the French Shore was redefined from Cape St. John to Cape Ray.

Notes

For a general discussion of the French Shore, see:
The French Treaty Shore: https://www.heritage.nf.ca/articles/exploration/french-shore.php

Most of the correspondence, including the letters from Trinity, are located at the National Archives of the United Kingdom:
http://discovery.nationalarchives.gov.uk/details/r/C7346159

Additional correspondence is found in the Colonial Records 194 series. The names of those leading the French fishing efforts in Bonavista are found in CO194, vol. 32, page 56.

PART THREE: THE GROWTH OF A TOWN

11 — THE BONAVISTA MAP AND REGISTER OF FISHING ROOMS

The eighteenth-century map "A View of Bonavista in Newfoundland" is something of an enigma. It appears in Prowse's *A History of Newfoundland*, which was published in 1895. The original map is housed at the British Library in London, England, and copies can be located at the Map Room and the Centre for Newfoundland Studies (CNS) at the Queen Elizabeth II Library at Memorial University of Newfoundland (MUN). The British Library has recorded that it received the map in 1881, but, through direct correspondence with them, they acknowledge that they did not record how they obtained possession. Neither the Map Room, nor the CNS, at QEII have any information on it. The author consulted with local historians, and searched through various information sources, both at local libraries and online, but with no success.

Dr. Gordon Handcock, formerly a historical geographer at MUN, believes that the map was probably developed by a member of Captain James Cook's team around the 1760s, and the British Library supports this opinion. It is a nautical map, as it denotes depths at various locations just off shore, and provides nautical information in the upper right corner. The outline of the coast is generally accurate. For our purposes, we will assume that the map was developed around 1765.

About forty years after we assume the map was produced, Sir Erasmus Gower, governor of Newfoundland, wrote a letter to the magistrate at Bonavista, John Bland, requesting the boundaries of "Ship's Rooms" in and around Bonavista. In his response, Bland noted that all of what are now called "Fishing Rooms" in Bonavista were once "Ship's Rooms." Gower was seeking clarity on laws pertaining to land ownership along the coastline and needed an inventory of infrastructure. By Bland's account, the "Fishing Acts of King William III" to which Governor Gower referred only applied to those rooms that ships of the migratory fishery from years ago visited on an annual basis, and since that era has long since passed, the Acts no longer apply. In fact, Bland noted that the Ship's Rooms have been abandoned by the ships of the migratory fishery and "their progressive possession and improvement by adventurers and planters have so confused and blended this sort of property that it is impossible now to say which were once Ship's Rooms. The remembrance of these things has passed away."

Bland was correct to say that the transition from Ship's Rooms to Fishing Rooms had been happening for some time. In 1722, it was reported that "there have not been a sufficient number of fishing ships to employ the Ship's Rooms" and that "several stages are possessed by the inhabitants of Bonavista, occasioned by the small number of ships coming to fish here . . . several of the inhabitants do and have possessed ship's rooms for several years past." Many years ago, then, even relative to 1722, the migratory fishery had succumbed to the process of settlement. Perhaps some of the plantations operated by the planters listed in the early census of 1675 and 1677 were once Ship's Rooms in the process of being possessed by those who would become permanent inhabitants.

Bland created a detailed account of the twenty-eight Fishing Rooms situated along the coastline of Bonavista, including occupant, claimant, "in what manner held," as well as additional buildings and detailed specifics of boundaries. The report is called the "Register of Fishing Rooms in Bonavista, 1805–06," and many of the details of the Fishing Rooms are contained in Appendix 2. The general locations of the Fishing Rooms have been added to the Map of Bonavista by the author based on the boundaries provided by Bland to the governor. The result gives us an opportunity to take close stock of Bonavista as it was in the mid-1700s through to the early 1800s.

When we look broadly at the map of Bonavista, habitation is clearly evident. The Fishing Rooms stretch along the coastline from Bayley's Cove, along Mockbeggar, Bonavista Harbour, and Canaille, as well as flakes or lodgings along the eastern side of "Shoal Pond" and inland at Canaille. This indicates what we would have clearly surmised—that settlement at Bonavista began along the shoreline, extending from Bayley's Cove to Canaille, and that it expanded inland, farther east, through the 1700s and 1800s.

If we look more closely at the map of Bonavista, a few details emerge. Bayley's Cove, clearly identified along the northern extent of Bonavista, is perhaps named after one of the early settlers. A "John Bayly" is noted at Barrow Harbour (near present-day Salvage in Bonavista Bay) in the 1675 census while "Richard Bayly" was settled at Bay de Verde. Old maps of Barrow Harbour denote Keat's Island and Tilly's Cove, both of which reflect names in the 1677 census for Bonavista. It is likely, then, that planters operated from both Barrow Harbour and

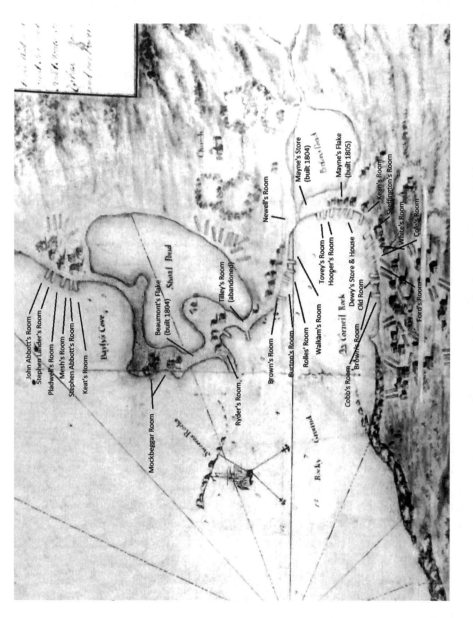

Bonavista (circa 1765). (British Library. Ms 31357 M.)

Bonavista in the 1600s. "Shoal Pond" is larger than the body of water we now call O'Dea's (or Old Days) Pond. The areas known as Mockbeggar and Bonavista Harbour are clearly identifiable. Burton's Pond was likely named by "Stephen Barton (or Burton)," who signed the 1742 and 1752 petitions (Appendices 3 and 4), or an ancestor or family member. Bland does not speak of Burton's Pond when describing boundaries of the Fishing Rooms but calls it Harbour Pond instead. The map does not indicate a bridge crossing the brook adjoining Burton's Pond with Bonavista Harbour, but forty years later, Bland speaks of "the bridge at Walkam's brook" when delineating boundaries.

The presence of "Corneil Rock" farther south is also worthy of note. Other documents of the late 1700s referenced "Corneil" or "Cornail" in southern Bonavista, while Bland's Registry refers to this area as "Corneil." Almost certainly, the southern area of Bonavista now commonly called "Canaille" was, at one time, spelled and pronounced differently.

Another interesting aspect of this map is the distinct building at the eastern edge of Canaille. It looks, to the untrained eye, like a schoolhouse. Although Rev. Jones clearly identified that two schools were initiated at Bonavista during his tenure in the 1720s and 1730s, it is unclear if buildings were actually constructed for that purpose or if school instruction was conducted in a building already built for other purposes. The other distinct building is the church located just east of "Shoal Pond." This would have been the building that had been in need of repair when Rev. Jones arrived in 1725 and which was ultimately completed in 1731. We will speak to those details in Chapter 12.

Looking northwestward from the courthouse toward Mockbeggar.
(Wilson Whiffen via Ross Abbott)

The delineation of separate buildings on the map of Bonavista provides the opportunity to match these structures with the list of Fishing Rooms provided in the Register developed by Bland. The author has examined the specifications on location, boundaries, and structures to identify where each Fishing Room is located. The identification of these Fishing Rooms from the 1905–06 Register has been added by the author to the 1765 map of Bonavista.

The Fishing Room farthest north in Bayley's Cove was John Abbott's Room, owned and operated by John Abbott, and passed to him through inheritance. He also owned Kate's Room in Bayley's Cove, which was being leased to William Hicks & Co. Stephen Lander's Room was owned and operated by Stephen Lander and had also been passed down through the family. Also situated in Bayley's Cove were Pladwell's Room, which was owned by Hannah Pladwell, Stephen Abbott's Room, operated and owned by Sarah Abbott upon her husband's death, and Mesh's Room, owned by Rachel Mesh and operated by Moses Keel and Richard Mesh. Thus, three of the six Fishing Rooms at Bayley's Cove were owned by women, whose husbands had died and left each wife his plantation.

Hannah Pladwell, Rachel Mesh, and Sarah Abbott could rightly be considered among the first female pioneers of the business community at Bonavista. Nonetheless, although the petitions of the 1700s and early 1800s were signed by the more prominent members of the Bonavista community, their names do not appear in any of them (see Appendices 3–5, 8–10).

The Mockbeggar Room, known more recently as the Mockbeggar Plantation, was the largest Fishing Room in Bonavista. It was owned by Samuel Rolles but was occupied by Benjamin Lester and Co. at Trinity. It was the only Fishing Room with three stages. In fact, "Plantation" is arguably a more accurate label, as these properties were relatively large production facilities. The Mockbeggar Plantation is now a Provincial Historic Site and is discussed in Chapter 26.

Beaumont's Flake was built in 1804 to cure fish brought to Bonavista from the French Shore, which at that time extended from Cape St. John to Cape Ray. Ryder's Room, located on Newman's Point, was owned by Benjamin Lester & Co. of Trinity. The name perhaps originated with George Rider, a ship's captain from the 1700s (see Chapter 9). Newman's Point may have been given that name by one of the early planters (Robert or William Newman) of the 1675 or 1677 census. Tilley's Room is not listed in Bland's Register, but Bland does make note of it as a "void room called Tilley's Room" between Ryder's Room and Brown's Room. The surname "Tilley" is found in the original 1675 census and frequently thereafter.

The Mockbeggar Plantation. (Glenn Mitchell)

Brown's Room was owned, in 1805, by Joseph Brown and his brothers and sisters. Their father was William Brown, Esq., former magistrate at Bonavista. Burton's Room was owned by Stephen Burton and his family, who we have already seen were present in Bonavista in the 1740s. Rolles' Room was owned by Magistrate Bland.

Walkam's Room was likely named for the early Walkam family. The first "manchild" of Bonavista was a Walkam (Appendix 1), and the surname appears in the census for 1708. Walkam's Room was located just north of the brook passing from Harbour Pond to Bonavista Harbour.

Newell's Room was located to the south of that same brook and along the stretch of land separating Harbour Pond from the ocean. Court records indicate that this was the first Room, or Plantation, not only at Bonavista, but in fact throughout Newfoundland. This is perhaps not surprising given the presence of the Newell surname in the 1675 and 1677 census.

According to a court challenge to ownership of Newell's Room, Thomas Newell was "the original proprietor of a fishing plantation on the island of Newfoundland." Based on the court records, he had four children: James, Edward, Jonah, and Nehemiah (Thomas, Jr. noted in the census records was perhaps the son of Jonah). James and wife gave birth to a daughter, Elizabeth, but he, James, died before his father. Upon Thomas Newell's death, his plantation passed to his second-oldest son, then to Jonah, and from there to Jonah's successive children and grandchildren.

In the 1760s, Elizabeth's son, Richard Abbott, contested the passage of

Thomas Newell's plantation to his second-oldest son, Edward, and from there to Jonah, arguing that Thomas's plantation should have reverted to Elizabeth, since James, her father, was the oldest son. The Abbott family ultimately lost this battle in 1779. Newell's Room in Bland's Register lists Thomas Newell and Giles Hosier as "claimants." As we'll see in Chapter 15, Thomas Newell and the wife of Giles Hosier (Grace Newell) were siblings descended from Jonah Newell.

Mayne's Store and Mayne's Flake were built by John Mayne in 1804–05. Mayne was the resident doctor at Bonavista and a good friend of Magistrate Bland. Tovey's Room was built by John Tovey of St. John's and was being rented to John Mayne. Hooper's Room was built by Stephen Hooper and rented to Richard and Thomas Ryder. Dewy's Store and Dwelling House was owned by John Green of Trinity.

Shambler's Room was likely also one of the oldest Rooms at Bonavista, as the name Shambler was evident in the 1675 census. It was one of the few Rooms with two flakes.

Kean's Room was owned by "Captain Kean of the Navy," descended from the original William Keen of Bonavista mentioned earlier during the French attack at Bonavista in 1704–05. This Room also had two stages and would be purchased by James Ryan in 1869 (Chapter 23) and is now a National Historic Site.

Bonavista Harbour looking south toward Canaille. The Ryan Premises (originally Kean's Room) are in the background, far left. (Wilson Whiffen via Ross Abbott)

Skiffington's Room was originated by George Skiffington, who, like Kean, was referenced in the battle for Bonavista in the early 1700s. Kean and Skiffington were business partners during the 1710s. White's Room was owned and occupied by Charles Saint, one of the early converts to Methodism at Bonavista. Cole's Room was owned by B. Lester & Co. and occupied by William Cole. It is worth noting that along with Charles Saint, another early convert to Methodism was Benjamin Cole. Ford's Room was owned by B. Lester & Co. and occupied by another Magistrate at Bonavista, Gerrard Ford.

Old Room was owned by B. Lester & Co. Brown's Room (the second Room so named) and Cobb's Room were owned by Joseph Brown and his brothers and sisters.

The Treaty of Utrecht of 1713 gave fishing rights to the French from Cape Bonavista northward toward Cape Riche along the west coast of the Northern Peninsula. The town of Bonavista, including Bayley's Cove, Mockbeggar, and Canaille, fall within that French Shore. We've already documented confrontation between the French and Bonavista in Chapter 10. Other evidence of a French presence, even for seasonal fishing, has been non-existent. It should, however, be noted that John and Joseph Foquet (various spellings) signed the 1742 and 1752 petitions at Bonavista (Appendices 3 and 4) and that William Browne purchased a plantation from "Joshua Foquet" in 1784. Although "Foquet" does not prove a French presence, the surname does not appear elsewhere in any records. Beaumond's Flake, situated at Mockbeggar, and owned by Jean Beaumond, was built in 1804. The description of the property states that Beaumond's Flake "consists only of a flake for curing fish brought from the North, or French Shore." A second property, Mayne's Flake, built by John Mayne in 1805, describes it as "a flake erected for the purpose of drying fish brought from the North Shore," or, as more commonly known today, the French Shore. In 1783, the French Shore was changed according to the Treaty of Versailles to extend from Cape St. John (west and north of Bonavista) to Cape Ray.

Notes

The Colonial Office 194 Series contains the detailed Register of Fishing Rooms 1805–06 and the court challenge to ownership of Newell's Room (vol. 16). The transcriptions of the 1742 and 1752 petitions are in the possession of David Bradley, Maritime History Archive, Memorial University of Newfoundland (MUN)—the originals of these petitions are obtained through the Society for the Propagation of the Gospel records at the Centre for Newfoundland Studies

(CNS), MUN. The author is grateful to Dr. Handcock, David Bradley, and staff at the British Library, CNS, MUN's Map Room, and The Rooms (St. John's) for their assistance in trying to add additional detail to the Map of Bonavista.

Barrow Harbour 18th Century Map:
http://collections.mun.ca/cdm/ref/collection/maps/id/319

Among many other sources, a good discussion of James Cook (and Governor Hugh Palliser) is found in the *Newfoundland Quarterly*, Vol. 69, No. 2, October, 1972. "James Cook, Hugh Palliser and the Newfoundland Fishery," by William H. Whiteley.

The discussion of Ship's Rooms in 1722 is taken from the Calendar of State Papers, Colonial Series. America and the West Indies, vol. 33. 1722-23.

12 — THE INTRODUCTION OF RELIGION

In a letter to the "Lords of Trade" of England in 1716, the merchants and masters of ships of Poole wrote that "since the true worship of Almighty God is the glory of all lands, a sufficient number of ministers of the Church of England may be sent to reside in the principal harbours of the island (of Newfoundland) to instruct the inhabitants and teach their children and servants . . ." Whether as a consequence of this petition or otherwise, a missionary presence in Newfoundland became firmly established in the 1720s.

i) Reverend Henry Jones

Rev. Henry Jones and his young family arrived in Bonavista in mid-May, 1725, likely on a merchant vessel either directly from England or via St. John's. He had recently been ordained and was working for the "Society for the Propagation of the Gospel in Foreign Parts," or SPG. This organization was formed in 1701 in an effort, as the title suggests, to promote the Church of England in the British colonies by sending missionaries and literature to "foreign parts," supporting education, and promoting the construction of churches and schools. Early supporters of the SPG were also concerned about "dissenters" (e.g., Quakers) or Roman Catholic missionaries and wanted to inhibit their impact on growing communities in the New World. The SPG still exists today.

As there was no residence at Bonavista for a local minister, Rev. Jones and his family settled into temporary accommodations during the summer. In an early letter back to the SPG, Jones reported that he received "a very kind recognition from the inhabitants of this place." In the next few months, Jones worked diligently in line with the goals of the SPG. He quickly circulated a series of questions around the community:

1. At what place shall divine service be performed this winter?
2. How shall the minister be provided with fuel?
3. Shall the old part of the church be rebuilt? If so, who shall undertake to see it done; and how shall the charges be defrayed?

4. Shall a dwelling house be built (at the public expense) next spring for the use of the minister? If so, shall it be made convenient to perform divine worship in, when the church shall be too cold to assemble ourselves in, on that occasion?
5. How shall poor people (who by sickness or otherwise are, or may be, incapable of supporting themselves) be assisted or maintained?
6. Shall a Charity School be begun to be founded in this place?

At a public meeting organized by Rev. Jones, and during further discussions over the course of the following year, the town committed to "rebuilding and enlarging the church next spring (i.e., in 1726) . . . and to provide all things necessary to be used in divine service (communion table, font)" and that it be large enough to contain 100 people, and to the construction of a schoolhouse and charity school. As well, "several persons promised to send one child each spring of the year and to pay for its teaching." Jones further noted that "we have fixed on a Dame who is very willing to make the teaching of them her entire business if it can be made a sufficient maintenance for her." Firewood and funds are also promised by some of the inhabitants to support the new missionary, his family, and his efforts. In the fall of 1725, Jones and his family moved into a "dwelling house" that would have been vacant for the winter.

Clearly, Rev. Jones had made significant progress during his first few months in Bonavista. He had established clear goals for the coming months. As well, it is clear that the residents of Bonavista were quite agreeable to and supportive of these aims. Nonetheless, Jones had some concerns from what he had seen living among the inhabitants. In a letter to the Bishop of London written in the fall of 1725, Jones noted that while he hoped that the inhabitants would be able to pay for their children's instruction, some "are very poor" and "I fear the poverty of the generality of people will be a great obstruction." Jones also noted that "it has been the custom in this place to be married without publishing the bans and we have here no licenses."

Rev. Jones continued at Bonavista through 1726 until December, when, for health reasons he returned to England "ten days before Christmas Day" with a "great cold." He and his family returned to Bonavista on May 31, 1727, and "was very courteously received by the inhabitants who had by subscription satisfied a school mistress for teaching all the poor children sent to her this year and have contributed as largely to me as usual." This is the first indication we have that school instruction was taking place in Bonavista, and for that matter in Newfoundland. Jones stayed in Bonavista through the summer and into the winter season and provided school instruction himself in "writing and arithmetick" and in discharging "the great truth." As Jones provided school instruction during the winter, it is probable that the schoolmistress either relocated inland during the winter (a common practice) or returned to England.

In 1729, England introduced the era of Naval Governance in Newfoundland by a local governor with a commission empowering him to appoint magistrates at the local level. Newfoundland's first governor was Captain Henry Osborne, appointed in 1729 and stationed in St. John's. The magistrate he appointed for Bonavista was Rev. Henry Jones.

Rev. Jones discovered very quickly that administering justice to a community that also provided for a portion of his income was not without problems. On December 8, 1729, in a letter to the Bishop of London, he stated that "the masters of families continue their subscriptions to me, but upon the punishment of some lawless persons for their offences . . . most of the servants have withdrawn their (subscriptions) to my no small detriment." He further indicated "for the future I may hope (with my associates) for less trouble; the first onset towards procuring a reformation being generally the most difficult." Jones was hopeful that he would be able to continue to perform his duties as magistrate and that the local servants would return to providing financial support (i.e., subscriptions) for his performance as a missionary.

From Jones's correspondence, we get some indication of the population of Bonavista. In a letter dated December 1, 1729, he indicated that "there will be resident this winter in Bonavista about 200 people and more than that number being removed for the winter." He also stated that about 100 persons in Bonavista routinely relocated to two particular locations about forty leagues (or sixty miles) "to the northward." To ensure that those people continued to receive spiritual guidance, Jones appointed "the most proper persons" to officiate as readers for everyone and gave them sufficient bibles and other literature to assist with keeping the Sabbath Day. Jones took particular care to note in a request to the SPG for more books that he was in need of "a few of good print for the ancient people."

Further to this, £130 had been raised for the rebuilding of the church and for glass work to be completed in England. Jones hoped that it would all be completed and delivered in the summer of 1730. Although "a gentleman of London has been pleased to present us with a neat set of vessels for the communion and a very handsome stone font," problems and delays resulted when "work has been much retarded by some hurt which three workmen received by the fall of one of the scaffolds." It was not until June 29, 1731, that Jones reported that "the church here is near finished," and in a letter dated October 8, 1731, Jones stated that the "church is fitted for use but not so well finished as it would be were our people able to bear the charge." For the record, then, while we do not know the date of construction of the initial church in Bonavista, we can fix as 1731 the year in which it was completed sufficiently for use by Rev. Jones and the inhabitants of the town. Meanwhile, Jones also noted in 1731 that "we have a school mistress that teaches between 20 and 30 children; she is very careful and writes a good hand and shall want no encouragement or assistance that I shall be able to give her."

Jones continued to flourish in Bonavista through the 1730s. He noted in 1734 that "I proceed cheerfully to perform all parts of my ministerial function (with) every family in this place constituting a part of my congregation. Though the number of our communicants is not great, yet, thank God, tis increasing among which are two that have been dissenters, one of each denomination." On July 8, 1734, Jones reported that he had baptized 114 individuals (seventeen of whom were baptized at Trinity, and among those in Bonavista, five were adults). We can conclude, then, that between 1725 and 1734, Jones baptized at least ninety-two children, an average of nine children per year. Among the five adults baptized at Bonavista, three were married women born of "annabaptist parents and bred up in that persuasion," and one was a father of a numerous family. Later, in 1741, Jones baptized eighteen children.

The "annabaptists" to which Jones referred were the Quakers of whom we've spoken in Chapter 6. Quakers, as with other annabaptists, did not believe in baptism by newborn babies, but rather in baptism as a personal choice. Baptism of an "annabaptist" was considered a victory by Rev. Jones. As we'll see, Peasely also referred to "Anabaptists" within the same context. Both missionaries were careful to record the number of baptisms during their tenures and to transmit those numbers to the SPG. We know that marriages and burials were also performed in Bonavista, but documentation of their numbers were not kept—or at least were not conveyed to the SPG as part of the official preserved documents.

The general problem with respect to making a living in Bonavista did not diminish through the course of Jones's tenure. As late as 1740, Jones references the "suffering through the poverty, removal or decease of many of the inhabitants," indicating not only the challenges for the inhabitants, but for the missionary as well. Although Jones doesn't document burial services directly, some headstones remain at the Anglican Church in Bonavista marking the death of individuals during Jones's period. William Dare died on August 23, 1725 (aged 46), Thomas Addams (of Frampton, near Dorchester, aged 26) died on August 13, 1729, and Roger Gantlet, aged 30, died July 12, 1734. Another, erected to John Dare (1727), bears the epitaph:

As you are now, so once was I,
Therefore prepare yourselves to die.
As I am now, so shall ye be,
Therefore prepare to follow me.

Before leaving the subject of early headstones in Bonavista, we should also note the inscriptions on two other headstones at the Anglican cemetery in Bonavista. The first records the death of Rose Amer, daughter of William and Tabitha Amer, who died on August 8, 1717, aged 6 years. The second is of Ann Burton, wife of John Burton and daughter of William and Tabitha Amer, who also died on August 8, 1717, aged 17 years. Burton (or Barton) is present as a surname on both the 1742 and 1752 petitions (Appendices 3 and 4), while William Amer's name is present on the 1752 petition. The surname Gantlett is present in both the 1677 and 1708 censuses.

In 1732, Jones wrote "though I have much affection for the people, and should be unwilling to leave them, if I could subsist here" he would benefit from some other place as "my bare fuel (costs) at least £15 yearly in this cold climate." In later correspondence he speaks of Fogo, where the people are "pretty numerous" and in want of a minister, and asks of the possibility of ministering in St. John's. He is also "hoping your Lordship (the Bishop of London) will grant me some settlement in England in a few years."

The SPG meeting minutes for 1739 indicate that Rev. Jones wrote a letter to "His Grace the Lord Archbishop of Canterbury" stating that "the inhabitants of Bonavista . . . are in the summer season somewhat numerous, when two or three hundred often attend the divine service, but their number of communicants seldom exceed ten or twelve, that there have been baptized in the two last years about twenty children and that the congregation is in a flourishing condition."

On August 19, 1741, Rev. Kilpatrick died in Trinity. Jones had written of Kilpatrick in earlier correspondence and had visited his fellow missionary on various occasions over the course of the past few years. They had likely developed a close bond, finding themselves in close proximity under similar circumstances. Jones wrote that "my dear friend Reverend Mr. Robert Kilpatrick departed this life the 19th day of August greatly lamented of all that know him. His disconsolate widow desires to present her humble service to you (the SPG Secretary) and request that you will represent her melancholy circumstances to the venerable society (i.e., the SPG) having five small children and she left not in a capacity to provide for them." Jones then requested to be removed to Trinity, which was granted December 18, 1741.

In testament to the importance of Rev. Jones to the community of Bonavista, a petition from thirty of the inhabitants of the town was sent to the SPG, dated June 10, 1742. In it they speak of "our lately being deprived of a minister by the removal of Rev. Mr. Henry Jones . . . it was the more unexpected to us especially as we are not conscious of ever giving our Minister any just grounds of complaint." They indicated that they usually raised £50 per year to support his efforts "by the voluntary subscriptions of masters and servants," an amount which compares favourably with the annual salary of between £25 and £40 sent by the SPG. The petitioners repeated the events reported by Rev. Jones with respect to losing the support of the servants as a consequence of his role as magistrate. They also highlighted the "sad state of the place in regard to the education of children, whereof there are not less than one hundred and fifty without the means of instruction or learning." The letter in its entirely is Appendix 3.

Before proceeding to events subsequent to Rev. Jones's departure from Bonavista, a few words are in order to summarize his tenure. We know that he arrived in Bonavista at a time of poverty for many, with no school and an uninhabitable church. With the support of a very agreeable and appreciative community, he succeeded in completing the church and in establishing two schools, in organizing workers and a teacher, and in collecting subscriptions from the inhabitants to pay for supplies, fuel, and salaries. He also continuously appealed to the SPG for funds and literature. Much of this was accomplished within the first six years of his tenure. He also provided for those inhabitants who left Bonavista during the winter season to go inland or farther north, and even took care to instruct the SPG to provide literature "for the ancient people," presumably because of failing eyesight.

When Rev. Jones first arrived in Bonavista in 1725, and for many years thereafter, he frequently referenced the "poor children" in the community. We know that he assisted the schoolmistress with school instruction during the winter season (when the schoolmistress had departed Bonavista). As best we know, he lived almost continuously at Bonavista from 1725 to 1741. He would have been perhaps touched as the children grew in age, just as he would have watched his own children grow. At the end of his tenure, in 1741, he wrote that "his congregation was increasing" and that "the many young people and children are growing up and I cheerfully proceed in my ministerial office." It was the first time he used words other than "the poor children."

Testament to Jones's integrity was Governor Osborne's selection of him as the magistrate for Bonavista. Osborne could have easily selected a member of the planter or merchant community but, instead, wisely chose someone who did not have a personal connection with the inhabitants and was not part of the merchant class. He could, therefore, presumably provide impartial judgment as necessary. And despite the fact that both servants and masters provided subscriptions to Jones, the schoolmistress, and to help defray the costs of construction, Jones did not let that interfere with his judicial responsibilities. As noted earlier by Jones himself (and as we saw in the Bonavista inhabitants' petition of 1742), servants in Bonavista withdrew their financial support to Jones following judgments by Jones, presumably against some of their friends. Jones was undeterred, merely hoping that, in time, residents would appreciate the circumstances and necessities.

Through the 1730s, Jones continued to increase his congregation, such that he could claim that he was able to provide the functions of ministerial responsibilities to "every family" of his congregation in the community. This would have involved a few hundred souls. Final testament to Jones's value to the community by its inhabitants is their reaction upon his departure. The decision to move Jones to Trinity was made in December 1741. We do not know when Jones was aware of this decision or when he transferred. But clearly reaction was swift, since a detailed and formal petition, signed by thirty senior members of the community, was sent in June 1742.

Some attention needs to be given to the historical record with respect to the first school and first teacher at Bonavista (and, as a consequence, in New-foundland). It has been variously reported that Rev. Jones established the first school or provided first instruction to children at dates ranging between 1722 to 1726. Close inspection of Jones's letters highlights that he was responsible for setting in motion a schoolhouse and charity school at Bonavista in 1725 (though it is unclear if new buildings were constructed for that purpose) but that the first instruction to children at Bonavista was provided by a schoolmistress in the spring of 1727. Some confusion may have arisen from summary documents from the SPG based on a Jones letter, which is dated 1725. This document incorrectly concludes that the Jones letter states that "he teaches the children there to read." This may have led to some of the erroneous conclusions about instruction in Bonavista during that decade.

Sadly, we know little of the first teacher, or "schoolmistress," in Bonavista. But we do know something of her character. Not long after Jones arrived, as we have stated earlier, Jones noted that "we have fixed on a Dame who is very willing to make the teaching of them her entire business if it can be made a sufficient maintenance for her." The words "sufficient maintenance" sound as if she was available if paid according to what she believed she was worth. In 1727, Jones further noted that the inhabitants "had by subscription satisfied a school mistress for teaching all the poor children sent to her this year" and in a separate letter notes that "all the poor children of this port whose parents would send them to school have been taught this year gratis (vis-à-vis, the SPG); the school Dame having been satisfied by the subscriptions raised here for that purpose." Again, Jones carefully noted that the schoolmistress provided instruction according to her own terms. Finally, in 1731, Jones wrote that "we have a school mistress that teaches between 20 and 30 children; she is very careful and writes a good hand and shall want no encouragement or assistance that I shall be able to give her." This observation lends credence to her level of education (as assessed by an ordained minister) and that she was as confident and assured in her management of her students that she had no interest in guidance or interference from the local minister/magistrate.

Jones's failure to record the name of his schoolmistress was not a practice exclusive to that gender. In fact, Jones never named any resident of Bonavista, choosing to refer in general to "the inhabitants" and occasionally to "masters" and "servants." This is unfortunate, since he occasionally spoke of Rev. Kilpatrick in Trinity, Rev. Fordyce in St. John's, and Governor Osborne.

The hierarchy within the fishery at Bonavista is first evident in the census of 1675, 1677, and beyond, whereby planters and their families are noted specifically, followed by an accounting of the number of servants. This is part of the general discussion of settlement in Newfoundland (see, for example, Handcock). We note here that Jones's letters left no doubt but that a two-tier class structure existed in Bonavista during his tenure. His reference to "masters" and "servants" as required to explain circumstances was made without explanation required as to the meaning of those terms. The discussion of the capacity of the inhabitants to help support salaries for himself and the schoolmistress and for the construction of buildings to support their responsibilities often made reference to the ability of the servants to support these activities. Even the requirement to build both a schoolhouse and a charity school implies the need to accommodate both tiers in the community. But the mistake should not be made that the servants were unable to play a significant role in the community itself. They were clearly paid for their work and in some cases were able to use their funds to support the construction of buildings and the education of their children. In fact, both Jones and the 1742 petitioners (Appendix 3) noted independently that some servants withheld their financial support as a consequence of Jones's judicial rulings. They were servants to the masters/planters of the community but were not incapable of exerting their own influence and were free to use their own resources as they chose.

Rev. Jones noted in a letter dated March 20, 1747, that he was fifty-six years of age and had lived in this "cold country" for "about 26 years." This would have put his birthdate around 1691 and his first arrival in Newfoundland at about 1721. There is no reason to doubt anything that Jones recorded in the numerous letters submitted by him over the course of his career, and it is difficult to imagine him making a simple miscalculation. The SPG, to whom the letter was written, would have known of his years of service in any case. It is possible, then, that he first arrived in Bonavista in 1721 as a "catechist" before being ordained as a Church of England minister, in England, in 1724. Under these circumstances, he would have not had need to correspond back to the SPG, as he would return to England in the fall. Although we have no proof, perhaps Jones, in 1721, helped to organize the initial construction of a church, since, when he arrived in 1725, he referred to "rebuilding and enlarging the church."

Jones was stationed in Trinity in 1747 when referencing his twenty-six years of service, and requested removal to a "milder climate." He returned to England in the fall of 1747 and was transferred to St. Anne's Parish, Jamaica, in the Caribbean, in 1750. The letter written by the secretary of the SPG for presentation to the governor of Jamaica noted that Jones was "venerable in his person and of tried virtue and abilities." Nothing is known of Rev. Jones and his family after 1750.

ii) Mr. William Peasely

In 1742, consequent to the petition from the inhabitants of Bonavista, the SPG agreed to send Mr. William Peasely of Trinity College, Dublin, as missionary to Bonavista. At that time, Peasely was under a "probationary term according to the standing orders of the Society." History books and articles typically reference him as "Reverend." During Peasely's tenure at Bonavista, he never signed his name as "Reverend," nor did the SPG reference him by that title.

Peasely arrived in Bonavista on June 15, 1743, via a merchant vessel from St. John's. He reported back to the SPG that "I have read prayers and preached to a large congregation twice every Sunday since my arrival and have visited most of the inhabitants, who seem well disposed to contribute towards support of a minister and are very willing to comply with the society's good resolution in appointing a house and glebe as, I apprehend, will appear by a petition next spring." He further indicated that "there is a handsome church here built of wood, which is kept in good repair and I really think the inhabitants to be in great distress for a clergyman." By October, Peasely had baptized nine children but was having great difficulty in persuading his parishioners to participate in Holy Communion . . . "they being very ignorant of the principles of their religion" . . . a comment which, intentionally or otherwise, reflected poorly on his predecessor. Peasely wrote that he set aside four hours each day to teach the children "of which there are a great number." He was also concerned about war between England and France, and felt that France would attack here first as it is "incapable of making any defence" and "must inevitably fall to the enemy." Despite (according to SPG meeting minutes) Bonavista having provided Peasely with a "good house for his residence that winter and proposed building a new one for him next spring," Peasely was already interested in leaving Bonavista, stating that he wished to be moved to another mission "where I may live a little more comfortably than I can here."

Between October 1743 and October 1744, Peasely baptized twenty children and two adults, one of whom "was bred an Anabaptist" and increased the number of communicants (those who can receive Holy Communion) from six to twelve. On December 2, 1744, Peasely reminded the SPG that "upon my disembarqueing for this disagreeable country" there was a promise of "something better" after two or three years. "I beg leave to remind you of it . . . I have a family." Peasely was transferred to St. John's in 1745.

A petition dated November 15, 1752, from Bonavista (Appendix 4) was sent to the SPG asking for another minister. They had no knowledge of Peasely's reason for departure and wrote that they had no one "to instruct us, which we want very much, for it's a miserable thing to see the people on the Lord's Day scattered abroad like sheep without a shepherd." In 1753, the SPG, in response to the Bonavista petition, recommended that "Mr. Lindsay, Missionary at Trinity Bay . . . visit the Church at Bonavista as often as he can conveniently" and that "an enquiry be made for a missionary at Bonavista."

iii) The Growth of Methodism

Although Lench indicates that a contemporary of his, John Swyers, informed Lench that his (Swyers's) mother had heard Rev. Laurence Coughlan preach in

Bonavista, in fact, given Swyers's family history details and the fact that Cough-lan made no mention of it in his records, this claim is unlikely. We do know with documented certainty that Rev. John Hoskins of Old Perlican paid a visit to Bonavista in 1784 (when Swyers's mother would have been seven years of age) and was likely the first Methodist missionary to the town. Hoskins's visit was a singular one, and no further missionaries arrived until 1794.

Rev. George Smith was born in Burton, near Nottingham, March 1766. He wrote (as recorded by his son William) that "at the age of sixteen or seventeen, some remarkable dreams served to awaken my conscience to deeper reflection. I then became more strict in watching over every part of my conduct, and in the faithful discharge of my duties. . . . My conscience grew more and more tender and my heart was very frequently engaged in prayer to God." Smith's early life was not without temptation, however. "My distress increased continually, till my life became an insupportable burden, and sore temptations followed me wherever I went. . . . They were suggested by the

Rev. George Smith. From Lench's *The Story of Methodism in Bonavista*.

wicked one, in order to drive me to despair of the divine mercy, and to put a speedy end to my wretched life." While in his twenties, he joined the Method-ists and began preaching to them. In 1790, at Newark, he was invited to preach in the large chapel. "It was with fear and trembling that I undertook it (the sermon) . . . but the Lord stood with me and great was the Holy One of Israel in the midst of us."

A few years later, Rev. Smith found himself in Poole, which at the time was the central link between Bonavista and England. "Some of the men who had heard us preach in Poole, and afterwards sailed to Newfoundland, spoke of our proceedings with approbation to Mr. Stretton, a gentleman of Harbour Grace." On May 1, 1794, Rev. George Smith was en route to Newfoundland. Over the next year and a half, he preached in many communities, including Bonavista. Life was difficult for a travelling missionary, though, so Rev. Smith resolved "to return to England, to obtain ordination from the Archbishop of

Canterbury, the President of the Society for Propagating the Gospel in Foreign Parts." William Bramwell Smith then relates the story of the petition and counter-petition from inhabitants of Bonavista in support of, and opposed to, the return of Rev. Smith to Bonavista. These details will not be repeated here, and are noted here simply to highlight that William Smith's account concurs accurately with the evidence we will see soon from the petitions and letters from John Bland (Chapter 13). Rev. Smith's request to return to Bonavista as missionary was denied.

Undeterred, Rev. Smith returned to Newfoundland around 1795. "I sailed from St. John's in a boat in the month of November . . . wet and stormy weather . . . the sailors thought good to put in at Bonavista, for which I was very glad. I was no sooner on shore, than I found myself obliged to take to my bed, in a poor tilt belonging to two poor men, where I lay about a month, seldom rising . . ." "I must have left the earthly tabernacle had it not been for the care of the Magistrate (likely John Bland) and the Apothecary (John Mayne) who both kindly and liberally ministered to my necessities. The latter gentleman, Mr. Mayne, sent me some bottles of port wine when I began to recover . . . I then began to teach the children to read, who were altogether destitute of any help of that kind, and many of them in rags, without shoes or stockings. . . . I sold some of my books in exchange for clothing which with what I begged from others for the purpose, served to relieve their present wants." Smith remained in Bonavista until the following May (likely 1796) and never returned. Of his time in Bonavista, Rev. Smith wrote:

"I would observe, to the praise of God of my life and of all my mercies, that in the discharge of my ministerial duties, I found the same gracious assistance and divine animation which I had experienced on my former visit to that poor, and in some sense, not-desired land. I had reason to believe that through the blessing of God, several souls were converted at Bonavista, and the children whom I taught gratuitously, appeared to be very hopeful. Their parents endeavoured to requite my kindness by bringing rafts of wood, which they cut and squared on the other side of the cove, on sleds over the ice, with the intention of erecting a chapel in the spring, if I had received, as I expected, remittances from England."

Lench called Rev. George Smith "the pioneer Methodist missionary of Bonavista." His tenure secured the beginning of the Methodist movement in the town, starting with Charles Saint and Benjamin Cole, whom Lench called "the first spiritual children" of Methodism in Bonavista. Lench also noted that Smith initiated the construction of the first Methodist church in Bonavista. A frame was built, but the church was never completed, and eventually the frame itself fell into decay. William Bramwell Smith records that Rev. George Smith married Ellen Strothard in England. They had two sons and two daughters. William Wilson notes that Rev. Smith died on January 25, 1832, aged sixty-six.

That period of time between Mr. Smith's departure from Bonavista in 1796 and the arrival of the next missionary is captured in a letter by Charles Saint to Rev. Smith, written in 1815 and recorded in Winsor's *Methodism in Newfoundland*. Saint wrote "You (Rev. Smith) were the first that I ever heard preach the Gospel sermon from, and under that first sermon that you preached . . . I was sore convinced of the truth . . . . It was then that I felt the want of the Gospel." After a short visit to St. John's, Saint continued to write that back home in Bonavista "we commenced meeting together for prayer and reading a sermon. The news soon spread far and wide, and our names rung in the mouths of the ungodly." Naboth Winsor, in *Hearts Strangely Warmed*, states that for the thirteen years that elapsed (1797–1810) between the departure of Rev. Smith and the arrival of Rev. Ward, Saint "was the leader in nearly all the services by which the sheep without a shepherd sought to strengthen each other." The early ministers (Remington, Ward, and Ellis) all stayed with Charles Saint during their ministry in the region.

A Methodist missionary did not visit Bonavista following Rev. Smith's departure until 1809, when Rev. John Remmington paid a short visit. According to Lench, Remmington found a "little band of followers were doing well and that Messrs. Saint and Cole had developed into useful laymen and acceptable preachers." Remmington's visit precipitated a renewed interest in a permanent missionary. Immediately following Remmington's departure, Magistrate Bland sent a letter to Rev. Thomas Coke, requesting a missionary. Rev. Coke instructed Rev. William Ward to depart immediately for the town. His instructions were clear: "I request that the committee will provide Mr. Ward a large quantity of flannel and fleece hosiery. If we don't, we may be unintentionally the cause of his death, for he is going to a part of Newfoundland that is exquisitely cold . . . let him have warm stockings and very warm clothes of every kind."

Mr. Ward stayed in Bonavista for two years, from 1810 until 1812. He drowned returning from a district meeting in St. John's, along with all others on board, in 1812. The Memorial United Church in Bonavista has erected a tablet in his memory:

Erected by the
Methodist Sunday Schools of Bonavista
In Memory of the
REV. WILLIAM WARD
First stationed Minister of the Bonavista Circuit
Came from England to Bonavista in 1810
Was drowned en route from Bonavista to St. John's, 1812.
"He being dead yet speaketh." — Heb. 11:4.

Charles Saint, in the letter noted above, described Ward's loss. "He (Rev. Ward) left this for St. John's in the year 1812, about the first of October. Returning from that place the 10th in Mr. Hosier's boat, his son, William, being in her, there was a gale of wind and they were never heard of afterwards. So I saw him no more, but hope to meet him in a better world." Lench also described the event and supports the version in the Saint letter that Ward drowned en route from St. John's to Bonavista.

In the course of Rev. Ward's stay in Bonavista, he restarted the construction of the Methodist church initiated by Rev. Smith. Rev. William Ellis arrived in Bonavista following Ward's drowning, in 1813. Lench notes that Ellis performed the first sacramental service on Christmas Day, 1813, and first preached in the new church in February 1814. The church was completed that summer. Lench details the financial records for the new church at that time, which were, by his account, "most accurate." Charles Saint, James Mouland, and Samson Mifflin were the chief creditors for the new church, while another twenty-eight families and individuals supported the church through subscriptions and payment of pews (Appendix 6).

Rev. Ellis stayed until 1814, the same year in which Newfoundland was added as a district at the Wesleyan Methodist Conference. In that year, Ellis wrote (as recorded in Winsor) that the population of Bonavista was "upwards of 1700," of which 1,200 were Protestants and the remainder Roman Catholics. He noted the presence of the original Anglican church and that those who had profited from the ministry of Rev. Smith had "put up the frame of a little chapel." There was no "Romish Chapel." Ellis wrote "I had not been long there (in Bonavista) before the Lord began to work upon the minds of many, by the preaching of His word; and before the end of the year, we had a class consisting of thirty members . . . when I left them in April, there were sixty in Society. Such a work of God, all things considered, I never witnessed before. It was impossible to see the change which was wrought in many, and in so short a time, without being convinced that the work was of Him . . . their love to the ordinances of God was remarkable; they were not deterred from attending them by any weather. I have seen men and women walk up to their knees in snow, on their way to class meetings and prayer meetings."

This is perhaps an opportune time to pause and reflect on religion as it evolved in Bonavista over the past century. We've seen that some settlement had occurred in the 1600s, and that by the early 1700s the residents (both among the planters and servants) wanted a missionary presence. Rev. Henry Jones was very well-received by the community in 1725 (and likely earlier) through the support of the Church of England through the Society for the Propagation of the Gospel in Foreign Parts, and considerable progress was made in the construction of the schools and the local church and in the formal and religious education of the children and adults. However, despite the various petitions following Mr. Peasely's departure in 1745, very little attention was provided by the SPG and others. Rev. Balfour visited for brief periods of time, while Dr. Clinch (before he was officially ordained) and Abraham Ackerman performed services in a lay capacity. Others may have contributed from time to time. But the Church of England had largely abandoned Bonavista from 1745 until the 1820s.

The introduction of Methodism into Bonavista with Rev. John Hoskins's visit in 1784 was successful in that it provided the seeds for the growth of a religious revival in a community that had been in want of religious leadership for several decades. His visit, and subsequent stays by others, served to establish Methodism as arguably the strongest religious force in Bonavista in the early 1800s. But the strength of Methodism did not arise simply from a ministerial presence, but rather on what the minister preached and to whom he delivered his message. Hollett, in *Growth of Methodism in Newfoundland, 1774-1874*, focuses keenly on this issue. "Populist Methodism in the bays of Newfoundland, continually energized through revivals, was in sharp contrast to the extremely hierarchical nineteenth-century versions of Anglicanism and Catholicism . . . emanating from St. John's. Methodism presented a vision of a people, not in contrast to the cruel land but in contrast to clerical mediation, through its proclamation of direct access to God." Hollett further spoke of the importance of ministers speaking directly to his listeners, in the vernacular, in a manner they could understand. Magistrate Bland made that same point in 1809 when, in his letter to Rev. Dr. Coke requesting a missionary, asked for a man "who will speak to the people in plain language, and appear to be in good earnest."

The important role played by the local inhabitants, and more specifically those who converted to Methodism in the late 1700s, led to the growth of the revival in Bonavista. Rev. Remmington's arrival in 1809 occurred twenty-five years after Rev. Hoskins visit in 1784, and Rev. Smith's stay was relatively short. Revs. Remmington and Ellis (and perhaps others) specifically highlighted the important work of Charles Saint and Benjamin Cole in keeping the flock intact. Hollett notes that when Rev. James Hickson came to Bonavista in 1815, he testified "Glory be to God. I have felt more of His love while I have been in this place than I ever did before. I received the blessing of sanctification when my dear friend Mr. Saint . . . was praying." Hollett further notes that "missionary Charles Bates" in the 1820s acknowledged the important role of "a local preacher (probably Cole)." We can see in Appendix 7 (Methodist Classes, 1823) the continued leadership provided by Saint, Cole, and others.

Charles Saint, in his letter to Rev. Smith in 1815, described the level of activity ongoing within the Methodist movement at that time. "We have public worship three times on the Lord's Day—one by candlelight, when we have tolerably large congregations . . . I have endeavoured to speak on these stated times. . . . On Tuesday evening we have class meetings, where we have sixty who walk in love. Thursday evening we have public worship; Friday evening a prayer meeting at some house. I cannot call it preaching, but the Lord gives me great liberty, and I trust that some have been brought to God. There is a young man here, Benjamin Cole, whom the Lord has owned, and he exhorts occasionally."

A final closing word is in order with respect to Charles Saint. When he was buried on August 12, 1840, a comment in the official registry records that he was "one of the first converts." His headstone in the churchyard on Church Street in Bonavista states:

> To the memory of CHARLES SAINT who departed this life on the 8th of August, 1840 aged 76 years. He, together with Thomas Bass, received the first Wesleyan Missionary into their house. When the first class was formed he continued one of its members, and for many years was a devoted and zealous class leader and exhorter and was made a blessing to many. The truth of the religion which he experienced and urged upon others, supported him under and enabled him to triumph in the midst of extreme sufferings with which his useful life terminated.
>
> "Mark the perfect man and behold the upright for the end of that man is peace." — Ps. 37:37.

While Methodism was growing among the local inhabitants, and was being provided leadership and funds by the larger Methodist church and some of the wealthier residents of Bonavista, the Church of England had been largely ignored since the departure of Mr. Peasely in 1745. While the church completed by Rev. Henry Jones in 1731 was falling into disrepair, the Methodists were constructing their own new church directly opposite it. Church of England services were conducted by Abraham Ackerman, a local "servant of the fishery" (as Bland described him) while the Methodists were being led by an ordained clergyman. An undercurrent of discontent had likely been brewing for some time. Hostilities boiled over in 1814.

The new Methodist church was completed in 1814. At that time, there were no bells in the church tower to signal to the inhabitants that church service would be commencing within the hour. Instead, a flag was raised one hour before church service, was lowered to half-mast thirty minutes before service began, and was lowered and removed as the minister entered the church. As the Methodists were erecting the flagstaff in preparation for the church service on the coming Sunday, they were approached by the local magistrate, Gerrard Ford, who felt that it would be an insult to the established Church of England to raise a flagstaff on Sunday morning in direct opposition to the Episcopal church. Ford perhaps felt that it was as much his responsibility to keep the King's peace as it was to support the Church of England. As recorded by Rev. William Wilson:

Ford: "What are you Methodists doing there?"
Answer: "We are putting up a flagstaff."
Ford: "What do you want of a flagstaff there?"
Answer: "To hoist a flag as a signal for divine service."
Ford: "What, directly opposite the church?"
Answer: "We are not aware that we are doing any wrong."
Ford: "I tell you it shall not be, and I forbid it."
Answer: "We think you have no right to interfere with us, and we shall not regard your prohibition."
Ford: "Well, I will allow you to hoist your flag on any day but Sunday."
Answer: "That is the day on which we intend to hoist our flag."
Ford: "If you dare to hoist your flag on next Sunday, I will certainly cut it down."

The Anglican (right) and Methodist Churches facing each other in the early 1900s. Each church would be replaced in the coming decades. (Gordon Branton via Ross Abbott)

On Sunday, the flag was raised one hour before service, and Magistrate Ford, with his son as constable, informed the Methodists that he (Magistrate Ford) had forbidden them raising the flag and instructed his son to cut the flagstaff down. According to Wilson, Mr. Saint intervened and said "Sir, take care what you do, for I have taken advice, and find we have done nothing wrong." The word "advice" perhaps caused the magistrate to pause, for he told his son to halt. There were no further challenges to the flagstaff and the raising of the flag prior to religious service.

Hostility between the Methodist Church (later the United Church) and the Anglican Church dissolved over time. Rev. Dr. Arthur Butt said Grace at the luncheon at Bonavista for the Queen on June 24, 1997. He was a United Church minister who served in Bonavista on two occasions. He wrote (*Telling It as It Was*) that in 1950, at a Masonic Service held at the Memorial United Church in Bonavista over which he presided, he invited Reverend Lewis Norman of Bonavista's Anglican Christ Church to sit with him at the pulpit and to share service responsibilities.

> While they waited for the service to begin, Norman said to Butt, "We are making history today, for, to the best of my knowledge, no Anglican priest has ever been in your pulpit before to share in a service!"
>
> Rev. Butt continued, "But things have changed. Thank God! During the week of prayer in 1986 when we were again serving Memorial's congregation, Father James Beresford of the Roman Catholic Church gave the message at the United Church; the following night I gave the message at the Anglican Church; the next night Rev. Eugene Abbott of the Anglican Church gave the message at the United Church in Elliston; and on the final night of our services Mr. Clayton Austin, our Lay Supply minister at Elliston, gave the message at the Roman Catholic Church. What a great week it was for clergy and people. We had been drawn closer to one another in a quarter of a century than we had in a century and a half previous to that period."

Rev. William Ellis was replaced in 1815 by Rev. James Hickson (1815–17), his brother Rev. Thomas Hickson (1817–18), and Rev. Richard Knight (1818–20). Rev. Ellis returned for a second term in 1820, followed by Rev. Ninian Barr (21–22) and Rev. William Wilson (1822–23). Rev. Wilson recorded the membership of the Methodist classes in Bonavista in 1823. The five classes, their leaders, and members are listed in Appendix 7. Rev. Wilson also recorded the first Methodism marriage to survive the years. It was between Martha Hicks and James Way, both of Bonavista, on December 12, 1822.

iv) The Church of England Revisited

In 1771, Rev. James Balfour, at that time stationed in Trinity, noted in a letter to the SPG that "Bonavista has opened a subscription for a minister." Balfour had been stationed in Trinity for six years and occasionally visited Bonavista. He would have been familiar with the area, so his comments about Bonavista are worthy of note below (though Handcock has recorded that Balfour was "frequently biased and exaggerated"):

I am much mistaken however much they may pretend, if they would not soon be more glad of [a minister's] departure than arrival; they are so notorious for swearing and drinking, in short, all manner of wickedness. Besides, most people here will as soon break their written agreements as they do their empty promises, unless compelled to keep them by force.

In 1775, Dr. John Clinch arrived in Bonavista, perhaps in consequence of the subscription Balfour referenced in his letter. Clinch was born in Cirencester, England, in 1749, went to medical school in England, and was a schoolmate and close friend of Dr. Edward Jenner, the discoverer of the smallpox vaccine. Clinch remained in Bonavista for eight years and, according to Gaylor, "perform[ed] the services of the Church." In 1783, he moved to Trinity, and four years later, he was formally ordained as an Anglican priest.

Following Clinch's departure to Trinity, Abraham Ackerman began to perform the duties of the church. He had no formal training but did his best to baptize children, marry couples, and bury the dead. He led church services as well. Magistrate Bland, however, did not think well of Ackerman. He called him an "ignorant, low bred man" and that "his habits of life . . . are too vulgar to command respect, and he is besides, so grossly illiterate as not to be able to read intelligibly." Lench was more complimentary. He noted that Ackerman "had full charge of the spiritual concerns of the community." He also recorded Thomas Gaylor's entry in the Church of England Register in 1840, in which Gaylor said that "Abraham Ackerman about the year 1780 took to reading in Church which was sometime without a reader . . . continued for nearly half a century to do the duties of the church. . . . I am happy to say that Mr. Ackerman did what lay in his power to keep the congregation steadfast even after the Wesleyan preachers settled here. . . . At so low an ebb was religion at this place about the time of Mr. Ackerman's death that he had often told me before I became resident, that if he should die, he did not know any persons who could read the burial service over him. It fell at last on the writer to perform the mournful service over him on the 27th June, 1822."

The flagstaff confrontation in 1814 between the Methodists and the Anglicans on what is now called Church Street may have led to a renewed interest on the part of the Anglican faith to enhance their church, especially since the Methodists had not only constructed a new church, but had, perhaps brazenly, chosen to build it directly across from the Anglican church. In November 1816, a number of prominent members of the Bonavista community sent a petition to the governor of Newfoundland, Francis Pickmore, requesting financial assistance for the construction of a new church. Noteworthy in the petition is their claim that "the church in Bonavista was the first establishment in the Island according to the rites and ceremonies of the Church of England and in that manner it has since continued being upwards of one hundred years old." They state that the old church has "from time become too much decayed to be repaired" and would cost "from eight to nine hundred pounds," of which the petitioners would be able to pay £500. They therefore "solicit the aid and assistance of Your Excellency to grant them such a sum as may be in Your Excellency's power to give for the purpose of their intention."

The reference to the church in Bonavista being upwards of 100 years old is noteworthy. We have already seen that there was a church in Bonavista when Rev. Jones arrived in 1725 and that it was in need of some repair. Rev. Jones oversaw the repairs—the newly rebuilt church was opened in 1731. So the "upwards of one hundred years" is certainly well-founded. The claim that it "is the first establishment in the Island" is historic within the context of the introduction of religion into the island of Newfoundland.

Nothing seemed to happen in Bonavista in those days concerning ministers, churches, and petitions without some level of controversy, and this latest petition was not without its drama. When Governor Pickmore received the petition, he immediately noticed that Magistrate Gerrard Ford's name was not among the signatories and, given his clear stance as shown by the episode of the flagstaff, wrote to Ford for clarification. Governor Pickmore's letter was Ford's first knowledge of the petition, and his response back to Pickmore makes clear why he, Ford, was left out. Ford writes, "I was out of harbour at the time it (the petition) was handed about. . . . I made inquiry into the business and found that the principal promoter was a Joseph Brown, an insulting, ignorant, common fellow, but having got a little money, wants to be considered of consequence, and to make himself popular amongst the lower order of the inhabitants of which its nearly all in these outports."

Pickmore did not provide any financial support to Bonavista for the repairs to the Anglican church in consequence of the petition. Instead, Joseph Brown took the lead himself. Thomas Gaylor noted in an entry in the Anglican Church records (dated 1840) the following:

"As I think the name of Joseph Brown should be known to posterity, and as there is no memorial of him in the church, I will just notify in this register that about the year 1812, the old church in this place was in a very ruined state. Some of the principal inhabitants proposed to raise a subscription to build the new church. But after many meetings and consultation . . . it came to nothing. In the old church when it rained there was scarcely a dry place in it.

In the year 1819, Joseph Brown said he would build the church himself and accordingly in that year he had the foundation laid . . ."

Joseph Brown died in 1819 but left £500 toward completing the church. A new petition (Appendix 8) to the governor was sent in 1821, stating that £660 had already been spent, and asking for a further 200. Among the signatories was Magistrate Ford. The new Anglican church was officially opened January 1, 1822.

Although an official account of the opening of the new church does not exist, we might assume that Mr. Ackerman led services until sometime before his death in June 1822. Thomas Gaylor performed the burial services for Mr. Ackerman on June 27. Rev. John Leigh, who visited Bonavista briefly in 1822, noted (again in the margins of the church records) that "Abraham Ackerman, Sr., aged 77, who for more than 40 years performed divine service in the established church, kept the congregation during the above period, was never absent by sickness or other causes, one Sunday but died almost suddenly." Rev. Leigh served in Bonavista at intervals in 1822 and 1833 and, in so doing, was the first ordained minister to serve the Anglican membership since the departure of Rev. Jones in 1842. Rev. Leigh died suddenly on August 17, 1823.

Before Rev. Leigh died, he wrote to Governor Hamilton (August 31, 1922) and described circumstances as he saw it, in Bonavista.

There is a new church which was begun by a worthy and pious planter, named Joseph Brown, but who shortly after its commencement died, not however without leaving a will by which he bequeathed the sum of £500 towards finishing the church which when finished he directed to be sold, and the money arising from the sale of the pews he directed to be paid to the poor . . . in addition to £100 he bequeathed to them.

There is no parsonage house nor are the inhabitants able to complete the church or to attempt to build a parsonage house, yet they are most anxious to have a resident clergyman amongst them, and they seem willing to do all in their power to make him happy.

Between the losses of Mr. Ackerman and Rev. Leigh, and the arrival of Archdeacon George Coster, Captain Thomas Gaylor conducted services. He was an ardent supporter of the Anglican Church and was strongly opposed to the spread of Methodism in and around Bonavista. The Methodist minister, Rev.

William Wilson, was stationed in Bonavista for a period of time. He wrote *Newfoundland and its Missionaries* and recorded a particular episode involving Captain Gaylor in 1824. He writes: "The store-keeper parson of Bonavista (by whom Wilson is referring to Mr. Ackerman—"parson" is in italics) was now dead, and he was succeeded by a man who had been a sea-captain, who was zealously opposed to Methodist preachers." Although Wilson only refers to Captain Gaylor as Mr. G., Nimshi Crewe (a provincial archivist), in a letter to the A. C. Hunter Library, confirmed Captain Gaylor as the person to whom Rev. Wilson refers. The story below is a composite from Wilson's own words and commentary from Crewe (himself originally from Elliston).

As Methodism spread throughout Elliston (at the time known as Bird Island Cove), Gaylor sent "Skipper Joe" and a choir to establish itself at the small church to serve to strengthen the Anglican presence in the town. This was to no avail, according to Wilson, as Skipper Joe and the choir all eventually "became awakened" to Methodism. Captain Gaylor, or as Wilson called him, "our nautical friend of Bonavista, who acted in this locality as a sort of rural dean," went to Bird Island Cove to address the fact that "the people (are) going mad." Skipper Joe replied, "Mr. G., I think your remarks are unkind and quite uncalled for . . . I have seen nothing improper here." Within a week, Skipper Joe "became a subject of the grace of God, and cast his lot among the despised Methodists of the place." Later, Captain Gaylor travelled to Bird Island Cove routinely to perform divine Anglican service and was forced on at least one occasion to threaten a "good woman" who wanted to join the Methodists to "bind her over to keep the king's peace, if she ever again so disturbed him while he was performing divine worship." Thus, according to the lady's version to Rev. Wilson, ". . . was I driven from the church, and compelled to be a Methodist." Wilson's final account (which Nimshi Crewe called "amusing anecdotes") tells of Captain Gaylor requiring a Bonavista clerk to accompany him to Bird Island Cove to help "reclaim the Methodists from the error of their ways." On his way home one evening, the clerk sprained his ankle, and as Captain Gaylor could provide little support, he, the clerk, lay on the ground in agony. He finally began to curse the Methodists, and exclaimed "If these Methodists will perish they must, for I will not go any more to save them." By Wilson's account, Methodism did not suffer opposition thereafter.

We will meet Rev. Wilson again later in Chapter 16. As we'll see, he was not without his own set of controversies.

Perhaps Rev. Leigh's plea for a resident clergyman in his correspondence in 1822 had some impact on the governor. Two years after Leigh wrote his letter, the first and most populous religion in Bonavista received its first resident and ordained clergyman since Rev. Henry Jones departed Bonavista. Rev. George Coster was born in Newbury, England, in 1794 and was ordained as a Church of England minister in 1819. After working in Bermuda for a couple of years, he arrived in Bonavista in 1824. During his time in Bonavista, Newfoundland was constituted an archdeaconry, and Coster was named the first archdeacon of the island.

When Coster arrived in Bonavista in the fall of 1824, he found that the congregation was considerable. He gave much credit to Captain Thomas Gaylor, as reader at the church, as a schoolmaster, and for maintaining the church in the absence of an ordained minister. In an 1825 letter to the SPG, Coster also noted that the new church was completely finished, had been painted, and was "really handsome and well-finished." Coster's stay in Bonavista was memorable, in that he made a concerted effort to provide support to the poorer members of the community during a difficult time. This story will be told in Chapter 16.

An iconic photo of Bonavista showing the United (left) and Anglican Churches in the background and Church Street leading to the foreground. Photo taken from the top of the courthouse, circa 1935. (Forbes Family Photograph Collection, Maritime History Archive, Memorial University)

Gaylor's diary noted the presence of Bishop Inglis of Nova Scotia in Bonavista on June 24, 1827. "The Bishop held a confirmation in the church this day (June 24) when 210 persons received that rite. The church and yard was consecrated in the morning." On the following day, a Captain Jones took the

Bishop, Archdeacon Coster, and Rev. Bullock to King's Cove. Between 1827 and 1830, Coster shared duties with Rev. William Bullock and Rev. James Robertson. In 1830, he left Newfoundland to assume archdeacon responsibilities for New Brunswick in Fredericton. Other Church of England ministers to serve Bonavista upon Coster's departure were Rev. N. A. Coster (1830), Rev. George Dodsworth (1830–32), and Rev. H. J. Fitzgerald (1832–40). Coster Street is named for Rev. George Coster.

v) Roman Catholicism

The first priest in the Bonavista area was Father Sinnott, who became parish priest in King's Cove around 1815. It may have been his presence that precipitated organization of the Roman Catholic Church in Bonavista. In a letter dated January 15, 1818, Magistrate Gerrard Ford acknowledged to Governor Pickmore that "I have received Your Excellency's letter giving permission for the erection of a Roman Catholic Chapel and I have told those concerned that they may go on with the building as soon as they please." The Roman Catholic Chapel in King's Cove was built around 1825. Perhaps the Roman Catholic Chapel in Bonavista was built around that same time.

Father Nicholas Devereaux came to King's Cove as curate, or assistant, to Father Sinnott in 1826 and assumed responsibility for the King's Cove district (which extended through Bonavista and Trinity Bays and included Bonavista) a year later when Father Sinnott left the region. Father Devereaux served the King's Cove, Bonavista, and surrounding areas for nineteen years. In the mid-1840s, he was accompanied by Father J. Scanlan, perhaps indicating that they shared responsibilities between King's Cove and Bonavista. Father Devereaux died around 1845 and is buried at King's Cove.

Father Thomas Waldron arrived in the King's Cove district in the mid-1840s, perhaps upon Father Devereaux's death, and served with Father J. Scanlan (who disappears from the record in the late 1840s). While serving in Bonavista, with Father Matthew Scanlan as his curate, Waldron visited St. John's in 1854, in the midst of a cholera outbreak. He contracted the disease, died a short while later, and is buried in St. John's. The epidemic ultimately killed 500 people in the capital city.

Father Matthew Scanlan took responsibilities for the district thereafter. He was variously supported by Father James Brown, Father James Cummins, and Father John Walsh. Lawton and Devine describe Father Scanlan as "a man of forceful character . . . stout, stocky and rotund, he ruled his parish by fear."

His energy, his sullenness, even the "pugnacious set of his lower lip, were sufficient to warn his interviewers to be circumspect in their speech and behaviour." He was not unlike a general set "to review his troops: everyone stood at attention." During mass, "he sauntered up through the chapel, looking leisurely to the right and the left to note the absentees—to the left where all the men, as was customary in these days, knelt together on the floor, and then to the right where the women occupied a similar position."

Father Scanlan lived in King's Cove until 1865, when he moved to Bonavista. A headstone in the cemetery adjacent to the Roman Catholic Church on Chapel Hill reads:

> Sacred to the Memory of the
> Rev'd Matthew Scanlan
> Parish Priest, Bonavista
> Departed on Dec. 11, 1871. Aged 68 years.
> May his soul rest in peace.

A new home for the resident Bonavista priest, St. Joseph's Presbytery, was erected in 1890. Stories related to the raising of funds, and laying the cornerstone, are found in excerpts from the James Ryan diary (Chapter 23).

St. Joseph's Roman Catholic Church, Chapel Hill, Bonavista, circa 1935. (Forbes Family Photograph Collection, Maritime History Archive, Memorial University)

Notes

The 1716 letter to the Lords of Trade is found in CO194, vol. 6, page 11.

David Bradley (Maritime History Archive of Memorial University of Newfoundland at time of writing) transcribed the many letters written by Rev. Henry Jones and Mr. William Peasely to the Society for the Propagation of the Gospel (SPG), as well as related documents written by the SPG with regard to Bonavista. The original documents are housed at the Centre for Newfoundland Studies at Memorial University of Newfoundland.

Occasional details during this era (e.g., the appointment of the JPs, correspondence in the late 1700s and early 1800s) are retrieved from the CO 194 records. Gaylor's diary, and the original church records, were also used.

The story of early Methodism in Bonavista was obtained through a variety of early sources, most notably Lench, Winsor, Wilson, and Hollett. The *Wesleyan-Methodist Magazine* for 1833 (Vol. XII of the Third Series) contains the memoir of Rev. George Smith written by his son, William Bramwell Smith.

Information on the early Roman Catholic priests resident at Bonavista was obtained from the *Newfoundland Yearbook and Almanac* with additional supporting information obtained from *History of King's Cove* by J. T. Lawton and P. K. Devine: http://ngb.chebucto.org/Articles/kc-chap-05.shtml.

13 — JOHN BLAND

John Bland was the magistrate in Bonavista for over twenty years. Because his correspondence is relatively well-recorded, his writings provide the first insightful picture of life in Bonavista since the writings of Rev. Henry Jones. His observations, as well, were often reasoned and wise, at times prophetic, and frank, even blunt. His work is referenced sporadically within this book, but a chapter devoted specifically to some of his efforts is also warranted.

In a letter dated September 26, 1802, while Bland had been living in Bonavista, he references "a residence of fourteen years in this place as Magistrate." If one assumes by "this place" he means Bonavista specifically, this would place his arrival in 1788. In an earlier letter, dated November 16, 1791, Bland refers to a role he played in signing a petition while in Harbour Grace for Rev. Coughlan as missionary for that community. Coughlan lived in Harbour Grace between 1766 and 1773, and the petition to which Bland refers was submitted in 1766—thus placing Bland in Harbour Grace in that year. When Bland arrived in Bonavista in 1788, he had already been in Newfoundland at least twenty-two years and had acquired, therefore, considerable experience and wisdom with respect to the area.

In 1788, the town had been without a resident minister, schoolmaster, or schoolmistress for over forty years. The inhabitants, as during the era when Jones and Peasely were in Bonavista, wanted to change that. Whether through Bland's leadership or otherwise, efforts to correct these deficiencies began in earnest.

On November 12, 1791, Bland wrote the cover letter for a petition (Appendix 9) to the Archbishop of Canterbury in England and "President of the Society for Propagating the Gospel in Foreign Parts," concerning the children in Bonavista and the need "to obtain a small salary for a schoolmaster, to enable him to instruct, gratis, poor children in reading and writing." There were thirty-two petitioners, whom Bland referred to as "the principal inhabitants . . . signed by all the proper in it of any consequence or property," including the three justices of the peace (Bland, Gerrard Ford, and William Brown), the signatures of another twenty-one, and another eight who made "his mark" indicating that they were unable to write.

It is worthwhile quoting a significant portion of the petition since it paints such a dismal picture of Bonavista for many of its residents: "There are at this time in the harbour of Bonavista upwards of three hundred poor children. That the parents of these children have themselves been bred in the most gross ignorance, and are not only wholly incapable of conveying instruction to their offspring but from their extreme poverty are destitute of the means of procuring for them so great a blessing. Thus yearly are multiplied numbers who have as little sense of the ends for which Providence has placed them in this world as the untutored savages of the woods. Deprived wholly of the assistance of a Missionary whose precepts and example might excite to piety and a moral life, the best cement of society, these poor people are also destitute of the most common means of attaining to that small degree of cultivation which the lowest orders possess in most civilized nations." The petitioners continue that a "George Bemister" presently lives at Bonavista and has provided instruction in the past.

In Bland's cover letter, he notes independently that "the number of poor children in the petition I believe not to be exaggerated." Bland perhaps felt a need to assure the Archbishop that this petition was driven by those same motivations upon which the SPG was based. He wrote, ". . . in truth, it reflects little honour on a great and enlightened nation that the population in Newfoundland should be making so rapid a progress without any system. It is a melancholy truth that the majority of the poor inhabitants of this place are in a very gross state of ignorance . . . how can we hope for the fruits of cultivation where the seeds have never been sown?" Bland delicately repeats the reference in the petition that a missionary is absent from this town, wholly a consequence of the fact that the SPG failed to replace Mr. Peasely when he departed in the 1740s. "It were indeed much to be desired that a Missionary resided here, whose life and morals might lend an example worthy of imitation." In closing, Bland suggests that "the respectable part of the residents here would be happy to see such a person established among them."

This petition was successful. Bland noted, in the fall of 1792, "our sincere acknowledgements for the attention which the society has been pleased to (grant) our request, and to assure them that their bounty . . . shall not be improperly applied."

Mr. George Bemister wrote to the SPG in the fall of 1793 indicating that he had been "appointed Schoolmaster for this place with a salary of £15 annually, commencing the 17th February 1792. . . . Since my residence of three years in this place I have had attending my school upwards of forty children."

Bemister noted that parents were insufficiently able to provide payment for his services, thus necessitating the need for a petition for SPG assistance.

Bland's capacity to stand on principle, even in the absence of support from the local community, became clear a short time later. As a consequence of the success of the petition for a schoolmaster, a second petition (Appendix 10) was circulated requesting a salary for Mr. Abraham Ackerman. This petition circulated without Bland's knowledge and included many of the same persons who had signed the petition for funds for a schoolmaster. In the absence of a missionary, Ackerman, a "servant of the fishery," had, in 1783, taken it upon himself to perform the duties of the church. As this second petition noted, "Ackerman voluntarily and without any reward or emolument whatever, undertook to do the duty of the church, which he has constantly served these nine years, to the entire satisfaction of the inhabitants of this town and district—that our children may be brought up in the knowledge and fear of God." The petition further noted the "declining state of the protestant religion and the rapid increase of Popery."

Why, then, was Bland ignorant of this petition? The answer became clear when Bland discovers its existence and wrote his own letter to the SPG. "I have learnt that a second (petition) has lately been smuggled through this settlement which has for its object to obtain a salary for one Abraham Akerman, for officiating as minister, or catechist." After pointing out that the petition should have sought out the "more respectable part of the inhabitants," Bland continued with a description of Ackerman. He calls him "an "inferior servant in the fishery . . . (an) ignorant, low bred man," and says that "his habits of life, as may be naturally supposed from his situation, are too vulgar to command respect, and he is besides, so grossly illiterate as not to be able to read intelligibly." Bland closed by again appealing for a Church of England missionary: "As Bonavista has lately much increased in respectability and population, the necessity of a public instructor in the religious and moral duties of life becomes every year more evident, and I shall hope that another season will not pass without some proposal for effecting so desirable an end."

Bland followed this letter in 1793 with yet another petition to the Archbishop of Canterbury and the SPG, formally requesting "to have established among them a truly Christian Minister, one whose life would be an example of the doctrine he taught." The inclusion of the word "truly" and the reference to living life as he preached were no doubt subtle references to the deficiencies inherent with Mr. Ackerman. Further, as many of the petitioners for this latest petition from Bland had also signed the earlier petition for a salary for

Ackerman, it signalled a clear victory for John Bland among the "principal inhabitants."

The 1793 petition for a missionary noted that "upwards of forty years have elapsed since a minister of the Gospel resided among them," thus only approximating the departure of Mr. Peasely in 1745. The petition highlighted that the inhabitants "have unhappily been deprived not only of the blessing of a public administration of the rites of the christian religion, but of spiritual assistance . . . (while) the increase of population . . . is a circumstance that renders the absence of an exemplary missionary a subject of particular regret." Previous points with respect to the poorer class are repeated: "the native inhabitants . . . are too generally to be reckoned among the lowest order of society . . . their offspring are bred in a most lamentable ignorance of the great concerns of religion." Bland notes that "it has recently been ascertained that few less than five hundred children under age are numbered in Bonavista."

Despite these best efforts, the SPG did not send a missionary to Bonavista. In 1795, another petition, and a counter-petition, was sent to the SPG. In the first, many inhabitants, including Bland and the local surgeon, Dr. Mayne, requested that Mr. George Smith, a Methodist, be supported by the SPG. Bland noted that there was precedent for this, insofar as Laurence Coughlan, a Methodist, had been supported by the SPG in Harbour Grace in 1766. According to Bland, "the application in favour of Mr. Smith has given much offence to some of the orthodox members of the established church (i.e., the Church of England)." These orthodox members had sent a counter-petition requesting the Anglican minister and surgeon, Dr. George Jenner of Harbour Grace, to be sent to Bonavista as missionary. In Bland's estimation, this application would have forced Dr. Mayne (the surgeon in Bonavista) out of work, as Dr. Jenner would have been expected to perform both responsibilities. As Dr. Mayne had a family with small children, including an infant, Bland described the counter-petition as being sent in "a spirit of jealousy." Bland further noted "I will ask you what opinion the present surgeon of Bonavista ought to entertain of a Christian priest who comes with his bible in one hand to show the things contained therein . . . while the other is thrust out to snatch from him and his family the means of their subsistence?"

The SPG were unconvinced by Bland's letter, but neither did they agree with the counter-petition. The SPG minutes:

A petition from Bonavista signed by 69 persons praying the Society not to consent to a prior petition signed only by 36 requesting that a Mr.

George Smith might be sent out Missionary from the Society to that place, was laid before the Committee. Whereupon they were decidedly of opinion . . . that the petition in favour of Mr. George Smith should be rejected as it appears that he is an illiterate unordained Methodist preacher and has already occasioned great confusion in that colony. Resolved to agree with the Committee that the Society are desirous to send a missionary whenever a proper person can be procured.

The reader may conclude that these various petitions had little consequent impact and were therefore of limited value within the historical context of Bonavista. In fact, we should pause and reflect upon the underlying messages hidden within the petitions themselves and the motivations driving these overt, and occasionally covert, operations of the leading citizens of Bonavista.

First of all, as we discovered through an investigation of the period of time during which Rev. Jones lived in Bonavista, the presence of a missionary and schoolmaster resident in the town was of deep concern. The two-tier class structure seen during Rev. Jones's time in Bonavista from 1725 to 1742 between the planters on the one hand, and the servant component on the other, continued to exist at the end of the century. The uneven distribution of wealth was also clearly evident, leaving the servant class desperately poor, uneducated, and perhaps even unaware of the basic tenets of English, Irish, and Christian society. The absence of a missionary since 1745 resident in the town (occasional visitation may have occurred from the minister in Trinity) undoubtedly meant that marriages, baptisms, and burials were either performed in the absence of rites or were not performed at all. The leaders of the community recognized the requirement for intervention and looked to the SPG for support.

Newfoundland in the late 1700s had been led by a governor resident in St. John's. Formal schooling funded by the Newfoundland government, as an official colony of England, was decades away. It is regrettable, then, to see that the people of Bonavista, born in the 1700s and raised by parents who themselves may have been born in Bonavista without schooling in either a classroom or church setting, continued to live without any education beyond that of their immediate surroundings as necessary to support the fishery and their homes. Also regrettable is that the leaders of the town could appeal only to the SPG, a distant society in a distant land with, perhaps, little appreciation or insufficient concern for the plight of the local inhabitants.

Care needs to be taken, however, that we do not exaggerate the conditions of the servant class in Bonavista or to judge circumstances inaccurately. Many were born and raised in Bonavista and supported themselves and their families through the fishery with little training other than that derived from their own families, neighbours, and natural inclination. Livelihood was derived from a point of land jutting directly into the North Atlantic. Bonavista had no natural harbour and was therefore exposed from practically all directions. Ocean conditions during the fishing seasons were among the most hazardous of anywhere in Newfoundland. Pack ice and icebergs caused havoc and even threatened lives. The landscape was relatively flat, with only marginal protection from surrounding hills. Woodland in the area when settlement began was quickly consumed in the construction of flakes, stageheads, homes, lodgings, boats, and fuel, leaving the inhabitants mostly exposed to the elements. They grew their own crops on relatively barren land. They were paid enough to survive. If they were poor and illiterate, they were, nonetheless, the backbone upon which Bonavista evolved.

It is Bland's observations of the Beothuk that are most often quoted in a historical context. As noted in Chapter 3, Bland made many candid, insightful, and prophetic remarks about the Indigenous peoples of the island of Newfoundland:

On lack of knowledge: I cannot help holding an opinion that we know almost as little of the Newfoundland Indian as we do of the inhabitants of the interior of Africa.

On injustice: They have been progressively driven from south to north and though their removal has been produced by a slow and silent operation, it has nevertheless had all the effect of a violent expulsion.

On inherent rights: It ought to be remembered that these savages have a natural right to this Island, and every invasion of a natural right is a violation of the principle of justice.

On the future: In proportion as their means of procuring subsistence became narrowed, their population must necessarily have decreased and before the lapse of another century, the English nation, like the Spanish, may have affixed to its character the indelible reproach of having exterminated a whole race of people!

The last Beothuk, Shanawdithit, died of tuberculosis, in St. John's in 1829.

Governor Waldegrave, when discussing with Magistrate Bland the circumstance of the Beothuk in Newfoundland, noted in a letter to Bland in 1797 that "As to your reflections they are such as to do honour both to your head and heart, and it gives me much pleasure to find that Bonavista possesses a Magistrate so amply qualified to fulfil the duties of that office. I shall have the honour to lay your letter before His Grace the Duke of Portland . . ."

In 1805, Governor Gower, in assessing means to tax the inhabitants of Newfoundland to help defray costs, proposed the requirement that anyone owning land should report same and to be granted leases "upon reasonable terms"—in other words, the introduction of a form of property tax. Bland was strongly opposed to this proposal and noted that "this measure . . . must be expected to be unpopular with the bulk of the people of Newfoundland. The poor class of this quarter urge that the ground is naturally unfertile and that to render it or a smaller portion of it fit to produce potatoes, their great article of food, has cost them years of labour." Instead of a property tax, Bland proposed a tax on rum. Apparently this notion had been proposed before, since Bland not indelicately noted that "the clamour . . . excited against the policy of this reasonable (rum) tax by a few interested individuals is so frivolous that one cannot help thinking it a pity that Government (meaning, by that, the governor) should have given it one moment's attention."

Bland further suggested that "in my humble judgment it would be gaining much could a legal authority be vested in a deliberative body at St. John's, however limited in number and however dissimilar to a House of Assembly." In fact, Newfoundland became a colony of England in 1825 (ending Naval Governance) and established Representative Government, including a House of Assembly in 1832.

In 1802, Bland requested of Governor James Gambier the construction of a jail. Bland knew of no place in Newfoundland as populated without a jail and noted that in one particular instance, "we have been compelled at a great expense to keep a guard throughout the winter over a prisoner charged with murder . . . and in many other instances for the want of such a resort, other offenders have been able to elude the punishment due to their crimes." Gambier responded a short while later consenting with the request and even including details to ensure "the comfort of prisoners . . . in separate accommodations for male and female prisoners . . . (and) . . . there should be air holes in the sides of the cells, close to the top, with valves to open and shut as may be necessary to cause a circulation and change of air." As discussion continued on funding, Bland's notes to the governor on need highlight circumstances in the community and in Newfoundland generally. "In a society comparatively large, yearly increasing . . . where the number of those who obey the laws through fear so much exceeds the opposite description, the Magistrates must ever be more or less obnoxious to many nor can he feel a more degrading mortification than when a want of power to execute the laws exposes him to the contempt of public transgressors." With respect to funding, Bland was frustrated by the fact that the planters and merchants were at an advantage, both with respect to the local servants and even relative to their counterparts back in England. "Why the inhabitants of this island, enjoying many privileges of a regular government, while they are exempt from the heavy burdens that bear down their fellow subjects in the mother country, should not provide their own jails . . . is beyond my comprehension." Polite banter between Bland and the governor of the day continued until 1807, when the jail was completed. When Bland asked Governor John Holloway for funds to pay for the jailer, Holloway replied that he had provided enough, and that £15 per year collected from the town should be sufficient "as I have great pleasure in being informed that good order and regularity prevails among the inhabitants of your district."

In the early 1800s, Magistrate Bland lobbied three governors of Newfoundland (Gambier, Gower, and Holloway) for a jail for Bonavista before he finally succeeded in seeing its construction in 1807. Given, as Governor Holloway observed, that "good order and regularity prevails among the inhabitants of your district," we might wonder why Bland persevered so adamantly. The answer might be found in letters several years later.

In a letter by Archdeacon Coster in 1825 to the Society for the Propagation of the Gospel, Coster noted that the "Court House," as he described it, had been destroyed by fire during the time of his predecessor, implying that the courthouse had burned to the ground sometime in the early 1820s. In a separate letter to the governor of Newfoundland (October 15, 1825), Coster noted that Bonavista had "neither Court House, jail, nor school room . . ." implying that the jail, schoolroom, and court functions were all conducted in that same building that had been originally constructed as a jail in 1807. Perhaps Bland had appreciated the need for a central building, close to the centre of the community, suitable for multiple functions. Bland may have felt that lobbying the governor of the day specifically for a jail would provide the best avenue for its construction.

Following the loss of the first courthouse in the early 1820s, another was constructed toward the late 1820s. As a reflection of the importance of this building, on September 27, 1830, James Douglas chaired a large meeting at the newly constructed courthouse to deal with the general distress within Bonavista and surrounding area (see Chapter 16). The new courthouse, as with the previous structure, continued to serve multiple purposes throughout the years. Magistrate Sweetland, as noted in his diary records for the early 1850s, spent most of his working hours administering justice at the courthouse, but noted occasional meetings with respect to road conditions or the establishment of a library. The November 20, 1851, entry indicates that Sweetland "attended a meeting at the Court House this evening to get up a library, which we accomplished, though on a small scale." The effort must have been successful, since a couple of years later, on March 17, 1853, Sweetland wrote that he visited the library and returned some books he had been reading. Sweetland even noted, in 1853, that the "potatoes . . . were planted on the 10th of May in the Court House Garden."

The courthouse, in addition to its formal responsibilities in the administration of justice, continued to play a role as a community centre, of sorts, through the remainder of the 1800s. James Ryan's diary noted that meetings of the Breakwater Commissioners and of the Agricultural Society were held at the courthouse, as were public meetings and occasional plebiscites. On August 10, 1888, the courthouse served as the focal gathering as a consequence of a visit by Governor Blake. Similar receptions were held at the courthouse on October 6, 1899, for Governor McCallum and on July 21, 1910, for Governor Williams.

On March, 18, 1897, at around 7:00 a.m., the courthouse was destroyed by fire. Nicholas Ryan wrote in his final entry for 1897 . . .

"No plague, fire, fever or famine has visited this community since last March when the Court House was burnt and mortality has visibly decreased of late according to the population of this town, and the needy poor of this place are few and far between, and on the whole we should be exceedingly grateful for all gifts bestowed upon us, and this Bonavista of ours, the Landfall of Cabot, should take a just pride in the welfare of her hardy sons of toil, the intelligence of her rising sons and daughters, and the enterprise and pluck of her many business and commercial men."

Construction of the new courthouse began in 1898 and was first used as the seat of justice for Bonavista on September 26, 1899. Nicholas Ryan wrote that "the structure has an imposing appearance from the site it is built upon—Court House Hill." A few months later, on January 20, 1900, a Miss Theresa Saint moved into an apartment at the courthouse, a section of which was assigned as the postal department. It was noted in the James Ryan diary that this was "rather an improvement on the old ramshackle tumble down office hitherto used."

The role of the courthouse as the centre for Bonavista diminished in the proceeding years as churches, schools, lodges, and other local and government buildings became established. But the courthouse remains a prominent, even imposing, fixture overlooking the harbour in the heart of Bonavista.

Bonavista Courthouse, early 1900s.
(Robert Abbott via Ross Abbott)

In 1809, Bland wrote to Rev. Dr. Coke concerning the proposal by the principal inhabitants of Bonavista that Mr. Remmington be sent to serve as preacher. As he had done on various occasions in the past, Bland was less concerned with orthodoxy than that the person residing in Bonavista and serving as minister should be "a man of simple manners, who will speak to the people in plain language, and appear to be in good earnest." Bland also noted that Mr. Smith "of your society" passed a winter in Bonavista . . . and that "Mr. Smith, or such a man as Mr. Smith, would find a very cordial reception from the inhabitants of this bay."

John and his wife, Sarah (Bayley) Bland, had three daughters and five sons: Arabella (born 1790), Elizabeth (1792), John Bayley (1794), Marcus Hill (1796), Edward Pakenham (1798), Fanny (1800), Horatio (1802), and Felix (1804). All children were born in Bonavista but were baptized by Rev. Dr. Clinch in Trinity. In 1809, John Bland was appointed High Sheriff for Newfoundland by Governor Duckworth. He and his family moved from Bonavista to St. John's in 1811. He retired in 1825, age seventy-seven, as a consequence of ill health.

Notes

The correspondence between John Bland and others is part of the Colonial Office 194 Series and in the D'Alberti Papers. Family information is based upon contemporary parish records in Bonavista and Trinity.

14 — MEDICAL PRACTITIONERS

The first medical doctor, as far as we know, to reside in Bonavista was Dr. John Clinch. He came to Bonavista in 1775 and practised medicine for eight years. Little is known of his stay in Bonavista, but upon leaving Bonavista for Trinity in 1783, he married Hannah Hart of English Harbour. In that same year, the inhabitants of Trinity petitioned the SPG on behalf of Clinch, and three years later, he was ordained. The Rev. Dr. John Clinch and wife, Hannah, had eight children.

Clinch is well-known as being responsible for bringing the smallpox vaccine to the New World. The person who developed the vaccine, Dr. Edward Jenner, was a student with Clinch in London, England, and they maintained contact after Clinch's move to Newfoundland, partly with the assistance of Jenner's nephew, George Jenner, who was stationed in Harbour Grace as both an Anglican clergyman and surgeon. In 1802, Clinch wrote to his colleague that "I began by inoculating my own children and went on . . . till I had inoculated 700 persons of all ages and descriptions, many opportunities soon offered at St. John's (where smallpox was making great ravages) which offered convincing proofs of the safety of the practice to the inhabitants and servants in Trinity Bay; they saw (at first, with astonishment) that those who had gone through the Jennerian inoculation, were inoculated with the smallpox, and exposed to the infection without the least inconvenience."

Clinch remained in Trinity for the remainder of his life and died in 1819.

Dr. John Mayne was Bonavista's second medical doctor. Although his arrival date is unknown, it was mostly likely sometime between Clinch's departure in 1783 and 1789, when a child of John and Elizabeth Mayne was baptized at the Anglican Church at Bonavista. Mayne's signature also appears on a Bonavista petition in 1791. He may have arrived with John Bland, who came to Bonavista in 1888, as they seemed to be good friends during the course of their tenure in Bonavista. Bland and Mayne, for example, were instrumental in supporting Rev. George Smith in Bonavista in 1795.

Georgina Ann Stirling, Newfoundland's "Nightingale of the North," is well-known in Newfoundland's history. She was born in Twillingate and became an international opera star. Ms. Stirling's grandmother was born in Bonavista.

Dr. John and Elizabeth Mayne had five children. John was baptized in 1789 and Henry in 1790, both in Bonavista, by Abraham Ackerman at the Anglican Church. Their next three children, Alfred, Elizabeth, and Emma, were all baptized in 1827 in Harbour Grace as adults. The Harbour Grace records are clear on the details of these baptisms—their parents were listed as John and Elizabeth Mayne, the records stipulate that they were born in Bonavista, and that they were respectively born in 1791, 1793, and 1796. The reason for not baptizing their last three children in Bonavista may have been related to the fact that Mr. Ackerman was not ordained, or as a consequence of John Mayne's, and Magistrate Bland's, efforts to find a more suitable minister for the town.

It seems clear that Dr. Mayne and Magistrate Bland were good friends. They likely arrived in Bonavista from Harbour Grace around the same time and either married local women at the town or were already married. They built or took possession of Fishing Rooms at the harbour in Bonavista (see Appendix 2). They both supported George Smith as Methodist missionary when he first arrived in Bonavista, and they both left Bonavista (Bland to St. John's and Mayne to Harbour Grace) around 1811.

A short while after John and Elizabeth Mayne and their five children arrived in Harbour Grace, their youngest daughter, Emma, married Dr. William Stirling, a surgeon of Harbour Grace who may have been a colleague of Dr. Mayne. When Emma and Dr. Stirling married, William was twenty-six, and Emma had just turned sixteen. In the following three years, Emma gave birth to two sons: John Mayne Stirling and William McClary Carrington Stirling.

Emma's husband, William, Sr., became a prominent member of the Harbour Grace community. He had been a surgeon in the Royal Navy, but upon settling in Harbour Grace with wife, Emma, and building his medical practice, he also served as magistrate, and as chairman for the Board of Commissioners for the Harbour Grace Grammar School, among many other functions. Meanwhile, their son, William, Jr., became a medical doctor himself and moved to Twillingate. When William, Sr. began to lose his eyesight, he and Emma left Harbour Grace for good to live with their son and his family.

Dr. William Stirling, Jr., married Ann Peyton—they had ten children in Twillingate. Their youngest, born in 1867, was Georgina Ann Stirling.

At an early age, Georgina's father took a special interest in her musical talents. He sent her to Toronto Ladies' College as a teenager to study music, then to Paris in 1888 for voice training. She joined a Milan opera company before returning to Newfoundland for a brief period in the early 1890s. In 1892, Georgina Stirling returned to Paris and adopted the stage name "Marie Toulinguet." Over the next few years, she toured England, then joined the New Imperial Opera Company based in New York. Her performances in New York, Philadelphia, and Boston were described as a "resounding success." She returned to Italy for a period, then England, before finally retiring back home in Twillingate. She died in 1935.

While in Bonavista, John and Elizabeth Mayne had five children. Though principally involved in his role as a medical doctor, Dr. Mayne also owned a store and flake premises at Bonavista Harbour. He and his family departed Bonavista for Harbour Grace in 1811, one year after Bland and family left Bonavista for St. John's. Dr. Mayne died in Harbour Grace in 1815, age fifty-four.

Dr. James Oakley followed Dr. Mayne to Bonavista shortly after Mayne's departure. He and wife, Mary, gave birth to Arianna Elizabeth Gill in 1813—she was baptized at the local Anglican church. According to Bonavista archivist information, Dr. Oakley settled in a home near Walkam's Bridge called the Oakley Cottage. While resident in Bonavista, he became paralyzed below the waist—local residents built a chair to transport him to his patients in the community. James died in 1829 at age seventy-four; his wife, Mary, died in 1844 at age seventy-five. They were buried next to each other in the Anglican cemetery on Church Street.

According to descendants of the Oakley family, when a new Anglican church was built sometime after Mary's death and burial, some of the headstones had to be removed. In protest, members of the Oakley family "moved their remains to the Wesleyan churchyard (now the United Church)" across the street. The headstone for James and Mary Oakley stands in the United Church today. Whereas most, perhaps all, of the headstones in the UC Churchyard face east, the Oakley headstone faces west.

The medicine cabinet and pestles owned by Dr. James Oakley. (Bruce Whiffen)

In 1964, Nimshi Crewe wrote to a descendant of the Oakley family. In part, he wrote ". . . your ancestor, Dr. Oakley was first buried in the Anglican churchyard and later disinterred and reburied in the Methodist yard—headstone and all, so I have heard." Crewe's files do not contain a response to his letter.

The veracity of this story is unknown. It is noteworthy that the story was related by a member of the family, that the respected historian Nimshi Crewe lent it sufficient credence to inquire, and that the headstone of two members of the Anglican faith should be found in the Methodist cemetery.

During at least part of Dr. Oakley's residence in Bonavista, he was assisted by Dr. John Skelton, whose presence is noted in the 1921 petition (Appendix 8). Skelton married Elizabeth Pittman, a native of Trinity, at St. Paul's Anglican Church in that place in 1823. They had eight children in Bonavista: Ann, George, John Gent, Pittman, James, Elizabeth Pittman, Mary, and Amelia. Both George and John received medical training in Scotland and returned to Bonavista. John married the daughter of an Anglican minister in Newfoundland, Rev. William Netten. George Skelton was the House of Assembly member for Bonavista from 1878 to 1885.

In the late 1870s, Dr. Robert Forbes and wife, Elizabeth (Cowan), moved to Bonavista from St. John's to establish his medical practice. Dr. Forbes was originally from Scotland and moved to St. John's in the late 1860s. In Bonavista, he worked for a time with Dr. John Gent Skelton before working on his own. Lench described Dr. and Mrs. Forbes as "a worthy couple." Lench described Dr. Forbes in particular as a "very highly respected and useful citizen. For a time (he was) Secretary-Treasurer of the Trustee Board (and) a Sunday School teacher (for the Methodist church)." Lench noted that he was a "regular attendant at church where his beautiful tenor voice was always in evidence in the church service. . . . We long in vain for a candidate to take Dr. Forbes' place as a man and a citizen." The reader will note that Dr. Forbes was the lead surgeon (Chapter 23, 1903) when it was

Dr. R. E. Forbes. From Lench's *The Story of Methodism in Bonavista.*

deemed necessary to amputate the leg of James Ryan's father, Michael Ryan.

James Ryan's diary 1918:

June 8, Saturday.
Dr. Robert E. Forbes breathed his last at 8:00 PM comforted by the presence of his wife, his daughter (Mrs. Jos Sellars), and his two sons John, now of Montreal, and Alexander, residing here following the footsteps of his father as a medical practitioner. The deceased was near unto 69 years of age, a native of Scotland, and a citizen of the very highest rank.

June 10, Monday.
The mortal remains of Dr. R. E. Forbes were interred this afternoon in the Methodist Cemetery by the Look-Out and near Big Brook. A large concourse of people followed his remains to the grave as well as the Odd Fellows Society of which he was a member.

Dr. Forbes's youngest son, Chesley Alexander, studied medicine at McGill University in Montreal and graduated in 1913. He married Irene Matthews in 1914—they moved into their new home just off Church Street and raised four children. When the Bonavista Cottage Hospital was opened in 1940, Dr. Forbes was named chief physician. He and his wife died within a month of each other in 1956. Like his father, Dr. Forbes was universally respected within Bonavista and throughout the area.

Dr. C. A. Forbes at his surgery, Bonavista. (From the Forbes Family Photograph Collection, Maritime History Archive)

Dr. C. A. Forbes and Irene (Matthews) Forbes, 1943.

Bonavista Cottage Hospital, 1947.

Notes

Some details on Dr. Oakley reside at the Bonavista Archives, Town of Bonavista. Bonavista Historical Society Fonds. A008.01. Series 5.

The letter by Nimshi Crewe is contained in the Nimshi Crewe Collection, Box 5, file 117.

Additional information on William and Georgina Stirling can be found at: clanstirling.org/william-archibald-stirling-of-newfoundland and www.tmacs.ca/ex_sterling.shtml.

Baptism and marriage records for the Mayne and Stirling families were obtained from the Bonavista and Harbour Grace parish records.

15 — THE HOSIER AND ALEXANDER AND MIFFLIN FAMILIES

Among the more established families in Bonavista in the late 1600s and through the 1700s, as evidenced in the census at that time, was the Newell family. Toward the latter half of the 1700s, the family had moved to Trinity, though they kept a strong connection to Bonavista via Newell's Room located near Walkam's Bridge. That connection was maintained in the early 1800s through marriages by Giles Hosier and William Alexander to Newell women of Trinity. The early Mifflin family maintained a close connection with the Hosier and Alexander families and similarly played an important role in Bonavista's early history.

i) Giles and Grace (Newell) Hosier

Giles Hosier was originally from Poole, Dorset, in southern England and had come to Trinity as an agent for John Jeffery. He married Grace Newell (a daughter of Jonah Newell at Trinity) in 1789. Lench described Hosier as "well educated, a man of refined tastes and superior attainments." Giles and Grace built a large home on the south side of what is now known as Coster Street, close to Walkam's Bridge and Newell's Room, which Hosier shared ownership of with his wife's brother, Thomas (Appendix 2). According to Lench, it was "a lordly home in good English style."

As we saw in Chapter 12, disaster struck the Hosier family in October 1812 when their eldest son, William, aged nineteen, was returning to Bonavista from St. John's with winter supplies. Their vessel sank, and all lives were lost. Lench wrote that "there was no insurance, and the loss spelled ruin to the Hosiers." Giles Hosier, Sr. died a month later. Then, in December 1812, Grace's youngest, and now only son, Giles, Jr., also died. Grace was left with four daughters and little means of support.

At the time, Methodist missionaries were visiting Bonavista routinely to provide support to the local converts. Grace opened her house to them as boarders, and in the process, two of her daughters married visiting preachers. Miss Jane (to use Lench's title) married Rev. Ninian Barr, and Miss Mary married Rev. Richard Knight. Miss Hannah married John Congdon, a graduate of Oxford University visiting Bonavista for a time, while the fourth daughter, Miss Bessie, taught some of the young children, then married a Mr. Fifield and remained in Bonavista. Jane's baptized name was "Jane Bland Hosier," undoubtedly in recognition of Magistrate John and wife, Sarah Bland.

The United Church Manse in the right foreground and the Methodist School behind it. (Wilson Whiffen via Ross Abbott)

Grace Hosier, in later years, turned her home, which Lench referred to as a mansion, to the Methodist Church in Bonavista. Lench described it "as a married man's parsonage, its fine garden and fields contributing to his convenience and that of his family." The building was torn down in 1958 and replaced with a new home for the visiting United Church ministers. Giles, Sr., Giles, Jr., and William Hosier are all buried at the Anglican Cemetery in Bonavista.

ii) William and Elizabeth (Newell) Alexander

The Trinity Church Records contain the marriage of William Alexander, from "North Britain," to Elizabeth (daughter of Thomas and Christian Newell of Trinity) on July 28, 1813. Thomas Newell was Grace (Newell) Hosier's brother—thus Elizabeth was Grace's niece. We don't know exactly why Alexander came to Trinity, but the witnesses to the wedding included a member of the Garland family, which was the major merchant family in Trinity at that time. Also possible is that William was living and working in Bonavista as an agent to the Garland family at the time of the wedding but had the marriage performed in Trinity because Rev. Dr. Clinch was the closest ordained Church of England minister.

In the early 1810s, Alexander Strathie constructed their new home close to Walkam's Bridge on Newell's Room. The house became known as the Bridge House and, in 1986, became a Registered Heritage Structure by the Heritage Foundation of Newfoundland and Labrador. The year of construction of the Bridge House is unknown, but Strathie's headstone, in the United Church cemetery on Church Street, reads:

> In Memory of Alexander Strathie
> A native of Greenock Renfrewshire Scotland
> and for 55 years a resident in this country
> who died May 22, 1869 in the 78th year of his age.

Since Strathie came to Bonavista to construct William Alexander's new home, it is reasonable to conclude that it was built in the year of Strathie's arrival, which, based on the information on the headstone, was 1814.

The home of William and Elizabeth Alexander, built by Alexander Strathie in the early 1810s. It is still standing and is commonly known as the Bridge House. (Centre for Newfoundland Studies, Memorial University, via CBC.ca)

Whether Alexander broke from Garland or (as Lench implied) came to Bonavista to start his own business, he eventually established "Alexander and Co." at Bonavista, one of the more prominent businesses through the late 1810s and early 1820s. Something of Alexander's character can be seen from a letter to the governor of Newfoundland by Archdeacon Coster in 1825. Coster was, at that time, engulfed in responsibilities and proposed Alexander as magistrate. His letter indicates that Alexander was "intelligent and upright" and also obtained the support of Mr. Samson Mifflin in his request, describing Mifflin as "the gentleman . . . who alone besides Mr. Alexander possesses the qualifications which the office demands and who alone, if another magistrate is requisite, could be recommended to the office." At the end of Coster's letter, Mifflin appends a note that "the appointment of Mr. Alexander of the Office of Justice of the Peace will be a measure very agreeable to me."

The success of Alexander and Co. toward the mid- and late 1820s is unclear. In Coster's letter to the governor in 1825 respecting the distress in Bonavista as a consequence of the failed fishery (Chapter 16), he notes that "there is now no large mercantile establishment at all in this place," though, in fairness, this commentary may have had more to do with the size of those establishments in Bonavista relative to Trinity or St. John's.

William Alexander died suddenly on June 22, 1828. The *Royal Gazette* in St. John's:

> Died at Bonavista on Sunday night, William Alexander, Esq., merchant of that place, aged 44 years. On the Tuesday preceding his death, he had occasion to arise at a very early hour in the morning to give some particular directions respecting a bait skiff, and after retiring from the window in which he stood, he had scarcely reached his bed when he was violently attacked by a paralytic stroke, which proved fatal. He was long and deservingly respected in the mercantile world, and has left a wife and five children to lament his premature death.

Archdeacon Coster buried his friend and fellow magistrate on June 25. Their children at that time were William, Jr. (born 1816, all years are approximate), Elizabeth (1822), Robert (1822), Isabella (1823), and George (1826). Alexander's wife was pregnant with their sixth child, John, at the time of her husband's death—John was baptized in early 1829.

In 1936, William Sweetland arrived in Bonavista as magistrate for the area. A widower himself, he met widow Elizabeth Alexander, and in 1839 they married at the Methodist church (witnesses Samson Mifflen and the bride's daughter, Elizabeth). Several years later, he recorded, in his diary, news of the death of his wife's son, George.

"We went to spend the evening at Doctor Skelton's with our two girls and whilst there received a letter from Mr. Bremner detailing poor George Alexander's death which took place on the 18th (December 1851). I did not break it to Mrs. Sweetland till on returning home. The scene was a dreadful one to all of them but to Mrs. Swd & poor Bell (Isabella) who looked like a petrifaction for neither of them could cry. It scattered Mrs. Swd's senses for the time. Bell and George were most tenderly attached to each other & God only knows what will be the result of it."

William and Elizabeth Alexander's other children, those first young inhabitants of the Bridge House, should also be chronicled. William, Jr. became a medical doctor and eventually moved to Mexico, as did John. Robert became a successful businessman and politician in St. John's. Robert's sister Elizabeth (they were baptized on the same day in 1823) married John Martin in Bonavista: their child "George Alexander Martin" was baptized in Bonavista in 1853. Isabella remained a spinster in Bonavista.

When Robert Alexander died in 1884, he left funds in his will for the poor of Bonavista to be distributed by the clergy of all denominations. It became known as the Alexander Charity Fund. When Isabella died in Bonavista in 1891, she similarly left funds for the widows and orphans of Bonavista, the Anglican Church, and a mortuary chapel. The Alexander Mortuary Chapel of All Souls in Bonavista was designated a Registered Heritage Structure in 1989.

Meanwhile, and as we've seen, William Sweetland's diary provides a glimpse into the life of the Sweetland family. It also provides a view into life in Bonavista itself. On June 3, 1851, Sweetland wrote "In the afternoon we had fine sunshine weather when Mrs. Sweetland & myself availed ourselves of it to take a walk upon the Bird Island Cove Road where we sighted our cow which appeared to be in good order tho she has been out for the last month—brought out some junipers for transplanting but they are of stunted growth." In fact, his diary references many walks with his wife . . . to Mockbeggar, Canaille, White Rock, Beaver Pond (among others), or just looking for "specimens of rock crystals." He also chronicled his and his wife's visits to both the Methodist and Anglican church services and happily offered his assessments to his diary of the sermons. He enjoyed the humour in life as well. On March 18, 1851, he recorded a race between him and the medical doctor to see who would reach home first. "We dined with Mr. B and after dinner walked home and almost beat Dr. Skelton with his horse and sleigh—he overtook me and cut me off—I think I reached home within ten minutes of him." On June 29, 1851, on his sixty-third birthday, he wrote that "I have enjoyed much of peace and happiness beside 'the still waters of comfort' at Bonavista." Can we detect a touch of sarcasm?

One tragic entry in particular is repeated here:

Anglican Christchurch, Church Street, Bonavista. Officially opened in 1931 and replaced in the late 1970s. One of the most beautiful buildings constructed in Bonavista. Some of the headstones of the first cemetery in Bonavista are visible in the foreground. (Forbes Family Photograph Collection, Maritime History Archive, Memorial University)

June 20, 1851 . . . called to Bird Island Cove to hold an Inquest on the Body of John Chant, an Englishman resident there, who this morning committed suicide by hanging himself. It appears the poor fellow has been suffering under a severe attack of influenza which reduced his strength causing frequent fainting fits, lowness of spirits, a feeling of weariness of life or of something hanging over him, terrified . . . that he should become an encumbrance (and) a hindrance to his family, a belief that his days were nearly run out . . . tied himself up . . . he had been missed about two hours by his son who on searching for him found him suspended . . . the kind-hearted Wesleyans refused his remains a resting place within their yard but fortunately he had, poor fellow, one of his own within his potato garden where he had interred some two or three of his children & where I directed they should place him.

Another entry is a lesson to any visitor to Bonavista with thoughts of descending into the Dungeon:

Oct. 2, 1851 ... Mr. Frasier ... went with Miss Shears and Isabella to view the dungeon and scrambled his way down into it without the assistance of a rope and in ascending narrowly escaped having his brains dashed out by a large loose rock falling on him which knocked his hat off and compelled him to descend again to recover it and seek a safer return.

Mr. Sweetland wrote a history of Newfoundland, but it was never published. Mr. & Mrs. Sweetland are buried together in the Anglican Cemetery.

iii) Samson and Mary (Ackerman) Mifflin

Samson Mifflin was baptized in 1770 at St. Paul's Anglican Church in Poole, southern England. His parents were Solomon and Jane (Randall) Mifflin. Solomon was originally from Warminster (just north of Poole) and worked as an agent for Joseph White, the principal merchant in Trinity, Newfoundland. Solomon frequently travelled between Poole and Trinity/Bonavista.

Solomon's wife, Jane Randall, may have been born in Bonavista. In a 1759 will by "Sampson Mifflin ... late of Warminster but now of Poole," Sampson left his "main estate" to his brother Solomon, but also references his goddaughter, Mary, daughter of Joseph Randall, Sr., of Bonavista. It is likely, though not certain, that brothers Sampson and Solomon referenced in this 1759 will were uncle and father to the young Samson baptized in 1770. Randall was a prominent name in Bonavista at that time. Joseph Randall's name is on the Bonavista petitions of 1742 (Appendix 3) and 1752 (Appendix 4). Samson Mifflin, baptized in 1770 in Poole, may actually have been born in Bonavista, but as there were no clergymen in Bonavista (nor possibly, at that time, in Trinity), Solomon and Jane may have chosen to have their child formally baptized by an ordained clergyman in Poole.

Solomon and Jane were married at St. Paul's Church in Poole in 1767. In addition to Samson, they also had a son Joseph Randall Mifflin (baptized in 1774), who drowned in Bonavista in July 1789.

Samson Mifflin worked, like his father, as an agent for the merchant firms in Trinity and, as evidenced by his signature among those leading citizens of Bonavista in the petitions of 1791 (Appendix 9) and 1792 (Appendix 10), had established a respected role for himself at an early age. On November 2, 1795, he married Mary Ackerman in Bonavista, who was likely related to Abraham Ackerman, the local lay person responsible for performing baptisms, burials, and marriages.

Samson and Mary had six children: Joseph (born 1796), Jane (1800), James Randall (1800), Thomas Randall (1801), Edward Ackerman (1802), and Mary Ann Pinner (baptized 1807). Samson's wife, Mary, died in 1807. Samson thereafter married Jane (maiden name unknown), with children Samuel (1812), George (1814), John, and Susan (1819).

Walkam's Fishing Room was identified in Bland's 1805 Register of Fishing Rooms (Appendix 2) as being owned by Solomon Mifflin and occupied by "S. Mifflin" (presumably Solomon, or possibly Samson). The Register indicates that the Fishing Room was partly purchased and partly built by the Mifflins.

Through the 1810s and 1820s, Samson Mifflin was frequently asked to be the executor of the will of some of the wealthier members of the community of Bonavista—a clear indication that he was looked upon with a degree of respect, confidence, and trust. When Archdeacon Coster, in 1825, recommended to the governor of Newfoundland that William Alexander be appointed magistrate, he wrote that he had obtained the support of Mr. Samson Mifflin, who "alone besides Mr. Alexander possesses the qualifications which the office demands and who alone, if another magistrate is requisite, could be recommended to the office." With the advent of Representative Government in Newfoundland in 1832, Samson Mifflin served as justice of the peace, returning officer, and as Commissioner of Roads in the Bonavista–Catalina area.

Although Joseph Randall, Joseph White, and Solomon Mifflin were Quakers, Samson Mifflin and his family, through the passage of time, became loyal members of the Church of England in Bonavista. But he was also supportive of the Methodist Church, helped finance the construction of the first church, and paid for a pew in the gallery (Appendix 6).

We don't know when Samson Mifflin's father, Solomon, died, but it may have been sometime around 1815. The death of Samson's mother, Jane (Randall), was recorded on April 7, 1833, by the *Dorset County Chronicle*, in which it was stated that she was the late wife of Mr. Solomon Mifflin (merchant, deceased), had died at the age of ninety-one after a few days' illness, was of a "mild disposition and goodness of heart," and that she "retained her faculties to the last."

Samson Mifflin died in September 1855, aged eighty-four. He is buried in the Anglican Cemetery, Bonavista.

The Honourable Fred Mifflin, the Member of Parliament in Ottawa for Bonavista–Trinity–Conception, a member of Prime Minister Jean Chrétien's cabinet, and formerly a rear admiral with the Canadian Armed Forces, helped escort Queen Elizabeth II and Prince Philip during their 1997 visit to Bonavista. He was a great-great-great-grandson of Samson Mifflin.

Notes

William Sweetland's Diary:
http://collections.mun.ca/PDFs/sweetland/SweetlandDiary.pdf.

A short biography of William Sweetland:
http://collections.mun.ca/cdm/landingpage/collection/sweetland

Family milestones were retrieved from the Anglican and Methodist Church records for Trinity and Bonavista.

16 — DISTRESS

The Napoleonic and Anglo-American wars of the late 1700s and early 1800s led to a reduction in fish harvesting in many countries throughout western Europe and in the New World, which, under normal circumstances, would have been competing with Newfoundland. In the early 1800s, then, both the fishing industry and the population of Newfoundland increased in response. From 1805 to 1815, for example, the population of Newfoundland and the volume of fish exports doubled. At the end of these wars, into the mid-1810s and beyond, the boom years at Newfoundland came to an abrupt end. Increased fish production elsewhere led to a dramatic drop in cod prices, and communities in Newfoundland, including Bonavista, did not have the means to support the increased population.

The Kelson and Slade diaries from Trinity, Trinity Bay, perhaps catch a glimpse of the influx of people into Newfoundland. On April 17, 1811, they wrote that "40 or 50 Irish youngsters came overland from Bonavista where they were put onshore from the Brig *Swift*," which had been lost in ice in Bonavista Bay earlier in the month. Four days later, April 21, another entry recorded that "a cargo of youngsters arrived in Bait's skiff from Ragged Harbour (later renamed Melrose), being part of those landed from the *Swift* lost in Bonavista Bay." This was just one incident, of course. Men and women, boys and girls, throughout England and Ireland were moving to Newfoundland.

The impact of the downturn in the economy was immediate. As early as 1815, "the inhabitants of Bonavista [are] very short of provisions . . ." as noted in the Slade and Kelson diaries. Two years later, in November 1817, the principal inhabitants of Bonavista, including Magistrate Ford and William Alexander, wrote to Governor Pickmore on the "unparalleled distress which many of the inhabitants of this Island experienced during last winter and from this place (Bonavista) was not exempted." Following the harsh circumstances of the winter of 1816–17, there was hope that the summer fishery would provide some relief. This did not happen. "The unsuccessfulness of the fishery this season has produced barely a sufficiency to maintain those employed in it . . . a great part of the population of this harbour are destitute of the common necessaries of life, and from this time until the return of the fishing season next year, there is no means by which the industrious poor can be employed so as to procure subsistence." The letter estimated that one-third of the 1,700 inhabitants of Bonavista were "in a state of actual want, and as many more will in a few months be in a similar situation . . . if some means of relief be not speedily devised many must inevitably perish."

A glimpse into the state of affairs in Bonavista, at a personal level, is provided by Rev. Ninian Barr, a Methodist minister in Bonavista on December 30, 1821. As recorded by Naboth Winsor in his *History of Methodism*: "The distress of many at this time is truly painful. I will state the case of one man as an instance. He came to one of our leaders lately, and begged to have the loan of a sail. He was asked what he wanted it for. He answered that he and his family had little or no food, as little firing, and that when they could suffer the cold and hunger no longer they went to bed, and having little bed clothing, they were almost perished there, and he wanted the sail to keep them warm. The weather is rough and cold now, almost beyond anything I have known in the island." The horror of this tale lies not only with respect to the specific circumstance of one family but that it was reflective of perhaps many families throughout Bonavista, that it was happening during what should have been a joyous time of year, and that it was happening at the onset of the long winter and spring season.

The Slade and Kelson diaries give further details of a circumstance that would last into the 1830s:

Saturday, May 7, 1825.

Skiff *Dart* bringing two constables who came from St. Johns with letters from the Chief Justice, indicative of the distress & misery prevailing in Bonavista, to which place they are bound, to relieve the indigent sufferers—the relief will be afforded by the bounty of a British Government, through the medium of the Chief Justice.

Monday, May 9, 1825.

William Morris and the Constable Butt went . . . to Bonavista with the dispatches from the Chief Justice at St. John's relative to relieving those in actual want.

Archdeacon Coster described the circumstance in Bonavista in a series of letters, in the fall of 1825, between himself and the colonial secretary, E. B. Brenton, to the governor of Newfoundland, Thomas Cochrane. Coster noted that "the fears I entertain . . . are not groundless, when I state that no quantity of provisions worth mentioning (not a single boatload at any one time) has even at this later period (October 25, 1825) entered our harbour with the exception of one schooner from Trinity. The boats of those who used to supply great numbers now return from St. John's in ballast, or at least with only a few articles for the private stock of the owner. All seem to declare with one voice that they will supply none who do not pay up their accounts for the year past, which cannot be after so bad a voyage, the case with many out of a population of 1500 souls . . . a great deficiency must inevitably occur."

Coster attempted to describe the circumstances that led to the conditions in 1825. "The catch of fish during the past two years has been unusually low while, and at the same time, the price of it unusually low, while provisions have been very dear. For thirty years previous to the last two, a bad voyage had not been experienced in Bonavista, the consequence of which has naturally been a redundant population and a want of preparation. . . . Till very recently the various little outharbours along the shores of the bay of Bonavista afforded a vent for the excessive population but these are now all stocked with living creatures as many as the fishery they have room for will maintain. All agree that the fishery carried on in Bonavista is not alone sufficient to support the people it contains and that they must direct their attention to some other profitable employment . . ." "Scarcely any seals were caught last spring of which great numbers are usually taken. Bonavista has always been a noted place for seals and the number of these valuable animals annually taken has been to the inhabitants a resource little inferior to the cod fishery itself." Without identifying the establishment, Coster also identified the "breaking up of a large mercantile establishment (which) threw great numbers out of a good employment (while) several minor establishments which to the people's misfortune have attempted to occupy the ground thus left vacant, have this year totally failed."

Coster recommended that "the most approved way of affording relief to a redundant and distressed population is to employ a portion of the people in works of public utility . . . we have in Bonavista neither Court House, jail, nor school room and any number of stout and tolerably skillful labourers might under present circumstances be engaged . . ."

As Coster had arrived only recently to Bonavista, he asked "my neighbours who are most likely to know what will be the extent of our distress" and stated that "they all with one assent to the truth of the statement in my letter of the 15th which has been confirmed by the enquiry at every point." Coster noted that some suppliers are obliged to contract their business in order to save themselves from ruin while others "have given up the business altogether." The governor sent provisions to Bonavista that fall. Coster thanked the governor generally, and noted that "the potatoes sent will prove a very acceptable gift for the excessive dryness of the past summer has been unfavourable to that crop in most parts of Bonavista and moreover the poor people have absolutely been obliged, for want of food, to begin digging them long before they were ripe or had arrived to half their size . . ."

Naboth Winsor (*A History of Methodism in Newfoundland, vol. 2*), through reports by local missionaries at the time, noted the bad economic conditions in 1826, as anticipated by Rev. Coster. He wrote that in 1826, "many of our people (in Bonavista are) moving in quest of new settlements because of the failure of the cod and the seal for two years. Some of our leaders and members have been under the necessity of crossing the bay for the winter."

Cochrane's support was provided with significant reservations. In a letter to The Right Honourable Earl Bathurst, Cochrane began by lamenting that "Perhaps no Governor ever assumed his government under more discouraging circumstances . . . than I did on my arrival at this Island. . . . Bonavista was described as being threatened with famine from an absolute want of a sufficient quantity of food to carry its inhabitants through the winter." While noting that other communities in Newfoundland suffered similar circumstances, Cochrane was suspicious. "I will . . . state that being full convinced, by experience, that it is most desirable in every case where it can possibly be attained, that a population should be thrown upon its own resources, and not encouraged in seeking a relief, the natural effect of which is, to make it, on a subsequent year, still more dependent on those who supported it. . . . I received with great caution the statements made to me."

Two years later, on October 30, 1827, Rev. Coster wrote that "I am happy to say that I do not think distress will be so generally prevalent among us, as it was during the last three winters, or would have been but for the timely assistance of the Government." Coster wrote that the past season was "very successful, and very little of the fish caught has proved to be of bad quality after curing." Measles visited the area in the midst of the fishery, which "occasioned a grievous interruption to the progress of many," while the potato crop was "a very abundant one." With respect to the population in general, Coster, perhaps in response to Cochrane's suspicions, wrote that "they (the inhabitants of Bonavista) are orderly and quiet and not a criminal case was brought before the court."

The extent of the measles outbreak that Coster references is indicated in the diary of Thomas Gaylor, Jr., a clerk in Bonavista for the firm Slade and Kelson in Trinity (which had branches in Catalina and Bonavista). Most of the diary from 1827–1829 has been preserved and transcribed. For the most part, deaths are mentioned only for those perhaps noteworthy individuals in the community—a total of ten deaths in all. But the measles outbreak from late August to early October, 1827, changed that. During that time, Gaylor noted the following:

Aug. 31.	Hannah, daughter of Joseph Abbott, departed this life this evening in the measles.
Sept. 2.	Two children buried this day that died in the measles.
Sept. 5.	A child of Mrs. Hopper's died.
Sept. 6.	Elizabeth Pardy died last night.
Sept. 7.	Henry Gale died last night and a child of N. Howlett's (?) this morning.
Sept. 8.	Three funerals this day.
Sept. 9.	Elizabeth, wife of R. Ryder, died last night.
Sept. 16.	The remains of the late Mary Oldford interred.
Sept. 19.	A child of J. Romaine died this morning.
Sept. 20.	A child of John Mouland's died this day.
Sept. 21.	Died last night Giles Little, Thomas Chaffey, Jr. And a child of T. Reader, Jr.
Oct. 3.	The remains of the late Jane Tucker interred.

In addition to the deaths noted by Thomas Gaylor in his diary, the Methodist burial records note that there were eleven burials among the Methodist flock between September 3 and October 7, and only four of them may be inferred to be among the deaths noted by Gaylor. Of those eleven Methodist burials, seven were children under the age of five.

The Church of England records also note, indirectly, the measles outbreak. There were eight burials recorded in 1827 up to July 11. Then, from September 8 to October 5, there were ten burials, six of whom were identified as infants. There were only two burials for the remainder of 1827.

Sept. 8.	Anne, infant child of John and Susanna Hopper
	George of John and Betsey Pardy
	Betsey, wife of John Pardy
Sept. 9.	Martha, infant child of Nicholas and Martha Howlett
Sept. 16.	Mary, wife of George Oldford, Bird Island Cove
Sept. 24.	George, infant child of Thomas and Jane Soper
	Thomas Chafey, son of Thomas and Mary Chafey (aged 26)
Sept. 26.	James, infant child of Thomas and Mary Pardy
Sept. 30.	William, infant child (illegitimate) of Mary Howse
Oct. 5.	Maria, infant child of Orlando and Elizabeth Hallett.

Gaylor ended his diary for 1827 with "And so ends this troublesome year."

Gaylor's diary primarily records weather conditions, the comings and goings of vessels and passengers, and, as we've seen, occasional deaths. Some events were recorded that provide a glimpse of the challenges faced by the community, even during a short period of time. On Thursday, April 12, 1827, Gaylor described a "most dreadful storm of thunder and lightning, hail and rain that lasted two or three hours" and which struck the house of Charles Fisher, causing considerable damage to the house and throwing "a large rock a distance of thirty feet . . . fortunately all the family (survived)." On October 2, 1827, Gaylor wrote that "all the stages at Canail and Gosling's (were) knocked down with the sea." On January 25, 1828, he noted that "Jane Weeks, in going to B. I. Cove (Bird Island Cove, now Elliston) yesterday missed her way and this morning was found a corpse. A boy that was with her escaped and was but little frostbitten."

Rev. William Wilson. From Lench's *The Story of Methodism in Bonavista.*

In 1830, distress (to use the word commonly employed at that time) returned to Bonavista with a vengeance. Rev. Coster had departed for Fredericton and was eventually replaced by Rev. George Dodsworth. The Methodist minister at that time was Rev. William Wilson—he had arrived from Brigus on June 9, 1829 (as noted in Gaylor's diary). In addition to poverty and famine, Wilson also recorded the impact of the diphtheria epidemic that struck the region at that time. In this own (edited) words . . .

"Many fell victims to this dire disease. The family of Mr. George Crew, one of our leaders in Bird Island Cove, who lost three members of his family by this disease in twenty-one days."

And from Wilson's journal:

July 8, 1830. This afternoon I interred two children; both died on the same day of the prevailing epidemic, one little boy, four years of age, was the son of Mr. George Crew, one of our leaders.

July 17. Saturday, Mary Minty, a married daughter of brother Crew, was taken alarmingly ill with sore throat.

July 19. Susannah, a girl of twelve, second daughter of brother Crew, was taken with the same complaint.

July 24. The girl Susannah died on Sabbath morning and was interred today. On entering the room, what a sight! The coffin containing the corpse of Susannah lay on the table, near which was her sister Mary Minty, struggling in the agonies of death, and in the interim of her pain, shouting "Glory to God." In another part of the room sat Joseph, suffering severely, and apprehending the fatal result of his disease; in an adjoining apartment was the poor mother, whose feelings can much better be conceived than described—bewailing the loss of two of her children and expecting every moment to see a third expire, while a fourth was in a very dangerous and critical state.

Wilson further wrote that "For more than a year, did this fearful plague . . . rage in Bonavista and Bird Island Cove. It seemed for a time as though it would depopulate the place; its victims were numerous; it seized persons of all ages, and no constitution was proof against its attacks. At length . . . the complaint entirely disappeared from the people." But no sooner had the plague disappeared from the region than famine reappeared among the communities. "Several families subsisted on nothing but potatoes and salt." From Wilson's (edited) journal two years into the famine . . . "I called upon a poor widow with six children. She uncovered a barrel containing two or three buckets of potatoes. 'This is all the food I have and all I ever expect to have.' She is reduced to a skeleton for want of food. 'When my children get up in the morning, I send them round to beg a potato from the neighbours; if they succeed I am thankful; if they do not succeed, I roast two or three . . . I find by this means the lives of my children can be saved until my potatoes are all exhausted; when my heavenly Father may yet smile upon us and send us deliverance."

As Rev. William Wilson played a leadership role in the distress of the early 1830s, a brief biography is warranted. He was described (T. W. Smith) as "a youth of short, slender figure and active temperament. In his native Lincolnshire village, a pious mother had led him in childhood to respect religion, but after her death he had entered into the follies common to his age and circumstances." While in London, "he heard the truth" and began to give addresses to the inmates of a London prison. He was recommended for the ministry, was "received on trial" in 1820, and ordained in 1821.

Rev. William Wilson kept a detailed journal on everything he saw. His book *Newfoundland and its Missionaries* not only articulates the history of Methodism in Newfoundland up to the mid-1800s, but also meticulously describes various aspects of life in Newfoundland. He goes into great detail, for example, in the process from landing fish on the stagehead to salting and drying the finished product. He describes everything from class structure (merchants, planters, fishermen) to the construction of a "tilt" during winter housing. After a year in residence in Bonavista, he chaired the "Committee for the Relief of the Poor in Bonavista and Bird Island Cove," even though he had only recently arrived in the community.

Rev. William and wife, Elizabeth Wilson, welcomed two children into their world during his stay in Bonavista. Arabella Martha was born on September 6, 1829 (baptized the following year by Rev. John Tomkins), and Matilda Faulkner, baptized in 1832 by Rev. Faulkner. According to Lench, Arabella was the fist child born in Bonavista of a resident Methodist minister.

Rev. Wilson was not without controversy. In the Minutes of the Newfoundland District for May 28, 1833, we find "several charges of imprudence being preferred against Brother Wilson and which have so oft been repeated even against the repeated admonition of the Board . . . we do mostly earnestly recommend his removal to England or at least from this Island to some other place." Hollett notes that the Wesleyan Methodist Missionary Committee had charged him (in Wilson's own words) "with having conducted myself so improperly that there is scarcely a place or Circuit in the whole District willing to receive me and that all the Societies shun me as a common pest." There were rumours of drunkenness— several witnesses testified "to having seen him inebriated." He was "extremely disliked," "absolutely held in contempt." He was even charged with engaging in fortune-telling, astrology, and the "black art" (Letters from the Methodist Newfoundland District Meetings, 1833), which he strongly denied.

Following the committee's admonition, Rev. Wilson spent a brief period of time at Trinity and Blackhead, and transferred to Prince Edward Island in 1834. He spent the remainder of his years in Nova Scotia and New Brunswick. Rev. Wilson died on September 26, 1869 (*Encyclopedia of Methodism in Canada*), on his way home from an afternoon service, in a small community in New Brunswick. "While riding in his waggon, the reins dropped from his hands, the horse moved slowly on, the material form was there, but the spirit had gone." T. W. Smith wrote that he "had been a man of much general information, well-tested loyalty and intelligent zeal" and continued with the rather intriguing note that "he had a quick scent for heterodoxy and a power to deal with certain forms of it which has not yet received proper recognition." Rev. Wilson had spent fifty years in the ministry and was seventy years of age.

On September 27, 1830, James Douglas chaired a public meeting at the newly constructed courthouse in Bonavista on the concerns for the poor. Attendees initiated the "Committee for the Relief of the Poor of Bonavista and Bird Island Cove." Rev. Wilson was named chairman; Michael Carroll was secretary. Other members of this committee were Dr. John Skelton, Capt. Thomas Gaylor, Sr., Joseph Mifflin, George Brown, Thomas R. Mifflin, Samson Mifflin, James Brown, Edward Mullally, James Douglas, George Robins, and Robert Brown. Rev. George Dodsworth, the Church of England minister, had just arrived in Bonavista and was not present at the meeting, but added his name to the consequent petition and was later named treasurer.

The intention of this committee was to obtain assistance from the governor. Before approaching him, however, the committee assessed the degree of distress and the available food supply. Bonavista and Bird Island Cove were divided into six districts—with one member of the committee assigned to each district to determine the number of men, women, and children in need of assistance and the amount of food each possessed. They ascertained that 90 men, 96 women, and 401 children, in possession of only 1,832 barrels of potatoes for the coming winter, were in desperate need of help from the government. The petition sent to the governor read, in part:

> At a public meeting held at the Court House, Bonavista, on Monday 27th September 1830, to take into consideration the distressed state of that harbour and Bird Island Cove adjacent . . . it was unanimously resolved:
>
> i) That this harbour is in a state of great distress, some hundreds of people being totally unprovided for, and unless some other means than the harbour is likely to furnish of obtaining subsistence be discovered starvation must be the inevitable consequence before the ensuing spring,
>
> ii) That a petition to His Excellency the Governor be prepared and that such a petition shall contain an exact statement of the situation of the inhabitants and a humble request to His Excellency for relief,
>
> iii) That the crop of potatoes though good is nevertheless inadequate to the want of the inhabitants during the winter.

An accompanying document stated "that the merchants' stores of Bonavista do not contain any provisions to meet the wants of the inhabitants and that the earliest time upon which they can calculate upon supplies is the month of June, and therefore when their stock of potatoes is exhausted, which from the above facts Your Excellency will see must be early in the winter, nothing but Your Excellency's bounty, which we now humbly solicit, can save many in this place from actual starvation." In return for provisions, the committee proposed improving the roads from Bonavista to Catalina and from Bonavista to Bird Island Cove.

Upon receipt of the petition, the governor's secretary, E. B. Brenton, decided to travel to Bonavista to see, first-hand, the extent of distress described by the petitioners. He stayed for a brief period of time at the home of Samson Mifflin, a local merchant who served additionally as magistrate, and prepared a report for the governor. Brenton wrote:

> [I solicited the opinion of] several of the most respectable inhabitants to the distress of the people arising from the failure of the fishery and to the steps which had recently been taken at the public meeting in order to convey to Your Excellency a correct statement . . . of relief required to save a portion of (the inhabitants) from perishing during the ensuing winter. . . . From all the information I have been able to collect on this subject from those best qualified to afford it, I have reason to believe that the statements which have been forwarded to Your Excellency are not exaggerated and that unless the bounty of government can be extended to this unfortunate part of the colony by providing for its wants during the approaching winter, the fatal results anticipated will assuredly happen. The distress I understand to be far greater than what it has been at any former period, exceeding either that of 1825 previous to Your Excellency's arrival in this island or to those of the subsequent years in which you afforded the relief so strongly called for.

With respect to the committee's proposal to improve the condition of the roads from Bonavista to Bird Island Cove and to Catalina, Brenton offered the following comments:

> I can from my own experience attest to the necessity of some improvement in the communication between this place (Bonavista) and Catalina. Not being able to reach Bonavista, I was obliged to put into Catalina on Monday, and in order to be on time at the former place for the discharge of my official duties, was compelled on Tuesday to proceed hither by land through paths and swamps which in any other country would have been deemed nearly impassable.

The Governor promised to supply 750 barrels of potatoes and two puncheons of molasses—a proposal which ironically initiated a couple of problems for the committee.

> We assure Your Excellency that it is utterly out of our power to provide a vessel to bring the potatoes to Bonavista and even if it were, now that the

season is so far advanced we feel they would be injured by the frost . . . Under these circumstances we most respectfully request that Your Excellency would be pleased to grant us bread in lieu of potatoes as it could be brought round with very little difficulty and freight free.

The governor later provided a large quantity of bread and molasses, which the committee distributed to those in need provided they agreed to be employed at improving the road conditions. In a report to the governor on April 6, 1831, the committee gave an insightful description of events during the winter:

The Committee . . . determined that the persons relieved in Bonavista should cut a new line of road to Catalina; and those relieved in Bird Island Cove should be employed in improving the road from thence to Bonavista; and that the men should receive four pounds of bread, the stout boys three pounds and the small boys two pounds per day and also that a small quantity of molasses be given them at the termination of their work.

In reference to the road to Catalina, the Committee has succeeded beyond their most sanguine expectations. They discovered a tract of country nearly in a direct line to Catalina and almost clear of marsh and hill; on this tract they have cut a road from six to eight feet in breadth; and have built bridges over the brooks, and it is presumed it will be quite dry in the summer season. It has been carefully measured, its angles taken, and mile boards put up at the expense of the committee. The distance is nine miles and a half.

The only means the Committee had of perpetuating their request for His Excellency the Governor was to name the road after him. They have therefore unanimously agreed to erect a board with an inscription expressive of their sense of His Excellency's humanity and kindness. The Committee hopes that His Excellency will be pleased to allow the road to bear his name.

On the Cochrane Road, there were employed 25 men and 8 boys, number of days worked 576. The aggregate of their families—153.

The Bird Island Cove Road has been considerably improved. On it, there has been employed 12 men and 8 boys; number of days worked 331. The aggregate of their families—64 individuals.

As soon as the frost set in, the Committee began to turn their attention to the timber His Excellency had instructed them to procure. In Bonavista, they have obtained 614 sticks from 36 men; the aggregate of whose families is 184 individuals. In Bird Island Cove, there were obtained 258 sticks from 15 men, the aggregate of whose families in 74 individuals.

The same report noted that on February 4, provisions were provided to "26 families, comprising 79 individuals," and on April 6 to "28 families comprising 85 individuals."

Rev. Wilson, in his *Newfoundland and its Missionaries*, stated that Governor Cochrane (appointed to the post in 1825) was responsible for construction of the first and second roads on the island—from St. John's to Portugal Cove, and from Harbour Grace to Carbonear. Perhaps the Cochrane and Bird Island Cove Roads were the third and fourth roads constructed on the island, and the first outside the Avalon Peninsula.

Hardship continued through the winter of 1831–32. Rev. Wilson's journal (quoted from Winsor's *Building on a Firm Foundation*):

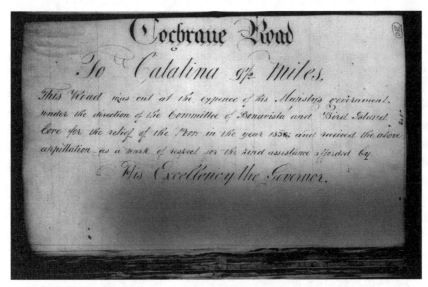

The sign proposed to be constructed on the road between Bonavista and Catalina in recognition of Governor Cochrane, contained in the letter from Bonavista to the governor of Newfoundland, November 25, 1830.

Saturday, Mary 5, 1832.
The past winter was certainly the most severe that I have ever experienced. It has frozen almost incessantly since last November, and the frost has been intense, the thermometer having fallen frequently to from fifteen to eighteen degrees below zero. The cold still continues, and the

ground is as impervious as in the month of February; whilst the bay and, as far as we can judge, the whole coast is completely blocked up with ice.

The severity of the winter, followed by a severe spring, and the general failure of the seal fishery; and this again succeeded by an ice-bound coast that prevents any supplies from being brought into the harbour, have all added to that poverty which has long oppressed the inhabitants of Bonavista; and they are at this moment in circumstances of great distress.

In fact, the cries of distress, bordering on actual starvation, are truly appalling. During the winter, whole families have been necessitated to live upon potatoes and salt, with scarcely any other article of food; and the extreme severity of the frost have destroyed a great number of potatoes. Two persons are reported to have fainted away from hunger; while the wan countenances, and debilitated constitutions of others, through in the prime of life, render them objects of the greatest commiseration . . .

Some families are now subsisting entirely on a small pittance of Government bread, issued under the direction of the Committee. But this resource must soon be exhausted; and as no provisions can be obtained from the merchants' stores, should navigation be interrupted only a short time longer, the consequences to many is likely to be serious.

. . . in the midst of poverty our members continue steadfast. Our chapel on Sabbath evening is well filled. Our prayer meetings in private houses, of which we have held two every week during the winter, have been usually crowded.

Sunday, May 27, 1832.
The ice is still in our bay; and in consequence of the impediment it offers to navigation, our people are reduced to great distress, and famine begins to be felt amongst us.

Sunday, June 3.
Another week has passed on, and no appearance of a clear coast. Yesterday, the wind came to the east and still continues to blow violently from east to southeast; so that the ice that was in the bay is driven up with greater force than before.

Monday, June 4.
Almost every day some instance occurs of cattle dying from want of food; and report states that nine horses died from the same cause last night . . . al-

most every stock of provisions is nearly exhausted. The Government provisions are all expended. The potatoes which were our only dependence, are also almost gone; and there is only one store that contains any provisions, and that only in a very small quantity.

There is now a schooner in sight that has been in the ice for six weeks. Some of the crew walked ashore today, and report that their companions are almost perishing from cold and hunger.

Monday, June 11.
The ice is still on our coast. The grass does not yet spring. Cows, horses and dogs are dying from want of food. The potatoes are almost exhausted. I asked a poor widow what she gave her children to eat; she replied: "I send my children out in the morning, and if they can get a morsel, well; if not, I give each of them two or three potatoes a day, as I have yet a bucket or two of potatoes left."

Friday, June 15.
In the midst of our distress, a kind Providence has supplied the wants of our almost perishing poor. On Wednesday, a letter was received from the President of His Majesty's Council, directed to the Rev. George Dodsworth, Samson Mifflin, Esq. and myself informing us that the news of our distress having reached St. John's, the Governor had directed the Magistrates of Trinity to purchase and send to our relief forty bags of bread, twenty quintals of fish and twenty gallons of molasses. Had it rained bread from heaven it could not have come more unexpectedly.

This morning I walked to Catalina, accompanied by nearly one hundred of our perishing poor, to distribute a part of the Government boon. We shall hold the remainder another week, if we can, as the ice is still on the coast. The total number of families relieved today, and that are to be relieved tomorrow is 176, comprising 914 individuals.

Wednesday, June 20.
Thank the Lord, the ice is leaving the coast and we expect relief in a short time.

Entries (edited) from the Slade and Kelson diaries (Trinity, Trinity Bay) for the same time are worth providing as they, in general terms, support the events as noted by Rev. Wilson in his diary. The reader is reminded that weather conditions and ice floes can vary significantly between communities.

Sunday, June 10.
Ten men from Garland's Schooner *Arrow* and William Verge's Schooner, laying in Conception Bay, travelled over the drift ice from New Perlican to Eastern Head Random and came by land from Heart's Ease, this day. Also, several planters who have been ice-bound for this fortnight past & upwards, were compelled to travel by land in quest of provisions. Harbour Grace, Carbonear & all along the south shore of this Bay, with King's Cove, Bonavista, Catalina, etc. are in extreme distress for the wants of provisions.

Tuesday, June 19.
Garlands Boat, Jasper Hiscock Skipper; with provisions for the relief of the sufferers at Bonavista, who are in extreme distress for the want of food of every kind.

Wednesday, June 20.
Bonavista Bay is still jammed with ice, so that no craft can proceed round the cape in that direction.

Thursday, June 21.
This day bears no appearance whatever to convince us of the approximation of mid-summer being close to our doors, with chilling cold atmosphere, drift ice still besetting us, which is the primary natural course, (or the only way in which the writer can account for it), for the long continuation of very cold weather.

Friday, June 22.
We are again flattered with hopes, undeserved, of the prospects of a change working effectually permanent. Afternoon and evening we have just reasons to suppose that our anticipations of a change are now actually realized. The wind continuing to blow from the southwest, a pleasant breeze accompanied with fine clear warm weather inshore, hazy, in the offing, the drift is driving rapidly out of the bay.

Saturday, June 23.
Commenced with moderate breeze from the southwest and at length, fine, warm weather. The drift ice moving out of the bay rapidly. There is yet some quantity drifting about in the harbour, but by far the greater part has melted, and is now consuming quickly. Afternoon & evening,

smart breeze continuing from the southwest, weather fine & warm, hazy in the bay all day.

Saturday July 7.
Government Schooner which brought potatoes, etc. here for the relief of the inhabitants of Bonavista sailed for St. John's this morning.

Mr. and Mrs. Meek, two teachers hired by the Newfoundland School Society, were instructing children and adults at Bonavista during this period. In his annual reports, Mr. Meek wrote of the "almost total failure of the fishery . . . starvation must in all probability be the inevitable consequence." The Annual Report for 1832 wrote that "Mr. Meek states that the sufferings of the people of Bonavista had attained a fearful height. In consequence of the failure of the fishery, the protracted winter and the entire stoppage of all navigation by the ice, multitudes must have perished had it not been for a timely arrival of relief from the government and a change in the weather."

The Committee for the Relief of the Poor disbanded in the spring of 1832. "The Committee in closing its business desires to express its most grateful acknowledgements to His Honour the President from the prompt and liberal assistance afforded to the distressed whom they have represented. It is resolved that as no further exertions on the part of the Committee appear at present called for, it be forthwith dissolved."

A letter of thanks to the Governor, signed by Rev. Wilson, Rev. Dodsworth, and Samson Mifflin, stated that "We respectfully tender our most grateful thanks to Your Honour for this very seasonable and unsolicited relief to the poor sufferers and trust that our endeavours in distributing it with the utmost parsimony will meet with Your Honour's approbation." This letter was accompanied by a list of the names of the 178 families who received assistance, and the amount of bread, fish and molasses each received. A letter from Rev. William Wilson to the editor of the *Royal Gazette* is found in Appendix 11.

A darker side of life in Bonavista during this difficult time was provided by Rev. H. J. Fitzgerald, a Church of England minister who arrived in Bonavista in 1832. After a few months, he informed the governor of his observations.

When I look around me, I see a moral desert . . . piety and religion scoffed at or abused. . . . The laws are most flagrantly violated.

The stores of Mr. Samson Mifflin have been twice entered by violence and articles stolen. . . . A small store house of Mr. Alexander, with whom I lodge, not five yards from my bedroom window was daringly robbed of the poultry which it contained . . .

When . . . that large supply of provisions was sent (by the government) such a spirit was at work among the people, it was deemed unsafe to have the provision conveyed to Bonavista . . . a few bags at a time used to be brought over to Bonavista by the Committee in order to be distributed to those who were unable to go to Catalina for it, the sick, the infirm, the aged, the orphans, the widows. Horrible to say, the store in which it was kept has been thrice broken open, and thrice has the bread been stolen . . .

The cellars of very many individuals (many poor widows among the number) have been robbed of the few potatoes which their gardens produced . . .

The people also in the most public manner threaten to kill the domestic animals of their neighbours . . . they openly say that they are justified in proceeding any extremity to satisfy their hunger.

Notes

A general discussion of economic circumstances leading up to the distress at Bonavista can be found at: https://www.heritage.nf.ca/articles/economy/19th-century-cod.php/ (retrieved January 27, 2020)

The information from Mr. and Mrs. Meek is found at the Centre for Newfoundland Studies, MUN. Newfoundland School Society. Microfilm A-322. 1823-1833.

The Slade & Kelson Diaries are online at MUN's Digital Archive Initiative and at PANL, The Rooms.

Minutes of the Newfoundland District are housed at the U.C. Archives, St. John's, NL.

The Cochrane Maps are located at the Archives, The Rooms, St. John's, GN2/2 1831 (1) vol. 7. Correspondence begins on page 272.

Further details on Rev. William Wilson are found at the:
United Church Archives, Elizabeth Avenue, St. John's, NL. Minutes, Newfoundland District Wesleyan Methodist Church, England. 1829-1850.
National Archives, Ottawa. Methodist Newfoundland District Meeting, 1833. Microfilm A-266 (letters 78, 79 and 80).

References:
Maritime History Archives: Names Files.
Parish Records at Bonavista and Trinity
Personal Records of the Mifflin Family, Bonavista.
Charles Lench, *The Story of Methodism in Bonavista.*

17 — WINTER HOUSING

As settlement became more strongly established in the 1700s and 1800s, the transition from summer to winter activities involved the settling of accounts between the fisherman and the merchant. Supplies for the winter season were accorded to the fisherman by the merchant according to the success of the fishery. Upon settling of accounts, many fishermen families resorted to what has been termed "winter housing"—living inland or in another bay away from the fishing location during the winter season, then returning once again in the spring season for the start of the next fishing season.

Smith (in *History Today*) described that as settlement began in the late 1600s, fishermen and their families, and servants, began to shift from returning to England to settling into inland residences for the winter. This occurred throughout Newfoundland in those early years, and no less so in Bonavista. When the fishing season drew to a close in the fall, there was little or no reason to remain along the coast. In fact, for Bonavista, it made more sense to move inland or to other coastal locations, for a couple of reasons. First of all, Bonavista is located near the tip of the Bonavista Peninsula and therefore exposed to the extreme winter storms that pass through the region. The removal of much of the forestation throughout the area for construction of fisheries infrastructure, homes, and firewood would have enhanced this exposure. Secondly, food would have been found more easily inland, through animal meat (e.g., caribou, bear) or fish (salmon, trout). Wood would have been harvested both as heat for the winter tilts in which they lived and to bring back to Bonavista. And finally, furs, salmon, and wood might be returned to the principal planters and merchants in springtime for compensation.

Captain James Story spoke of this is 1681. "The fur trade is further north, towards Bonavista . . . the planters go a furring about the middle of September and take no provisions with them but bread and salt, finding beavers, otters and seals enough to feed on. They carry guns, and kill also a great deal of venison, which they salt down for the winter. They return about 1st May."

Captain Ogle, in 1719, gave another account, again describing "winter housing" in one of its various forms:

The furring trade the last year proved of very great advantage to the inhabitants of Bonavista many persons having taken to the value of £40 sterling per man for the winters' season, all the furs so taken is sent to Great Britain by the Poole and Livington ships using that trade, the seal fishery to the northward is likewise to very great advantage and greatly encouraged by Mr. Keen who yearly purchases all of that commodity. Recommends Christopher Sheppard as a good person to help police Bonavista during the winter season.

Hollett described winter housing as a means by which settlers not only addressed the need for wood production, but communication between settlements, and even resettlement to other communities. Winter housing, in time, supported the population growth of coastal Newfoundland. Rev. Charles Bates (from Hollett) reported in December 1826 that because of poverty, many had left Bonavista that fall to go "across the bay," where food was more plentiful. Archdeacon Coster references the same pressures in a 1825 letter to the governor (Chapter 16), in which he writes, "Till very recently the various little outharbours along the shores of the bay of Bonavista afforded a vent for the excessive population but these are now all stocked with living creatures as many as the fishery they have room for will maintain."

Wilson explained that a number of families, not only in Bonavista but elsewhere along the northeast coast, worked in the woods "to do a winter's work," collecting firewood, building boats, and hunting wild game. A sled or catamaran was used with a horse or dog team to bring wood from the country. A portion of the firewood was reserved for the clergy. The winter houses were called tilts, made of spruce studs, with moss wedged between the studs and bark as an overlay. Holes were left to allow a vent for smoke and for the sun's rays to penetrate. Stones were used to form a fireplace. Wilson said that he and his family lived in a tilt near Burin (which he called Wesley Vale) in the winter of 1827–28.

In Winsor's *Building on a Firm Foundation*, an excerpt from a letter by Rev. Adam Nightingale in 1836, while stationed in Bonavista, described his visit to Keels, near Bonavista, where there was a small church consecrated by Bishop Inglis. Nightingale wrote "the whole of the inhabitants, with the exception of three or four families (according to Nightingale, 186 Protestants and 110 Catholics lived there) leave this place in the fall of the year for different parts of the bay, where they live in small houses called 'tilts,' and return again to the harbour in the spring."

The habit of moving inland and to other harbours was easily accomplished in the 1600s, as fishermen and their families had already made the trip from England and Ireland to Newfoundland, where they had constructed the necessary infrastructure along the shoreline from scratch. Winter housing continued into the 1700s and 1800s for a variety of reasons, all motivated, ultimately, by survival during that time of year when the fishery was shut down. The custom died out in the latter half of the 1800s and in the early 1900s.

Notes

Captain James Story: Calendar of State Papers, Colonial Series, America and West Indies, 1681-85.

Captain Ogle: Colonial Office 194 Series. Vol. 6. 1719.

18 — SEALING

We know that early settlers to Bonavista were engaged in the seal fishery as early as 1681, as noted by Captain James Story (Chapter 5). In the 1600s and 1700s, many inhabitants were "winter housing" into other coastal areas of eastern Newfoundland. The seal fishery in winter and spring helped to supplement their livelihood before the cod fishery recommenced after the ice had departed in late spring or early summer.

In 1802, Governor Gambier asked Bonavista's Magistrate John Bland to describe the seal fishery along the northeast coast of Newfoundland and into southern Labrador. Bland's response to Gambier was several pages long and provided a detailed insight into the working lives of the people of Bonavista at the time.

Bland described the seal fishery as an "adventurous and perilous pursuit" that is prosecuted during the winter months by nets, and during the spring in "ice skiffs, decked boats or schooners." The nets used during the winter were about fifty pounds in weight, forty fathoms wide (one fathom = six feet) and three fathoms deep. Four to five men in each boat attended to about twenty nets. In Bland's letter, he wrote in detail about the nets themselves and how they were positioned in the ocean. He also spoke of the difficulties in disengaging the seals from the nets and noted that "none but men active and inured to hardship can be qualified to engage in it." Bland further described the types of seals and those that provided best yield of oil.

Bland then related circumstances specific to Bonavista Bay in the winters of 1791–2. "A succession of hard gales from the northeast brought the seals in great numbers before the middle of January, unaccompanied by any ice . . . a circumstance that rarely occurs. In Bonavista, about two hundred men might have been employed in attending the nets . . . and the number of seals caught amounted to about seven thousand. The entire catch at Bonavista Bay may be taken at ten thousand . . ." Over the course of the next few years, from 2,000 to 6,000 seals were caught each year. "In the spring of 1801 we may count about twenty thousand, the greatest part of which were dragged on the ice by men, women and children with incredible labour."

"The sealing adventure by large boats, which sail about the middle of March, has not been in general longer than nine years. It has been pursued with various success . . . from two to three thousand men have been employed in this perilous adventure, and it may excite surprise that so few fatal accidents have happened." Bland clearly understood the dangers inherent in the seal harvest and foretold the sealing disasters to come.

William Sweetland's diary, in *Occurrences at Bonavista*, record one such harrowing sealing circumstance in Bonavista in 1839.

March 30.
Morning, light airs from the east-southeast. About 9 o'clock it commenced snowing with a little more wind. Noon, wind southeast blowing fresh, afternoon blowing smart from the SSE with snow and very thick. Evening, blowing from the south and less snow. A great many seals seen today and a great distance in the northwest and several hauled onshore; but 14 men and 7 boys were not onshore at 10 o'clock, but we hope they may reach Mr. Brown's schooner or the schooner "Mary."

March 31.
Morning, blowing smart from the west by north and very cold. Noon, blowing smart from the north-northwest with snow. Evening, blowing smart from the northwest by north with drift. Arrived this day at 12 o'clock, 19 out of the 21 poor fellows (to the great happiness to those to whom they belonged) that were driven off yesterday, leaving behind them two poor fellows, Thomas Mealey and L. White. It appears that young Thomas Dyke happened to be one of the party and had more courage than the rest; according as he came across them, he advised them to keep beating up the bay and accordingly they did so, and fortunate for them Mr. Wm. Brown's two schooners, "Rebecca" and "Thomas," happened to be jammed up off Broad Cove, and some of the men belonging to the "Thomas," being aloft, observed the men, who had themselves arranged along the edge of the ice, it being about one and one-half miles from her. They launched three punts and took them all on board, and as the schooners drove down the bay off Blackhead and the ice being into the shore, properly safe all hands left her and landed all well in Brown Head Cove."

Bland's concern for "fatal accidents" was well-founded. Tragedy escaped these men, and boys, in 1839. We'll see a different result in Chapter 24.

Notes

Bland's 1802 letter is contained in the D'Alberti Papers.

19 — WOMEN IN THE EARLY YEARS

The history of a country, a region, or even a community is typically based upon the written word of those who lived during that time. We rely upon the documented accounts of explorers, missionaries, merchants, and politicians, to name a few. We search through their diaries, journals, and letters. We access government documents and newspaper reports. Invariably, these documents are written by men and are usually about men. Women, when noted, are often nameless.

Although women, individually, were generally not acknowledged in original source documents for Newfoundland and Bonavista in the early centuries of the New World, there is no doubt but that women were as instrumental, if not more so, in establishing settlement. Rev. William Wilson gives a detailed account of life in outport Newfoundland, and given that Bonavista was a significant part of his stay (and was perhaps the largest community during his tenure in Newfoundland), it is reasonable to conclude that his description applies as well to Bonavista as elsewhere. He detailed the three well-known classes of "men" in the outports during the 1800s: the merchants, the planters, and the fishermen. The planters were the owners of the fishing boats that supplied fish to the merchants. They hired the young men who worked on their boats. The wife of the planter, in Wilson's words, "is generally the skipper of the shore crew (who are mostly female." This would include the daughters of the planter and his wife, as well as any girls brought over from England to help. The shore crew was responsible for taking the fish from the boats and preparing it for sale or credit to the merchant. Wilson commented that "the labour of the females is quite as incessant, and even more exhausting, than the labour of the men. When the men have thrown the fish upon the stage-head, it is put upon the splitting-table, by one of the females." Wilson describes in great detail (as was his habit) how the women passed the fish from one person to another (from splitting to salting) until the entire catch of fish is processed. If the catch is large, the work "will occupy the whole night." "Often I have heard the women complain for want of sleep, and say 'If I had but two hours' sleep in twenty-four, I could stand the week's labour; but to do without rest for nearly a week is too much for my strength.'"

John Bland, in a letter to the governor in 1802, noted that "In the spring of 1801 we may count about twenty thousand (seals), the greatest part of which were dragged on the ice by men, women and children with incredible labour." Wilson made a similar observation: "Sometimes the drift-ice will come into the harbours with thousands of seals, when men, women, and children will go to get a haul. It is said that, in the spring of 1843, near 20,000 seals were thus taken by the people from the shore." Hollett similarly noted that "working on the fish flakes was a labour common to women, and in many cases exclusively so." We may even take it a step further. As noted in Chapter 11, of the six plantations in Bayley's Cove in 1805, three of them were owned by women: Sarah Abbott, Rachel Mesh, and Hannah Pladwell.

Hollett described the manner in which the work of women within the Methodist movement was generally ignored or only grudgingly acknowledged. Maria (Palmer) Nightingale, husband Rev. Adam Nightingale, Jane (Garland) Hickson, husband Rev. Thomas Hickson, and Martha Downes all played important roles in supporting Methodism and yet were given only passing reference, or no reference at all "but for her obituary." The *Wesleyan Methodist Magazine* recorded that Jane Hickson had the ability "both to feed and guide the flock of Christ," which Hollett noted "is close to stating that she was a preacher."

More recently, Hilda Chaulk Murray, in *More than 50%*, described the role of women in Elliston, an outport community not far from Bonavista. She wrote "No woman in Elliston went catching cod, but this was the only part of the operation in which she was not involved . . . any of the operations performed in 'putting away' a boatload of fish might be done by a woman." Further, "in summer, fishermen's wives were expected to combine homemaking with long hours of work outside the home, either at the fishery or at the gardens." The conclusion that "it was universally accepted that the matriarch was the driving force in meeting the family's and indeed the entire community's needs" is not difficult to accept. And although Murray's work was specific to Elliston in the early 1900s, her description is consistent with our understanding of the work of women in Bonavista from the time, in the 1600s, when they first arrived and settlement first began.

PART FOUR: INTO THE TWENTIETH CENTURY
20 — HARDSHIP AND HEROISM

Winsor, in *Building on a Firm Foundation*, wrote that growth in Bonavista through the 1820s to 1850 was difficult. As a consequence of the failure of the cod and seal fishery, many moved from Bonavista around 1826 in quest of new settlements. "Great suffering" was again noted in the early 1830s, as a consequence of the bad fishery and failure of the potato crop. "Positive starvation would have been the consequences had not God inclined the heart of the Governor." "Great poverty; a lack of clothing" was again prevalent in 1847, when "members moved to another harbour" in search of better conditions. In 1848, of 750 members of the Methodist church in Bonavista, "550 are paupers."

Magistrate William Sweetland of Bonavista painted a somewhat different picture to the colonial secretary. On May 13, 1839, he wrote:

> I beg to congratulate His Excellency on the prosperous state of this district at the present time. The last season's prosperous fishery, the economical method of catching and curing their fish, their agricultural pursuits, the employment afforded them on the road from hence to Catalina, the productive seal fishery with nets during the winter and the spring haul of seals, by what are denominated the sharemen added to the success of the sealing schooners, all contribute towards that honest independence which the inhabitants of this place in particular appear to be aiming at and are desirous of achieving.
>
> During the past winter, though a long and severe one, we have not had more than one case of distress at this place and that arising from the loss on the sea of the father and oldest son of the family who perished through the inclemency of the weather.

Philip Tocque (*Newfoundland, As it was . . .*) gave another account:

> "There is no part of Newfoundland where I have seen so much poverty as in Bonavista, in 1841 and 1842 . . . were it not for their gardens, the fisher-

men of Bonavista could not live." Later, Tocque says ". . . notwithstanding the poorness of the diet, a hardier, healthier or better looking race of men are not to be found upon the face of the globe!" One is reminded of Lench, who said of the people of Bonavista ". . . good stock it was (the earlier settlers at Bonavista), judging from the splendid physique of their present day descendants, of which there are no finer specimens of physical manhood in the Colony."

While economic conditions improved in Bonavista in the latter half of the 1800s, hardship was always on its doorstep. Nightingale wrote (as quoted by Winsor, vol. 2) in 1851:

Last September and October (i.e., 1850) we were visited with two strong gales, which are said to have done damage to the amount of some thousand pounds; more than two-thirds of the fishing-boats were driven from their anchorage to the shore, where twenty-one were totally wrecked, and others greatly damaged. All the fishing-stages, with the exception of four, came down; and all the fish, oil, and salt that were in them, together with most of the utensils of the stages, were lost. Fences not a few were levelled by the gales; ours did not altogether escape. The fish on the flakes in large and small piles, was considerably scattered, and rain in abundance came down upon it.

The first gale took place in the night, which was very dark, and which will be long remembered by those who rose from their beds to secure their property, but with little success. It is the general opinion, that there never was such a wreck or loss of property, in one year, in Bonavista before.

Magistrate William Sweetland provided similar details in his diary.

Tuesday 10th September 1850.
The gale which was raging at midnight continued to blow with increased violence until daylight when it began to abate and veered northward— The harbour presents a scene of desolation again. Several boats bottom up at their moorings—a great number on the beach and many a total wreck. A great number of stages down and our own in a dilapidated state—a great number of garden fences laid prostrate—in fact the loss is incalculable to the poor people.

These storms were undoubtedly hurricanes that had developed in southern latitudes, then tracked northward toward Newfoundland. This is not uncommon. Hurricanes require very warm ocean waters in order to form and intensify—conditions which are most prevalent in the Caribbean in late summer and early fall. Usually, these storms will dissipate as they pass over colder waters near Newfoundland. Occasionally, however, they will re-intensify if atmospheric conditions are supportive of redevelopment. The two storms of October and September 1850 were likely intense hurricanes crossing eastern Newfoundland.

Many of the most severe storms in Bonavista through settlement in the 1600s and 1700s were never recorded, while those of the 1800s occasionally found their way into the journals and diaries of residents and visitors. The diary of James Ryan, a merchant in Bonavista, records (below with minor edits) three such storms, in 1880, 1885, and 1907.

1880

Saturday, November 20.
Fine day. Wind west-northwest, blowing a stiff breeze.
9 PM. Wind considerably lulled and veering southerly. Fearful sea rolling. Anxiety felt for crafts in the harbour. John Powell's boat came ashore this afternoon. R. Ford's came ashore 7 PM.

Sunday, November 21.
Blowing a gale from south accompanied by a mixture of rain and snow.

Monday, November 22.
Wind blowing fits from west-northwest. The "Penguin" and "Pearl" are total wrecks. The "Scud," Sam Carroll's boat, and the boats of Richard Hicks and Samuel Hicks ashore all more or less damaged. At Noon, the schooner "Paragon," having begun to drag her anchors as early as 9 AM, finally went ashore at Mockbeggar. Seas running so high and wind so strong as to prevent any attempt at boarding her.
5 PM. The "Flying Arrow," "Joy," and the boats of Sampson Mouland & Robert Little are ashore. Later on, Keel's boat ashore.

Tuesday, November 23.
The gale was tremendous during the night and the cold severe.

9 AM. Aneroid barometer 29.5. "Paragon" still holds together but it is evident that unless the wind lulls she will break up today. D.A. Ryan with a large crew and every conceivable means at their disposal are preparing to board her if they find it possible. Commissioner of Wrecked Property and posse of police in attendance.

1885

Monday, June 8.

A gale of momentous and unparalleled severity visited us yesterday, causing a loss to property to the amount of five thousand pounds.

Baine Johnston & Co's barquentine "Christabel" drifted from her moorings at Swerry Head and held on at a cable's length from Caplin Cove. One man lost. Schooners "Sunburst," "Minnie," "First Trial," Saint's craft of Goose Bay, and "Ida May" totally lost. Joy's, Paul Hampton's, Clarke's, Goodland's (2), Russell's, Groves', Skiffington's, and several other small boats, came ashore. The beach presents a sad appearance and is strewn with debris in great quantities.

Tuesday, June 9.

Fine day. Wind variable. Water smooth.

The beach presents a scene of mutilated wreckage—boats, pieces of them, stage material, and other necessaries for the fishery are strewn in all directions.

A great many fishermen have no means nor boats to fish in, and what they will do sorely puzzles them.

1907

Tuesday, September 17.

Wind northeast this morning, but very light. Weather still dull. At noon the wind veered to the south, and the weather became wet. Weather dry enough to handle dry codfish. Discharging dry fish in lighters from "Grace" & "Sweetbrier." Flakes covered with fish out drying.

"Snorre," new vessel just off the stocks, arrived at 5 PM laden with flour for this firm. She is chartered to load a cargo of shore fish in bulk.

Wednesday, September 18.
Wind northwest, a stiff breeze with rain at intervals.
Rain of unusual severity set in after dinner from a northwest direction and continued incessantly for several hours when the wind veered to north-northeast and it lulled away but again at 9:15 PM a hail of rain came down & the wind blew violently.
Some of the craft at Swerry Head may suffer during the night.

Thursday, September 19.
During last night's storm, the Norwegian Schooner "Snorre" was driven ashore west of Canaille Point and became a total wreck. Two seamen drowned. Four rescued. Four schooners driven ashore at Canaille—one a total wreck, others severely damaged.
Wind continues from the northeast today, blowing a gale with heavy seas. A large quantity of wreckage floating around the shore which tells of the fearful destruction of property at this place.

Lewis Little. From Lench's *The Story of Methodism in Bonavista.*

Friday, September 20.
Wind north, a good breeze, but not so high as yesterday. The sea that raged yesterday has also abated.

James Ryan's diary does not record the heroic efforts of the six Bonavista men who risked their lives to save the crew of the *Snorre*, though it does record the medal presentations the following year. Lewis Little, Robert Brown, James Little, William Ford, James Ford, and Eli Paul managed to rescue four of the crew. They were recognized by the Government of Norway, the Carnegie Hero Commission, the Royal Humane Society, and the Governor of Newfoundland. The Carnegie Fund Commission Report (as recorded by Lench) described the heroic event in great detail, which is repeated in Appendix 12.

James Ryan's diary recorded the reception the following year.

1908

Saturday, May 9.
We are to have here on Monday or Tuesday next His Excellency of the clan MacGregor and Tasker Cook, vice-counsul for Norway, the Governor's Lady and daughter and his aid-de-camp. His Excellency comes for the sole purpose of pinning and presenting the silver medals of the Norwegian Government and the testimonials of the Royal Humane Society upon the breasts of those prominently distinguished for their heroic bravery in saving the lives of the Captain and two mariners of the Norwegian sloop "Snorre" in the gale of the memorable night of 19th September 1907, which caused such destruction of life and floating property over the island, especially in the district of Trinity where a score of people were lost or drowned and after some days the bodies were recovered and brought to Trinity Harbour and buried in the precincts of consecrated ground there.

Monday, May 12.
His Excellency Governor McGregor, lady and daughter, aid-de-camp Goodridge, and vice-consul Tasker Cook arrived here per SS *Dundee* at 8 AM. A deputation of citizens met His Excellency on landing and escorted the party to their lodging house. An address from townspeople will be read at 3 PM by Magistrate Roper and afterward the medals of the Norwegian Government and testimonials of the Royal Humane Society will be presented by His Excellency to the gallant rescuers of the Captain and crew of the ill-fated Norwegian sloop "Snorre" on the memorable and disastrous night of the 19th of September last.

21 — CAPE BONAVISTA LIGHTHOUSE

On April 8, 1841, the Government of Newfoundland passed "An Act to make Provision for the Establishment of a Lighthouse at Cape Bonavista." Shortly thereafter, Ambrose Shea, the secretary to the Lighthouse Board, travelled to Bonavista to select the best location for the lighthouse. Shea was a young man at the time but, through his responsibilities with Royal Mail Steamships, was well-versed in marine requirements. Ambrose Shea is well-known to Newfoundland historians. He was elected to the House of Assembly and 1848 and was a prominent figure in business and politics throughout his life.

Shea had two choices for the location for the lighthouse at Cape Bonavista: that part of the mainland of Cape Bonavista farthest north toward the sea, or the small island known as Cape Island, just offshore. According to Molloy, Shea wrote that if Cape Island were chosen ". . . a suspension bridge would be necessary for this purpose, and I doubt much even if the Commissioners felt disposed to sanction so large an expenditure as this would involve . . ." For reasons of safety and cost, then, Shea chose a site on the mainland, just adjacent to the island. Shortly thereafter, John Saunders of Bonavista began construction of the lighthouse as well as the tower embedded within the dwelling needed to support the light. The design was based upon the Cape Spear lighthouse near St. John's.

Meanwhile, the Newfoundland Lighthouse Board had learned that the light at the Inchcape Rock in Scotland was being replaced. They described the light as "of a very superior character—unequalled by anything of the kind on this side of the Atlantic" and decided that it would be used for the Bonavista lighthouse. Although the building itself was completed by the end of 1842, Robert Oke, the chief inspector of the Newfoundland Lighthouse Service who also oversaw installation of the Inchcape Rock light, rejected the tower built within the lighthouse as inadequate and insisted it be rebuilt with nearby stone and topped with granite. When completed, the tower was four metres in diameter. Finally, on September 11, 1843, Thomas Bennett, chairman of the Commissioners of Lighthouses for Newfoundland, ordered the lighthouse into operation. In his letter to the colonial secretary for the governor, he noted that the Cape Bonavista lighthouse, "at an elevation of one hundred and fifty feet," would revolve at "regulated intervals of two minutes, exhibiting alternately a red and white light."

The light sitting atop the lighthouse was comprised of a series of sixteen Argand burners, which were each centred inside a curved reflector so as to reflect light outward from the lighthouse and toward the ocean. These were mounted on a metal frame that revolved continuously. Power was provided by a weight-driven mechanism that had to be loaded every two hours.

Cape Bonavista lighthouse. (Glenn Mitchell)

The first lightkeeper was Jeremiah White. Jeremiah was born around 1792 in Taghmon, County Wexford, Ireland, and according to family tradition, his wife died at an early age. Jeremiah moved with his two oldest sons to London and then, in 1842, to Newfoundland. His youngest child, a baby girl, remained in Ireland. In St. John's, he worked as groundskeeper for Government House and was reassigned to the lighthouse at Bonavista. He first spent three weeks training at the Cape Spear lighthouse near St. John's, then moved into the living quarters of the Cape Bonavista lighthouse with his wife, Mary, and their four children: Matthew, Nicholas, Johanna, and Thomas.

It is unknown when Jeremiah married Mary, his second wife—perhaps they met in either London or St. John's. Presumably Matthew and Nicholas were children of his first marriage, and perhaps Johanna was the young baby girl from his first marriage as well, sent across to Newfoundland when she was old enough to travel.

In addition to keeping the light in operational status and maintaining the lighthouse itself, Jeremiah White also served to inform the local community about passing and approaching vessels, the movement of pack ice, and the presence of seals.

In 1871, at age 79, Jeremiah passed responsibility for the lighthouse to his son, Nicholas, who had been assisting his father for the previous fourteen years. Five years later, James Ryan's diary records the following:

1876

March 7, Tuesday.
Mr. Jeremiah White, died today about noon aged 84 years.

March 9, Thursday.
The late Mr. Jeremiah White was buried today at 3:30 PM.

Less than two years later, on New Year's Eve, 1877, Nicholas died. He was forty-two. Ryan's diary noted that "Mr. Nicholas White's remains were buried this afternoon (January 1, 1878) and followed to their last resting place by a large and respectable concourse of all classes of this community."

Responsibility now fell to the remaining two sons. The elder, Matthew, became lightkeeper, and his younger brother, Thomas, was his assistant. Johanna moved to St. John's. Ten years later, Matthew became ill, and he died two years later:

1889

August 26, Monday.
Matthew White passed into eternity this evening at 7 o'clock. Deceased was suffering acutely for the past two years until stern death came yesterday, and bore him to the realms of the Great Unknown. May he rest in peace. His age is 60 years.

August 28, Wednesday.
The funeral of Matthew White took place at 2:30 PM. The last tribute of respect was paid him by his friends and followers who assembled in

goodly numbers to do honour to one whom they loved in life and whom they mourn in death. May God have mercy on his soul.

Responsibility for the Cape Bonavista lighthouse now fell to the youngest, and only remaining male of the original family. Thomas White served until 1895.

The Inchcape Rock light, which had served Cape Bonavista since 1843 and had been in operation since 1811 (beginning in Scotland), was finally replaced in 1895. The new light, with nine parabolic reflectors, kerosene lamps, and tall chimneys, had originated in Scotland and had operated at Cape Pine and Harbour Grace. It remains at the Cape Bonavista lighthouse today.

<u>1895</u>

Sept. 11, Wednesday.
News of the death of Thomas White, lighthouse keeper of Bonavista, reached us this forenoon by telegram. The deceased died at his sister's house in St. John's at the Tremont Hotel.

Sept. 12 Thursday.
A message from D.A. Ryan says that the remains of Thomas White are being conveyed here by craft, leaving this afternoon.

Sept. 14, Saturday.
Today the mortal remains of Thomas White were laid to rest in the Roman Catholic Graveyard at Bonavista, in the presence of a large concourse of people of all denominations. A short time ago he took passage on SS *Virginia Lake* to St. John's, hoping change of air and surroundings would do

Margaret Ryan White was the wife of Thomas White. She was a sister of James Ryan, owner of the firm James Ryan Ltd. (Courtesy of Ross Abbott)

him service. Whilst there, additional medical advice was taken but all proved unavailing and he died at the Tremont Hotel, St. John's on the 10th September. The body of the deceased was brought hither for interment by Captain Robert Brown in the Schooner "Cleopatra." The gentleman referred to was Keeper of the Cape Bonavista Lighthouse at the time of his death.

Following Thomas's death, responsibility for the lighthouse passed to his oldest son, Fred, aged twenty-one.

James Ryan took special care in referencing Jeremiah White with the title "Mr." (which was not typical) and in speaking of each of his sons with dignity. The entire family, Jeremiah and Mary, all four children, Nicholas, Matthew, Johanna, and Thomas, grandson Fred (and perhaps others), all played a role in supporting the lighthouse in many ways in providing protection to vessels, fishermen, sealers, and other travellers in their oceanic and coastal pursuits. The attention to which Ryan's diary spoke of the death and funeral of the lighthouse keepers over the years also spoke of the respect afforded the family and the importance of their role to the town.

On December 23, 1895, Captain Samson Mifflin, born in Bonavista in 1844, who had been a master mariner for over twenty years for schooners owned by James Ryan Limited, retired from service and was appointed assistant keeper of the Cape Bonavista lighthouse. He served for seventeen years and died in 1912 at age sixty-eight. The reader will recognize the name "Samson Mifflen" from petitions of the late 1700s and in the early 1800s. The senior Samson Mifflen was an agent for a merchant firm in Trinity and had been born a child of Solomon and Jane (Randall) Mifflen in Poole, England, in 1770. He was the assistant lightkeeper's grandfather.

<u>1912</u>

March 13, Wednesday.

The remains of Samson Mifflin were interred this afternoon in the C.E. cemetery. The S.U.F. walked in procession to the Church and grave side.

Although lighthouses were invaluable for assisting mariners in the identification of their location, they could prove to be ineffective in the dense fog that frequented the shorelines of Newfoundland. Although firearms were normally used in dense fog to help mariners, the advent of the fog alarm provided a more permanent and reliable solution. In 1913, an official with the Government of Newfoundland visited Cape Bonavista and, unfortunately, chose Cape Island (that same location rejected earlier for the lighthouse itself) as the location of the fog alarm. The fog alarm, a footbridge to the mainland, and a dwelling place were all constructed on Cape Island, and Hubert Abbott, a native of Bonavista, crossed the footbridge and took up residence in his new home in 1913. He was soon joined by his new wife.

Hubert and Sarah Abbott

For my grandparents, Hubert and Sarah Abbott, living at Cape Bonavista was mostly a life of hard work and struggle against the elements to survive and to raise a family of 11 children. They weren't the first lighthouse keepers at the Cape but with more than 46 years, they hold the distinction of being the longest-serving, and for those years, dedication and pride ruled. Grandfather never took a holiday or sick leave.

My grandfather had an innate ability concerning all things mechanical or electrical and no problem ever arose that he could not handle. With his family's support, he kept things running smoothly. It was crucial that the beacons and foghorn operated like clockwork because lives depended on it. He didn't have a whole lot of schooling but he had a whole lot of common sense, logic and intelligence. He never judged anyone's character and no one was a stranger after the first greeting. To his family and friends, to his job, to the fishermen and anyone who needed him, he was dedicated and loyal, generous and loving to the very end. He had a terrific sense of humour, too, and especially loved to tease grandmother in a loving way. The sparkle in his eyes was only for her. In later years, his eyesight failed him but the twinkle was as bright as ever and with it he welcomed everyone into his presence. And he dearly loved the gathering of family and friends enjoying music, dance, and card playing.

One day during a heavy rainfall, Grandfather arrived home from the town looking forward to drying off and settling into his brand new long johns only to be told by Grandmother that she had given them to a visitor earlier in the day! My grandparents were truly selfless and generous. His smile for her was free and genuine. You could feel the love flowing from them. They were so very happy together.

Grace Butler Difalco

Hubert and Sarah Abbott with five of their eleven children.
(Photo courtesy of Grace Butler Difalco)

The choice of Cape Island for the fog alarm proved to be a bad one. In 1919, an intense storm, as related by Molloy, passed over Newfoundland with prolonged northerly winds and high waves. Seas eventually destroyed the home and footbridge, but not before Hugh and his young family had departed for the mainland. Lesson learned: the new fog alarm, and new home, were built near the lighthouse itself.

Hubert Abbott and his wife raised a large family at Cape Bonavista. In 1923, Hugh took on additional responsibilities as lighthouse keeper. He retired in 1960. In the 1960s, the switch was pulled on an automated electric light perched atop a steel tower near the lighthouse. In the 1970s, the Bonavista lighthouse was transferred from the federal to provincial government, was restored as a museum to the 1870s, and was designated a Provincial Historic Site. It is visited by thousands of tourists each year.

Notes

The history of the Cape Bonavista lighthouse related here is based upon books by Molloy, Chubbs, and Kearley, and Sam Ryan's article in the *Evening Telegram* (Saturday, September 11, 1993).

The act to establish a lighthouse at Bonavista is found in the Journal of the House of Assembly, 1841, at the A. C. Hunter Library, St. John's.

Much of the early history of Jeremiah and Mary White and their children was related to the author from Catherine (Kay) Dusseault, Gertrude Karapita, Sharon Murza, and Ken Stelmack, in part thanks to Bill Doody, late of Bonavista.

Family milestones are found in the parish records for Bonavista.

22 — EDUCATION

When speaking of education for the children of Bonavista, we may be inclined to begin with the first schooling of children in a formal setting. In fact, children resided in Bonavista almost certainly about seventy years before that first school, and perhaps even earlier. The first "manchild," John Walkam, was born in Bonavista around 1654, while first formal schooling did not begin until 1727. And there were many children in those early days. There were 14 sons and daughters and 76 servants in Bonavista in 1675, while the census for 1677 lists 34 sons and daughters and 97 servants. Although we can't be certain how many of those sons and daughters were children, we can reasonably conclude that husbands and wives were, in many cases, beginning a new family. Many of the servants were young men and women. By 1715, the census records indicate that there were 70 children living in Bonavista.

These children were most likely born either in England (or possibly Ireland) or in Bonavista. They may not have received a formal education, but they certainly were expected to learn how to live and survive in Bonavista. They helped with the fishery: from catching, through landing, gutting, and salting in preparation for transport back to England. They had to learn how to construct homes, stageheads, flakes, and small boats. Development of the soil to grow root vegetables was important as a food source. Some planters owned farm animals, such as cattle, sheep, and pigs, and everyone needed to know how to care for them. In winter, many residents removed inland or farther north for the fur trade, the salmon fishery, seal harvesting, and log cutting, all of which required new and labour-intensive skills.

Rev. Wilson described how, in the 1800s, women and men, sons and daughters, all helped in the detailed process of catching and preparing fish. Wilson wrote "the labour of the females is quite as incessant, and even more exhausting, than the labour of the men." Both male and female servants were brought over to help with the fishery. John Bland noted that when seals came into the harbour at Bonavista, "men, women and children with incredible labour" helped with the harvest.

The history of Newfoundland invariably records that the first school on the island began in the 1720s (different years have been quoted) by Rev.

Henry Jones. If we look closely at the actual letters written by Jones during his stay in Bonavista (as transcribed by Bradley), we can conclude that while he set into motion the steps necessary to begin that first school, actual first instruction for some of Bonavista's children began in the spring of 1727 by the schoolmistress.

Jones frequently referred to the "masters" and "servants" in Bonavista. During his stay, he initiated two schools, which he refers to as a schoolhouse and a charity school. Although never explicitly stated, we may conclude that these schools respectively provided education for the children of the masters and servants. Both classes of residents, as well as the Society for the Propagation of the Gospel (SPG), provided funds (then called subscriptions) to support the costs associated with the schools.

Jones never recorded the name of that first schoolmistress of Bonavista and of Newfoundland. Based upon Jones's writings, she was a remarkable lady. We've already discussed what we know about her in Chapter 12.

The departure of Rev. Jones in 1742 led to a petition to the SPG by some of the inhabitants of Bonavista (Appendix 3) for a minister to replace him. Additionally, they noted that they had lost the capacity for instruction of their children, noting that "we beg leave to offer to your Lordship's further consideration the sad state of the place in regard to the education of children, whereof there are not less than one hundred and fifty without the means of instruction or learning." The petition of 1752, upon the departure of Mr. Peasely (Appendix 4), perhaps not differentiating between church and school instruction, noted that "we have not now any one to instruct us" and are "deprived of the benefit of the Gospel and . . . live in ignorance . . . for want of a teacher."

No documentation of school instruction in Bonavista following Rev. Jones's tenure exists until a petition was sent in 1791 to the SPG requesting funds to support George Bemister. According to the petition, and a letter sent by Magistrate Bland to the governor of Newfoundland, Bemister had already been teaching students at Bonavista "for some time past." There were "upwards of three hundred poor children" in the town "who have little sense of the ends for which providence has placed them in this world . . . (and) . . . destitute of the common means of attaining to that small degree of cultivation which the lowest orders possess in most civilized nations."

The petition was successful, and George Bemister became the schoolmaster for Bonavista. He retained a salary and was provided with books to support his instruction. His initial class comprised forty-seven students. Rev. Dr. Clinch personally conveyed to the SPG, in 1796, his admiration of Mr. Bemister in instructing his students. In 1798 (the SPG Journals), Bemister recorded that he has "30 scholars, nearly half of whom belong to persons of necessitous circumstances."

We don't know much about George Bemister (or what became of him), but he was probably born in Bonavista. Thomas Bemister signed his name on the 1752 petition (Appendix 4), and Mary Bemister is buried in the Anglican Cemetery (headstone reads: Mary Bemester, wife of Thomas Bemester, d. o. William and Sarah Cornes, died 1759, aged 64 years).

On December 12, 1810, Mr. Edward Mullally appealed to the SPG as schoolmaster for Bonavista. There was, however, some concern that since Mullally was Roman Catholic, he might introduce Catholic students, or Catholic teachings, into his classroom. Rev. Dr. Clinch, in Trinity, wrote the SPG regarding Mr. Mullally, "that he has no Roman Catholic pupil in his school— that he has not, nor does he intend to introduce any tenets except those of the Established Church; to which he assured Mr. Clinch that he will conform in every particular." This was agreeable to the SPG, and Mullally was hired.

We know little else of Edward Mullally. A headstone bearing his name rests in the Roman Catholic Cemetery on Chapel Hill in Bonavista. The *Harbour Grace Standard* records the death of Ellen Dowsley, second daughter of the late Edward Mullally, Esq., of Bonavista, on April 29, 1882.

Other teachers at Bonavista in the 1810s and 1820s were Bessie Hosier (daughter of Giles and Grace Hosier) and Thomas Gaylor. Thomas Gaylor, with Abraham Ackerman, performed duties in support of the Church of England in the absence of an ordained minister. In an 1825 letter to the SPG, Archdeacon Coster wrote that the courthouse was destroyed by fire during the time of his predecessor (therefore sometime in the early 1820s), so that Sunday school had to be moved to the homes of Thomas Gaylor (boys) and Coster (girls), the latter being taught by the females of his family. The total number of students was seventy, though when fishing began, the boys did not attend.

As Methodism became more firmly established in Bonavista in the 1800s, it began Sunday school instruction as well. Rev. Ninian Barr, in 1821, wrote in his journal (as recorded in Winsor's *Hearts Strangely Warmed*):

Our Sunday School is a small institution of great promise and utility. The number of children is almost eighty; most of whom have no other means of instruction. I laboured two years in one of our schools in Glasgow, containing 500 scholars, and I do not recollect any of those with whom our first class would not bear a comparison. We have a good supply of teachers. I attend regularly with them on Sunday afternoon; and with the tracts you sent me, I have formed among them a little Reading Society. By this means, the tracts are much more extensively read than if given away; and in receiving the last week's tract, and giving a new one, I have an opportunity of questioning them on what they have read, also of ascertaining whether they have read their little books to their parents, neighbours and fellows.

On June 30, 1823, a meeting held in London established the "Society for Educating the Poor of Newfoundland," which led to the formation of the Newfoundland School Society (NSS). In 1826, the assistant secretary, Mr. Willoughby, visited Bonavista and received "a most cordial welcome from William Alexander," the magistrate for Bonavista. Willoughby noted that the population was "reckoned to be 2317 souls" and, due to its size, "is therefore likely to become in a short time one of our most important posts." Willoughby, through Alexander's support, also met with Archdeacon Coster and others and was greeted warmly, and generously, by the community. During Willoughby's visit, a school location was determined: "a very desirable spot of ground adjoining the church yard." The land was donated, as was a "Canadian stove."

On November 6, 1826, under the NSS, Mr. and Mrs. John and Susanna Hopper began a day school, with an enrolment of 169 by the end of the year. A Sunday school and adult instruction were also provided. At a public meeting of the inhabitants, a committee was appointed to supervise the construction of the school, and on December 15, "Mr. Hopper had the gratification of seeing the frame put down."

In the following year, 1827, as was recorded in Chapter 16, "Anne, the infant daughter of John and Susanna Hopper," died on September 5, in the midst of the measles outbreak, and was buried three days later. In the following year, 1828, John Hopper died. Mr. Willoughby, while visiting Bonavista, found Hopper "so ill as to render his immediate return absolutely necessary." He wrote that "Mr. and Mrs. Hopper had been there scarcely two years but in that time had accomplished much. Two hundred and eight children had been under their instruction . . . . Mr. Hopper continued to labour even longer than his health justified; and Mrs. Hopper, notwithstanding her anxious duties as a wife and mother, kept up her school in excellent order to the last."

The following was filed to the NSS in 1828 with respect to Bonavista:

To read the parables and discourses of our Lord:	58
To read on boards of three and four letters:	11

To write on slates:	60
To write on copy books:	10
To knit and sew:	64
To plot straw:	25
To mark:	12.

The Annual Report for 1828 of the "Newfoundland and British North America Society for Educating the Poor" recorded that "Mr. Hopper was in every respect a most valuable Master and in this death the Society has sustained a great loss."

The Hoppers were replaced in 1829 by Mr. and Mrs. Meek. The *Royal Gazette* (May 4, 1830) reported the construction of a schoolhouse in Bonavista, built by the Newfoundland School Society. Later issues listed the donations made by various community leaders throughout Bonavista. The June 28, 1831, issue writes:

The new school room [in Bonavista] is in progress [under the care of Mr. and Mrs. Meek].

Mr. Meek remarks: "It gives me great pleasure to inform you that the state and prospects of our school are very encouraging, much more so than on our arrival, we could have anticipated, and the greatest difficulty we now appear to have is the want of room for the number of children in attendance. The dimensions of the room are only 40 feet by 20—the average attendance of some time past has been from 150 to 160. I fear this is not likely to continue through the winter [unless] shoes and clothes are obtained. We have now many more on the books who are desirous of coming, but who are in so destitute a condition as to be unable to get out." Mr. Meek continued, "In the Sunday school, there were generally from 100 to 110 children present, the Adult Evening School contained 48 scholars, all of them diligent and rapidly improving. A Friday Evening Bible Class had also been formed, [attended] by about 100 children and young persons."

Mr. Meek also reported on the broader issue of economic conditions in Bonavista during his tenure. Those comments are included in Chapter 16.

The introduction of Representative Government in Newfoundland in 1832, and the various Acts that were passed over subsequent years to provide for funding and structure to the denominational school system in Newfoundland, marked a significant turning point in education for the people of Newfoundland. Prior to 1832, education was left to the whim and generosity of distant organizations, such as the Society for the Propagation of the Gospel, or the Society for Educating the Poor of Newfoundland. Whether a single community received support may have depended as much on the capacity of a local minister or magistrate to build a case, or to know someone of influence, as on need. And when educational support was provided, it was invariably sufficient only for a fraction of the children in the community. Further funds were needed locally to cover the cost of additional students. Prior to 1832, many, perhaps most, children received little or no education.

The passage of the Education Act in 1836, followed by further Acts of 1843, 1850, and 1858, provided the basis for an island-wide approach to education. A denominational school system run by the Roman Catholic Church, the Church of England, and the Methodist Church became established throughout the country. The Methodists and Church of England were already entrenched in Bonavista at the start of Representative Government, and the Roman Catholic school system soon followed.

It is not surprising, then, that those young men and women who came to Bonavista in the 1600s, 1700s, and as part of the heavy migration of the early 1800s, had received more schooling in their original homes in England or Ireland than their children received in Bonavista. Some of the early settlers could sign their name to a petition or a marriage certificate. Their children, and even grandchildren, could not. It was not until a stabilized school presence throughout the island of Newfoundland began to develop following Representative Government that the education of the children of Newfoundland began in earnest. Even then, family responsibilities often took precedence.

The denominational school system expanded to include the Salvation Army and Pentecostal Church in later years, but most Protestant schools amalgamated in 1970. Then, in a referendum on September 2, 1997, seventy-three per cent of voters opted to end the denominational school system in favour of secular school instruction.

Notes

The Journals of the Society for the Propagation of the Gospel are contained at the Centre for Newfoundland Studies (CNS), Memorial University of Newfoundland, St. John's. Microfilm 567. Vols. 25-27.
Official records of the Newfoundland School Society (NSS) are also found at the CNS. Microfilm A-322, A323. 1823-1836.
Generic website information on the NSS:
https://www.heritage.nf.ca/articles/society/education.php

BRUCE WHIFFEN

https://en.wikipedia.org/wiki/Newfoundland_School_Society
http://faculty.marianopolis.edu/c.belanger/nfldhistory/NewfoundlandEducation.htm
The *Harbour Grace Standard* is found at:
http://sites.rootsweb.com/~cannf/cbnorth_norstandard_1882.htm
The *Royal Gazette* is found at: http://collections.mun.ca/cdm/

23 — THE RYANS

In Bonavista's early years, fishing was conducted by planters from England who visited the shoreline during the summer season and returned in the fall. Later, merchants and their agents living in Bonavista, nearby Trinity, or elsewhere ran extensive enterprises with headquarters in southern England. It was not until the 1800s that those born, raised, and educated in Bonavista began to establish their own commercial enterprises in their hometown.

Michael Ryan was born in Callan, County Kilkenny, Ireland, on January 6, 1814, and arrived in Bonavista around 1835, with his mother, Catherine Ryan. Michael married Ellen Fleming—they had eight sons and three daughters.

The Ryan Premises. (Alick Tsui)

On October 20, 1857, Michael and his oldest son, James, who was fifteen years old at the time, started a fisheries business in the Bayley's Cove area of Bonavista. In 1869, they purchased the Fishing Room formerly owned by William Keen and listed in Bland's Register of Fishing Rooms for 1805–06 in Appendix 2. At that time, Keen's Room was claimed by "Captain Kean of the

Navy" and occupied and leased by Thomas Street, Poole, stationed in Trinity. It was described as having two stages, bounded to the south by Skiffington's Room (toward Canaille) and to the north by Shambler's Room and Dewy's Store & Dwelling House (in the area of the present-day fish plant).

In 1870, the company was incorporated as James Ryan and Company. As their father removed himself from the company, James, along with brothers Dan and Nicholas, expanded to communities throughout the area, and eventually farther west and north to Labrador.

Nimshi Crewe wrote that Michael Ryan's wife, Ellen Fleming, was "a Bonavista girl," and that he, Michael, "used to swear on the moon for giving him rheumatism." Crewe remarked that, excepting Michael, Jr., "the sons were all men of strong, forthright, dominating character and speech . . . all were tall, robust men. I recall them all . . . they received the best of local schooling and were engaged, in one capacity or another, in business." Of James, in particular, Crewe wrote that his chief characteristic was his "grim countenance . . . it was an unflinching insistence upon conservative frugality, solidity and high quality . . . they (he and his brothers) were only satisfied with the best."

James Ryan. From Lench's *The Story of Methodism in Bonavista.*

As we'll see from the diary, James married Katherine McCarthy of Carbonear in 1897. In 1905, St. John's became their place of residence, and in 1911, they moved into an imposing structure on Rennie's Mill Road, at that time the wealthiest part of town. Known at the time as "The House," it boasts a grand staircase built at the same time, and by the same company (Harland & Wolff), as the grand staircase for the *Titanic*. At the time, Ryan was known as one of the wealthiest men of Newfoundland.

In 1913, James Ryan was appointed to the Legislative Council of the Government of Newfoundland. He died in 1917. The business he built with his father and brothers continued until 1978, when it closed its doors with the death of James's son Herbert. The Ryan Premises is now a National Historic Site.

James Ryan, like many contemporaries, kept a daily diary during the course of his life. For the most part, entries spoke of weather conditions, winds and seas, and the comings and goings of vessels around the harbour. Events of particular importance to business, and discussions with local fishermen, also comprise a significant part of his diary. There are, however, many entries that speak to the personal life of James Ryan and his immediate family. Births, deaths, and family visits illustrate a family not unlike many others. Other events, such as trips to see the inauguration of the President of the United States, or to St. Peter's Shrine in Rome, reflect a family quite different than his contemporaries and from his neighbours and workers in Bonavista. We also see in his diary historical events in Bonavista (visits from dignitaries, the introduction of the railway, the departure of young men to work elsewhere), or tragedies on a small and large scale (measles, the vessel *Snorre*, and the passage of the SS *Greenland*). There are even the occasional philosophical musings of James's brother, Nicholas, as he vents on the frustrations of the day.

Your author has scanned James Ryan's diary and has extracted those entries, either by James or Nicholas (in James's absence), that have been most revealing of the times. There have been only minor edits as necessary for clarity. The more philosophical, colourful, and even entertaining entries were invariably written by Nicholas.

1878

January 1.
Mr. James Ryan left Bonavista on the afternoon of December 31st 1877 for Catalina—there to await the "Plover" (SS) bound to St. John's. He is travelling to Great Britain & probably to the United States of America and Canada.

1885

March 11, Wednesday.
A cablegram from James Ryan yesterday informs us of his visit to Washington to witness the inauguration of President Cleveland. The former has not yet made his transatlantic trip.

<u>1887</u>

March 1, Tuesday.
A virulent type of measles abounds here just now. Yesterday eleven deaths were recorded from the effect of that fell disease.

<u>1888</u>

October 10, Wednesday.
This morning at 8.15 AM meeting of the Road Board was held in James Ryan's Office. Present: A. Vincent, Chairman. Thomas Harris, Robert Brown, Alan Ryder, John Roper & James Ryan. Proposed by John Roper, seconded by Alan Ryder & agreed to unanimously, that $80.00 be paid to James Ryan for a piece of land opposite J. Ryan's fish store required to widen Water Street.

At a meeting held at the Court House at 4 PM yesterday, it was proposed & agreed to without a [dissenting] voice, that the main street known as Water Street be widened in the Town of Bonavista. Present at the meeting: A. Vincent, Chairman, Alan Ryder, Thomas Harris, Robert Brown and James Ryan.

<u>1889</u>

September 7, Saturday.
Copy of Telegram sent this day.
To Right Reverend Bishop MacDonald, Harbour Grace:
"Mail arrived confirming reported destruction of Cathedral by fire. I beg to express my Sympathy. Promising substantial aid to rebuild. Would have telegraphed earlier but could not credit rumour.

James Ryan"

<u>1890</u>

December 20, Saturday.
Profound and universal regret is expressed in the community today on hearing of the sudden dissolution of Mr. J.T. Daly. The deceased complained of being sick during the early part of summer and did his usual accustomed work up to the 2nd October when he betook himself to bed,

and there remained until the 26th of October which time he was advised by Doctor John Skelton to repair to St. John's to seek medical advice. Forthwith he went and yesterday we hear, with astonishment, that he is no longer of this world.

The departed was, for the past eighteen years, manager or rather, agent, for the proprietor, James Ryan, and during those many years of service by his kindly disposition and suave manners, gained for himself a name that will be long remembered for its strict integrity.

1894

January 6, Saturday.
Mr. Michael Ryan, Sr. celebrated his 80th birthday today.

1897

March 2, Tuesday.
Received news the 29th that the proprietor, Mr. James Ryan, had married at Boston by letter written by him. Previously he had cabled from Queenstown that he had arrived "hearty" at that port of call, but he had forgotten to have wired from Boston or New York of his union in connubial bliss to his fair Miss Katherine McCarthy.

1898
March 26, Saturday.
The SS *Greenland* is now at Cape Bonavista pushing her way south. The writer's opinion leads him to believe that this steamer has already procured many young seals this season—a full load—had 14,000—lost 48 men—and has gone home to discharge.

Measles are prevalent in town, especially in that locality named Bayley's Cove and on the New Road. The malady was brought from Goose Bay by one Butler who was en route to St. John's for the ice fields and collapsed at the above named place and had to return after his father had gone to take him back. They are also prevalent on the West Coast.

May 7, Saturday.
Joseph Fisher's of Thomas wife at Cape Shore died at one o'clock PM—the result of measles but she was rather delicate in health for some years past.

The ploughing of land, with modern and ancient implements, is being attended to daily.

August 17, Wednesday.
Mr. John McCarthy and sister, who were visiting their sister, Mrs. James Ryan, took passage by her. The proprietor and his wife accompanied them to Catalina by vehicle.

1899

February 13, Monday.
Fine morning, clear sky, and a little cold. The bay is quite covered over with slob.

James Sweeney and James Keats hauled out from the country a load of firewood.

This is the first day for a long time that has been mild and besides the sudden break from intense cold the sun was shining out which added a lustre and brilliancy that made it delightful.

Mrs. John Cole of Bonavista and Mrs. Alfred Street are just now dead.

"Lagrippe" is still prevalent here and elsewhere and at Newman's Cove typhoid fever is at the home of one Keates. One young man in the full bloom of manhood succumbed to its ravages. On the whole, mortality is not heavy in this town.

Joseph Thompson is not yet recovered from his illness.

February 20, Monday.
Theresa Ryan died this morning at St. John's whither she had repaired for the winter. The deceased had not a robust constitution at any time, and she was in failing health for many years. Her kind and endearing nature was generally acknowledged. She was generous to a fault, sympathetic to the poor and queenly and hospitable in her home. Her husband D.A. Ryan who is just now in Rome, Italy, will be heart stricken by his bereavement as he was the kindest of husbands. His only consolation will be the offering at St. Peter's Shrine in Rome of prayers for the happy repose of her soul.

Rather mild weather. Wind south and snowing just a little in the afternoon. The premises was closed—shop and store—on hearing of the decease of Theresa and many flags around the harbour were hoisted half mast high—"Grave where is thy victory: Oh Death where is thy sting?"

A telegraphic dispatch from the Revd. William Jackman, St. John's to Mr. James Ryan says that he prepared Mrs. D.A. Ryan and administered the last sacraments of the Church on Thursday last.

June 4, Sunday.
The reverend A.E.C. Bayly, Church of England clergyman, celebrates today his golden jubilee as priest—the fiftieth anniversary of his ordination. Many and various are the changes that have taken place since he first worked in this portion of the vineyard. Steam and telegraphy were unknown factors—church music and choirs were out of the question—dissemination of knowledge through the aid of the press was quite limited— the means of propulsion was aided by oars—letter writing was almost unknown—journeys had to be performed on foot, horses being not introduced . . . one common cemetery was the receptacle for the dead of all creeds. That was a time when an opposing minister of the Gospel would be imprisoned for holding contrary views against the national church.

Today the scene is changed. All are united in professing to attain the object of the life of Man—in this mundane sphere all the civilizing influences of religion are worked harmoniously for Man's betterment. Today there are clergymen from many places in the island gathered around him who was the pioneer of the Church of England religion in Bonavista—to congratulate him and to do him honour on the attainment of this his jubilee day. May many years be yet spared him to give his guiding hand and lend his wise counsel to those who need them.

The writer's parents tendered the reverend and venerable old gentleman their congratulations. [written by Nicholas Ryan]

June 6, Tuesday.
Michael Ryan Senior—(the writer's father)—drove the Revd. R.M. Walker to Catalina. Father is somewhere in the neighbourhood of 86 years—a venerable age which he bears admirably.

1900

March 18, Sunday.
Today at the insistence of our young and energetic pastor, the Reverend P.W. Browne, P.P., of Bonavista, a meeting of the catholic parishioners

was called to donate funds for a new parochial residence, and, in ready response—before the elapse of five minutes—the credibly respectable sum and magnificent sum of $1307.00 was subscribed by a score members of this sparsely populated parish.

Mr. James Ryan of this town headed the list of subscribers with the munificent donation of $1,000.00. As this princely gift (the amount being then unknown) was about to be ratified by the signature of the donor, a pleasing little incident occurred between father and son in which the former now verging on his ninetieth year administered a paternal admonition to a worthy son in the following true-hearted and inspiring words—"Come, my son, don't be afraid; don't let your hand shake or fail you." Needless to say when the figures were appended and these figures were four, and the result was announced by the reverend pastor that that father felt an elated proud and grand old man bearing his ninety years of infirmity with an elasticity of step, a buoyancy and exuberance of spirits which well may be the envy of a much younger scion. The old gentleman said in Anglo-Saxon conservative style "put down £8.0.0 for me." That the worthy son of a worthy sire who first saw the light in the Emerald Isle acted well and nobly their respected parts on the spur of the moment the praises and thanks of those present amply testified. Right heartily and cheerily did other subscribers come to the front among them being Mrs. T.W. Stabb with $20.00 and Mr. J.T. McCarthy—a comparatively new resident—with the handsome sum of $50.00 and all others called upon responded right nobly and well.

So impressed was the esteemed pastor by this exhibition of generosity on the part of those whom he has just known that in rendering thanks language which but a few minutes previously was ready and glib earnest and eloquent as an electric spark now failed him—even Gaelic or Latin— and as he expressed it "he was beside himself," his joy was unbounded, the town failed to hold him and he betook himself to the precincts of a vehicle to cool off and sum up the measure of his supreme happiness. An excellent beginning in a noble cause.

March 20, Tuesday.
The corner stone of the new catholic presbytery was laid yesterday with impressive ceremony and the privilege of laying the stone was accorded Mr. James Ryan who tendered some appropriate and well chosen remarks on the occasion.

July 23, Monday.

His Lordship, the Rt. Rev'd Dr. McDonald, Bishop of this Diocese, accompanied by the Reverends Veitch and Murphy arrived here on SS *Dundee* at 3 PM and were immediately, on landing at our wharf, driven to the Chapel, where the Sacrament of Confirmation was engaged in. Some 40 candidates presented themselves.

His Lordship and accompanying clerics were well and hospitably entertained by Mrs. James Ryan, after which the party left for Catalina about 7 o'clock.

Bunting was freely and very generally displayed by the town's people, while our premises, the Chapel—inside & outside—and St. Joseph's Presbytery were, by willing and loving hands, made particularly attractive by the decorative display lavished upon them.

The Principal arrived from St. John's, via King's Cove, about 10 P.M.

1902

January 22, Wednesday.

SS *Ethie* from the north arrived here at 5 PM. Mr. D.A. Ryan came passenger by her—from King's Cove. Mrs. James Ryan left here by sleigh for Catalina—there to embark on *Ethie* for St. John's where she will be joined later by her husband previous to their departure for United States and Europe. Weather is as fine as could be desired at this season.

Magistrate Stabb, Dr. Forbes and several witnesses in the Pardy case are also proceeding to St. John's by *Ethie*. It is arranged that the government will send them back by SS *Fiona*.

February 11, Tuesday.

The immortal remains of Mr. Robert Ford were this afternoon conveyed amidst a large concourse of townspeople to the sacred asylum of the grave where the last rites were read in articulate solemn tones by the Revd. A.G. Bayly of Christ Church. The deceased—Robert Ford—was a man of sterling worth, high principle and goodness of heart. His kindness and acts of charity were not shouted from the house tops, but performed in a quiet unobtrusive manner, and many will miss the kind genial smile of him who has gone before.

February 21, Friday.
Mrs. D.A. Ryan, James Ryan Jr., repaired to King's Cove—Mr. D.A.R. coming half way from the other end to meet them. Mr. J.T. McCarthy drove his sister and James, Jr. thither.

A mass meeting was convened at Bird Island Cove on Tuesday night last by the citizens for the purpose of changing the name of the place. After resoluting and debating the question the more euphonious cognomen of Elliston was decided upon almost unanimously save and except the single exception of the venerable Samuel Tucker who protested most strenuously against the proposed alteration.

February 28, Friday.
A message from St. John's dated today from Mr. James Ryan says he leaves Saturday per SS *Glencoe* for Halifax en route to Boston.

March 20, Thursday.
A cable from Mr. James Ryan at Liverpool, England simply says "arrived" which means that he and his wife reached there from New York sometime this morning early or yesterday late.

March 29, Saturday.
A cable dated today from the city of Seven Hills says "Roma—28th March. Happy Easter—twelve chartered. 'Cecelia' loading." Which means that Mr. James Ryan and wife are at the seat and centre of Christendom taking in the ceremonies and functions of the Church where dwells its Visible Head the August Pontiff, Leo XIII.

June 16, Monday.
A cable from Mr. James Ryan intimates his present whereabouts is Glasgow, Scotland.

July 23, Wednesday
Mr. J.T. McCarthy proceeded to Catalina at 7:30 PM of yesterday to convey home by vehicle his sisters—Mesdames James and Daniel Ryan, Master James Ryan and D.A. Ryan—all from St. John's via Carbonear by rail. Mrs. James has been touring Italy, France and Switzerland during the winter months with her husband Mr. James Ryan who remains at St. John's for a few days to arrange some matters of business.

August 2, Saturday.
A message from Mr. James Ryan requisitions the horse and carriage to be at Catalina tonight for himself and a culler (McDonald)—to convey them to Bonavista.

November 8, Saturday.
Crowds of young men are emigrating to Westville, N.S. and other points where labour is obtainable, and it is the elite of the town in youth courage and endurance who are emigrating. (author's note . . . these men would presumably have been working at the coal miles at Westville)

Mr. James Ryan who has been in St. John's some six weeks or so returned per SS *Ethie* via Carbonear. He arrives here about midnight.

Typhoid fever is still a strong hold here in some quarters. A son of Philip White's lays unconscious while one other succumbed last week to the ravages of this fell disorder.

November 20, Thursday.
An electoral vote For and Against Prohibition was held here today and votes were recorded at Bayley's Cove, the Court House and Canaille booths. Needless to say the good sense of the townspeople with a majority voted in favour of the measure and in future the temptation will be hypothecated to the surgeries of the dispensing medical fraternity—Doctors Forbes, Rutherford and Kent. The vote resulted thus: 402 registered in favour of Prohibition, 58 registered against the measure—thus are the saloons knocked out unanimously.

1905

January 3, Tuesday.
Nicholas Fleming is very ill with, it is alleged, typhoid fever.

March 13, Monday.
Mr. James Ryan and wife and Mr. D.A. Ryan and wife left St. John's per SS *Rosalind* for Halifax and New York.

March 29, Wednesday.

Mr. James Ryan and wife left New York on Saturday for Liverpool in the crack greyhound Lucania. He says he has the schooner "Grace" bought.

The overland mail from St. John's and Clarenville—the first by railway to Clarenville since the 5th of February left Trinity at 11:30 AM. This means that 53 days have gone and passed by into oblivion since a northern mail has been received here from St. John's by rail. It looks really as if we had reverted to the dark ages. Anyway we have been submerged and rip-van-winkled into the white darkness of a Newfoundland winter by the boobies who signed or formulated the Reid Railway Contract.

May 23, Tuesday.

A cable dated Liverpool today says "Sabrosas—we will sail today." That is Mr. James Ryan and his wife intend sailing during the day.

Tomorrow known as Empire Day throughout the British Dominions will be observed as a commercial holiday.

June 8, Thursday.

Mr. James Ryan arrived home in the wee small hours from Catalina per "Portia" from St. John's returning lately from England. The two wee laddies returned as well.

June 11, Sunday.

Mr. James Ryan from St. John's via Carbonear arrived this morning. He is lately from England where he spent the winter.

July 28, Friday.

Dull foggy morning—will be bright about noon and after.

At 4 PM, the SS *Dundee*, Captain Darius Blandford steamed into Bonavista Harbour, gaily decorated with bunting in honour of Bishop MacDonald who was passenger accompanied by his Secretary Father Murphy. Rev'd P.W. Brown P.P., James Ryan, N.B. Ryan, Frank Kough, Leo O'Dea, Clement Fennell & John Thorne went off from Ryan's Wharf to welcome the Bishop, who then came on shore with them in a boat fitted up very neatly and landed at Ryan's Premises which were profusely decorated with bunting indicating a hearty welcome to his Lordship.

Several carriages were in waiting to convey his Lordship & others to the Roman Catholic Church.

Michael Ryan, Sr. drove up in his carriage to meet the Bishop upon landing—this occasioned great pleasure to his family and friends as he is now 94 years old.

The weather was ideal—calm with beautiful sunshine and the sea in the bay and harbour like a mirror. Bunting was flying in all directions. The writer is of opinion that everyone having a flag hoisted it. An immense crowd gathered upon the wharf, the galleries and the public streets.

September 21, Thursday.
A daughter of Joseph Thompson and a brother of Joseph Swyers succumbed to croup and typhoid this morning. The latter was buried this afternoon.

October 4, Wednesday.
Michael Ryan out to Cape Shore, Rolling Cove and Spillars Cove advising agents of price of dried cod.

1906

January 3, Wednesday.
Mrs. James Ryan gave birth to a bouncing baby boy at about 9 PM—a most interesting event of the New Year. The mother is thriving well and the baby lusty.

January 11, Thursday.
My father Michael Ryan, a veteran of over ninety-three years, had his leg amputated above the ankle today at eleven o'clock in the forenoon by Doctors Forbes and Rutherford of Bonavista and Le Visconte of King's Cove. The chief Forbes sawed the leg; Rutherford attended to the arteries and their tieing up while the main and most important of all the acts the administering of the proper supply of chloroform devolved upon doctor Le Visconte by order of the chief. This surgical operation was done in a most scientific way, and the feat of a man so venerable in years surviving this ordeal is marvellous indeed.

February 4, Sunday.
E. J. Ryan left for King's Cove at 6.15 AM and Father Scully arrived here at 6 PM to administer the last rites of the Church to Father Michael Ryan

who is on his death-bed. The Rev. Father came from King's Cove by sleigh around Black Head Bay.

February 7, Wednesday.
At 1:30 AM, my father Michael Ryan departed this life at the ripe old age of 93 years. Up to four months ago he was hale and hearty and but for meeting with an accident may have reached in years the century mark. While out driving in early October he turned around the horse and carriage himself and in doing so the beast trod upon his foot which afterwards grew sore and required the surgeon's knife to lance it. It grew gradually worse despite the utmost care and attention of Dr. Robert E. Forbes who was at his bed side during his illness by day and by night until finally he decided to amputate the decaying leg and on the 11th of January that member was cut off.

February 10, Saturday.
The Premises Shop & Store closed for the day.

The remains of father were consigned to the sacred asylum of the tomb in the Catholic cemetery near the Chapel at three o'clock yesterday and laid beside those of his wife, his mother and other members of his family who pre-deceased him. His bier was followed by his seven surviving sons James and Daniel, Patrick and Michael, John and Nicholas and Edmund. The concourse of mourners and friends who followed all that was mortal of Michael Ryan to his last resting place in God's Acre was large and representative. With those of the town flocked many from Elliston, Spillar's Cove and Lance Cove and beyond Black Head came men from the coves to honour the memory of him who came to the town of Bonavista some 72 years ago. Born at Callan, County Kilkenny, Ireland he immigrated here about the year of Our Lord 1813 (?). He was then above twenty-two years of age in the full prime and vigour of manhood and immediately began to carve out his future. What that future was, is better known by the older members of this community. To my knowledge, and certain it was, that he were a remarkable man in many respects. When he died on Wednesday last, his age was bordering on the century mark; he was the distinguished father of eight sons and three daughters; nine of whom survive him to mourn their loss; and he amassed sufficient wealth by his own strenuous life and exertions to educate his children and bequeath them at his death a goodly portion of this world's goods in money and in lands. He possessed an indomitable will, a keen clear intellect, and his bravery was proverbial. What higher encomium could be rendered a man of his advanced years than his own words when he told the doctor R. E. Forbes to cut above an old sore on his shin; advised the doctor to make a good job of it and be quick about it when he began operations. Younger hearts would have quailed.

Author's Note: There is no headstone for Michael Ryan in the Roman Catholic Cemetery. There is a headstone, presumably of Michael's mother (as noted above), which reads:

Of your charity, pray for the soul of
Catherine Ryan who died December 15, 1863, aged 75 years
Also her granddaughter
Catherine Ryan died August 20, 1846 age 7 months.

Another headstone reads:

In memory of Ellen, beloved wife of Michael Ryan
who died at Bonavista Aug. 22, 1901 aged 79 years.

1908

February 14, Friday.
Mrs. James Ryan and her eldest son James to join the Portia for St. John's. They are en route for Boston, and afterwards will visit Britain.

March 2, Monday.
Mr. James Ryan left here for Catalina about 12 o'clock to join the SS *Adventure* for St. John's. He will spend the remaining part of winter in England first visiting the United States. The Adventure passed the Cape about noon bound south touching Catalina on the way.

July 11, Saturday.
The proprietor, Mr. James Ryan, his wife and their son James will arrive to Catalina some time tonight per SS *Ethie* from St. John's via Carbonear. They have been on an extended trip to Britain and Mr. Ryan visited Portugal during the interval about some fish cargoes.

1909

January 24, Sunday.
Mrs. James Ryan and her two sons, James and Herbert, drove to Catalina to take passage to St. John's where the masters Ryan are to attend college.

1910

October 17, Monday.
Mr. James Ryan, Mrs. Jas. Ryan, James Jr. and Herbert Ryan drove to Catalina to join the SS *Ethie* for Carbonear en route to St. John's. The masters Ryan—James & Herbert—resume their studies at St. Bonaventure's College, St. John's.

1911

July 1, Saturday.
Mr. James Ryan and wife sailed from Liverpool for St. John's this forenoon.

July 6, Thursday.
Most of the fishermen unfortunately have a holiday—an unwilling one—as there is no bait procurable. The Canaille and Mockbeggar men are all viewing the construction work of the railway which is now out almost within a few hundred feet of Walkham's Bridge.

July 7, Friday.
Some bait is procurable at Black Head Bay and Catalina and some of our men (Bonavista) have been at the latter place in boats and got back this morning.

Construction train passed along by Walkham's Bridge and the Court House at 11:30 AM. We congratulate the government and the People's Party on the consummation of such a great boon to the people of Bonavista especially and to the public generally.

Silver Jubilee of King George V and Queen Mary, May 1935. Note the calm waters, the banners, and the parade marching across Walkam's Bridge. There is also a hint of the train tracks, which, at the time, ran westward from the train station in front of the Bridge House and the courthouse toward Mockbeggar. (Photo courtesy of Sandra Durdle)

August 19, Saturday.

It is also announced that a general tie-up in all trade in Great Britain has taken place; that 50,000 soldiers are guarding the railway trains leading to London; that many cities are on the verge of starvation; that a battleship is conveying food-stuffs to the Isle of Man where the people are starving; and that 50,000 men are idle in the collieries of Wales. Things have assumed a very serious aspect apparently and Great Britain seems to be in the throes of conditions amounting almost to Revolution. Parliament will not adjourn till the Labour troubles and disquietude have subsided and completely adjusted.

Thus Socialism has projected its hybrid monstrous head and Labour is fighting Capital to the Death.

August 28, Monday.

A disastrous fire is raging at several places on the Catalina Road and all traffic (i.e., by vehicle) is suspended for the time being. John Walsh's Half-way House is in danger of being destroyed and the wooded country is demolished. At Maberly, Elliston a fire is also in progress and is making big headway approaching very near the houses there.

It is said that some two to four miles of railway track—sleepers— have been burnt between here and Catalina.

September 9, Saturday.
Sir E.P. Morris (Premier) and W.D. Reid, Esq. of the Reid Nfld. Railway Co. paid the town a visit by rail and alighted near the Breakwater and proceeded on foot to a point where the terminal railway wharf is supposed to be built. The town was decorated with bunting in honour of their visit. They remained about an hour or so.

September 14, Thursday.
Mr. James Ryan, James Ryan Jr., Mrs. James Ryan and master Herbert Ryan took passage to St. John's per SS *Prospero* and all embarked on her here in Bonavista Harbour.

1912

January 19, Friday.
SS *Prospero* from the south passed up the Bay at 11:30 AM. Mr. James Ryan came as passenger by her to Catalina and came here hither by the train which arrived about the above hour. The Writer left St. John's on the SS *Prospero* yesterday morning and arrived at Catalina at 5 AM to-day. Then traveled by train from Catalina and arrived here at 4:30 AM. This was my first journey on the Bonavista Branch of the Railroad. James Ryan.

July 1, Monday.
Caplin are plentiful at Walkham's Bridge. They are rolling on the beach.

By train this morning arrived Mrs. James Ryan and sons James and Herbert and Mrs. John T. McCarthy. Masters James and Herbert are from St. Bonaventure's College and are now having their vacation.

<u>1913</u>

August 13, Wednesday.
Mr. James Ryan, wife and the two masters Ryan, James and Herbert, left by train at 10:15 PM en route to England—Master James will enter college over there.

August 29, Friday.
Hon. James Ryan, wife and son, sailed for Glasgow this afternoon per SS *Carthaginian.*

<u>1914</u>

January 9, Friday.
Hon. James Ryan arrived here from St. John's by train.

March 28, Saturday.
Hon. James Ryan left for St. John's by train at 6 PM.

July 13, Monday.
The warship SS *Essex* was scheduled to arrive here at 9 AM with H.R.H. the Duke Of Connaught—who was to land at 11 AM and proceed to the Orange Hall—receive an Address of Welcome and then meet the Survivors of the SS *Newfoundland* sealing disaster and prominent citizens. It was then arranged that he would, with his party and others, drive to the Light House, return and take luncheon at the House of Hon. James Ryan, then take a stroll around the town and embark.

The merchants of this town closed their stores and shops today and gave a holiday to all their employees to give them an opportunity of seeing and hearing the Duke of Connaught speak at the Hall. From an early hour, large crowds paraded the streets and gathered about the premises of Ryan and Templeman which were gaily decorated with flags. A beautiful Arch was built on Water Street midway between the road leading to the Roman Catholic Church and the Catalina Road— and another very fine Arch on the Main Street opposite the Court House.

1917

September 15, Saturday.
News from S. John's by telegrams intimate that Hon. James Ryan is seriously ill there.

September 19, Wednesday.
Hon. James Ryan passed to the Great Beyond at 8 PM.
    May his soul rest in peace. Amen.

September 20, Thursday.
Mr. & Mrs. McCarthy and Messrs. N.B. & M.J. Ryan left for St. Johns at 2.30 PM by train.

September 21, Friday.
We arrived in St. John's at 7.30. PM.
After supper M. J. Ryan, E. J. Ryan & N. B. Ryan and Walter N. White proceeded to the residence of the late Hon. James Ryan where his remains lay. Edmund and Walter White remained all night while Michael and I retired to the Osborne Hotel at 11 PM.

September 22, Saturday.
A kind of showery day in St. John's.
The funeral of James Ryan took place at 3 PM and a representative gathering of citizens attended.

1918

July 6, Saturday.
Dull foggy day with East wind. Sea smooth.
    Mrs. James Ryan arrived at some unknown port in England or France after a protracted passage of sixteen days from New York. This was a long passage and gave uneasiness & anxiety to her relations and friends. A cable of no origin was received by her brother J.T. McCarthy this morning announcing arrival.

The *Evening Telegram* (September 20, 1917) wrote (with some errors) the following:

> We regret to record the death yesterday of the Honourable James Ryan, for years one of the foremost personalities in the country. For some time in poor health, he became worse a few days ago and had not strength to rally, the end coming at eight o-clock last evening. He leaves a widow, nee Catherine McCarthy, of Carbonear, two sons now resident in England: James an officer in the British Army, and Hubert; and two brothers Daniel and Edmond.
>
> James Ryan was a native Newfoundlander, being born at Bonavista in 1841. From modest beginnings and aided only by rare personal qualities of thrift and industry, he rose steadily in the commercial life of the country until he became one of its first and dominant figures. The small business which he established in his native town grew under his management to large proportions and branches were extended to Trinity, Catalina, Labrador and other places. His remarkable success, which left him one of the wealthiest merchants in the Island, was due mostly to the possession of two indispensable qualities: a love of his business and the ability to save; and as is the invariable rule, it has been reflected beneficially upon the country in which it was won.
>
> In 1913, he was appointed to the Legislative Council where he made no pretense to oratory, but was always ready with advice that was both pertinent and valuable. In him, the country loses an exemplary citizen and Newfoundland commerce a master mind.

Crewe further noted that "In my opinion, they (the Ryan brothers) formed the biggest outport fishery firm in Newfoundland history—they aggregated more profits than did any fishery firm in our history."

From his estate, James Ryan left "a permanent fund for the benefit of the poor of the town of Bonavista . . . to be paid over in equal thirds to the Parish Priest of the Roman Catholic Church at Bonavista, the incumbent of the Church of England at Bonavista, and the principle minister of the Methodist Church at Bonavista, to be distributed by them amongst the most needy and deserving of the poor of their respective congregations."

Notes

James Ryan diary and the *Evening Telegram* are online at Memorial University's Digital Archive Initiative: http://collections.mun.ca/cdm

Nimshi Crewe's comments are taken from the Nimshi Crewe Collection, The Rooms, St. John's. Box 1. File 2a.

James Ryan's will: http://ngb.chebucto.org/Wills/ryan-james-11-3.shtml

24 — THE SS GREENLAND DISASTER

John Bland described the sealing industry as an "adventurous and perilous pursuit" and that "it may excite surprise that so few fatal accidents have happened." And yet it provided an important source of subsistence for the people of Bonavista, especially during those years when the cod fishery was insufficient to meet a family's needs.

Elizabeth Mouland was born in Bonavista in early May 1846. When she was twenty-six, she married William Russell, aged thirty-two. They had five children—all boys. In early March 1898, at age twenty-two, Elizabeth's second-oldest, Archibald, travelled to St. John's and won a berth on the SS *Greenland* for its seasonal journey to the ice floes north of Newfoundland.

The *Greenland* was under the command of Captain George Barbour, a member of the well-known Barbour family from Bonavista North—as that part of the bay to the north and west of Bonavista is generally known. George Barbour was an experienced and respected member of the fraternity of sealing captains. With a crew of around 200, the *Greenland*, on March 10, in the company of six other sealing vessels, left a wharf in St. John's harbour, sailed through the Narrows, and headed north. Many other vessels sailed in the following days.

The crew of the *Greenland*, as was the practice in all sealing vessels, was divided into four teams, or watches, each led by a master watch. The master watches of the *Greenland* were Jesse Gaulton, Jesse Knee, Nathan House, and James Norris. On the morning of Monday, March 21, Captain Barbour ordered all four watches to work. They had already been on the ice for almost a week, work that was interrupted frequently with severe weather and drifting ice floes. The first watch was instructed to head off in a southeasterly direction, after which Barbour steamed about three miles toward the northeast to drop off the remaining three watches.

In late afternoon, the falling barometer and darkening skies indicated that a storm was approaching, and by sunset, a full-blown blizzard had overtaken everyone. The *Greenland* returned to the first watch and retrieved everyone. As Captain Barbour headed back to the remaining three watches, which included Archibald Russell, the ice had shifted in the storm, and the open channel that had permitted the *Greenland* to manoeuvre between its watches had closed around the vessel. At the same time, an open channel had been created between the vessel and the three watches on the ice, stranding them. Captain Barbour and his crew were divided with no way, in the midst of a raging storm, to reach one another.

It is difficult to appreciate the severity of this circumstance. Over 100 men find themselves on the North Atlantic Ocean, hundreds of miles from shore, unable to return to their vessel. Their home is a sheet of ice, moving under the influence of the wind, the ocean currents, and the forces of the other, surrounding ice floes. They are exposed to high winds, blinding snow, and the bitter cold.

The three watches each tried as best they could to find a means to survive. The watch led by Jesse Knee found itself in "rough ice" that had crested upon other sheets, providing a makeshift shelter against some of the wind. Others tried to start a fire from the ropes and gaffs. But more young men, as the hours dragged on, and as they grew colder, became confused and dazed and walked through the cracks in the ice or tried desperately, and in vain, to reach their ship.

Eli Hall of Newtown later recalled his experiences:

> Coming on dark, it commenced to blow and snow was so thick that it was impossible to see five feet ahead. We remained together all night, huddling together and running around at times to keep warm. In the morning, the wind had increased to a hurricane. Some of the men got separated, having gone in gangs to look for the steamer. I passed fifteen men lying on the ice, some of them apparently dead, and others making futile attempts to keep themselves alive by jumping around on the ice.

In the edited words of Enos Squires:

> We had not been gone very long when a sudden gale and blizzard sprang up without warning, and we became separated from ship. A large body of water had formed between us and the ship which was several miles wide. We were trapped. There was no way we could be reached. All that day and early night, glimpses of men could be seen on the ice from the barrel of the ship; and during a lull in the storm, one hundred men were rescued. We tried to keep together in groups. This was very difficult as we could

only see a foot or two. About the only way you knew a man was near you was by touching him. Sight and sound were practically nil.

About 11 PM, the temperature dropped sharply and the wind chill must have been thirty to forty degrees below zero. We were on smooth ice, and there was no possibility whatsoever of building shelter. The ice was also very loose which would make a shelter useless even had we been able to erect one. My father had said to me: "Enos, you are going to take part in one of the most dangerous occupations known. There are not many precautions you can take, but there are a few . . . one of them is never leave without your oilskins." How glad I was that I had them on this awful night. They prevented the wind from blowing through my under-garments and kept me dry from the thick snow. This prevented me from getting frost-bitten.

Up to now, my brother Stephen Squires and I managed to keep together. But I missed him and did not see him again. He must have fallen into one of the many holes of water that abounded in the ice.

We sang songs, later we sang hymns. Most of us prayed. Many who went to their knees did not arise again. The moment movement ceased, you were frozen—the cold was so very intense. I had already decided that my only chance was to keep moving. I tried to go in circles. Every so often, I would stumble over someone who was frozen as solid as the ice around him.

Shortly after dawn, when I came across several others who had survived the terrific ordeal, we decided to try to walk to our ship. When I saw my comrades, I almost thought they were ghosts. They were encased in icy snow from head to foot. It was not until 7 PM that we finally reached our ship. When the roll was called, forty-eight of my comrades did not answer. Among the thirty-two who were rescued, many lost their fingers and toes, and a few even their feet.

Nathan House, master watch:

The three watches (when we were dispatched from the *Greenland*) walked away like spokes from the hub of a wheel. A sudden storm came out of the north, making visibility impossible. Night came down—no food, no shelter, no ship in sight. I ordered my men to try and build a shelter out of snow. After a long, long night, morning came, still stormy. We could not see how to walk, there were dangerous holes in the ice. Then, the storm went just as it had come, with a suddenness. We could then see our ship away in the distance. Then it was every man for himself!

(Upon reaching the *Greenland* and . . .) after four hours of sleep, I was awakened by the sobbing of Captain Barbour over the loss of his men. Forty-eight were either frozen or drowned. It was my job to call the roll. We had recovered 23 bodies. Twenty-five men were never found. It was necessary to pack these bodies on deck, until we could get them to the undertaker.

We have already noted that James Ryan knew of the disaster as the SS *Greenland* passed north of Cape Bonavista. From that diary:

March 26, Saturday.
The SS *Greenland* is now at Cape Bonavista pushing her way south. The writer's opinion leads him to believe that this steamer has already procured many young seals this season—a full load—had 14,000—lost 48 men—and has gone home to discharge.

The *Greenland*, in fact, had stopped farther south, where they radioed the tragedy to the ship's owners and the Newfoundland government.

"W. B. Grieve, St. John's.
SS *Greenland* arrived at Bay-de-Verde.
Too heavy so to run. Sad misfortune
LOST FORTY-EIGHT MEN in heavy gale;
more badly frozen and will need hospital care.
Twenty-five dead bodies on board.
Remainder could not find.
Advise where to go."
Capt. George Barbour.

Premier Winter and Mr. Grieve wired Captain Barbour immediately:

To Capt Geo. Barbour, Bay-de-Verde.
"My heartfelt sympathy to you and the poor men.
Come on here where arrangements are being made
for living and dead . . . " W. B. Grieve.

Shortly after 2:00 p.m. on Sunday, March 27, the SS *Greenland* sailed back into the Narrows with its flag at half-mast. It docked at the premises of Baine Johnston & Co, its owner, where doctors and nurses awaited to help the injured, followed by those men tasked with removing twenty-five frozen bodies.

Archibald Russell's mother, Elizabeth, received the news on Monday. James Ryan's entry reads:

> A special message to (Magistrate of Bonavista) John Roper from A.B. Morine says "*Greenland* lost 48 men: 25 bodies recovered, 23 not obtained. All Bonavista men safe, including Thomas Little, Richard Tilly, Archibald Russell and Henry Etsell—tell their friends."

Morine was the member for Bonavista in the Government of Newfoundland's House of Assembly. He was in St. John's at that time. Archibald Russell was, in fact, the only man from Bonavista on the SS *Greenland*.

An article in the *Evening Telegram* on March 28 noted that Archibald Russell, along with five others, suffered from frostbite on his face and behind his ears. He returned home, and a few years later, he married Elizabeth Hicks at the Anglican Church in Bonavista. He was listed on the marriage certificate as a fisherman, aged twenty-five. Elizabeth was twenty-three. They built a home on Lawrence Lane (near Coster Street and Church Street) around 1907, raised three children, and lived the rest of their days in Bonavista.

Notes

The personal accounts are taken from *The Greenland Disaster of 1898* by Danny Roberts (1998): http://ngb.chebucto.org/Articles/dis-greenland.shtml

The *Evening Telegram* and James Ryan's diary provide specific detail as noted and are found on Memorial University's Digital Archive Initiative: http://collections.mun.ca/cdm

Family history milestones were found from church, census, and cemetery records for Bonavista at http://ngb.chebucto.org.

25 — WORLD WAR II

Newfoundlanders answered the call from England for both the First and Second World Wars. This is the story of one young man from Bonavista who, in joining the war effort, returned to the home of his ancestors.

Philip Swyers, of Fordington, Dorset, in southern England, like many young men of his era, crossed the North Atlantic from Poole, England, to Newfoundland in search of a better life. The year was 1797, and Philip was twenty-one years old. He arrived in Bonavista, settled in that part of the community known as Bayley's Cove, and began a lifelong career as a fisherman. He and wife, Temperance (Abbott), raised a large family. The list of the members of the Methodist classes in 1823 (Appendix 7) includes Philip Swyers as the leader of the Bayley's Cove class—indicating that he was both a devout and respected member of the local community.

One of Philip's great-grandchildren was Joseph Thomas (J. T.) Swyers, born in 1876. Joseph's father, George, had expected Joseph, who was his oldest, to be, like him, a fisherman. Joseph, however, frequently succumbed to seasickness while working with his dad. Finally, on yet another day at sea in the midst of winds and waves, Joseph told his father to head toward the nearest wharf. Joseph would not spend his life on the sea. He was about fifteen years old.

James Ryan offered Joseph work with his own firm, but the young Swyers had other plans. In 1892, he began his own business buying fish from the local fishermen from a building not much bigger than an outhouse. Over time, he built it into the largest retail and wholesale enterprise not only in Bonavista, but throughout the better part of the Bonavista Peninsula.

Joseph married Alice Keel, and between them they raised a large and prosperous family. While many of Joseph's sons chose to support their father in his business pursuits, James saw the world differently. And just as Joseph could not follow in his father's footsteps and become a fisherman, James could not follow in his father's footsteps and become a businessman. So, when James was nineteen, he decided that he would join the Royal Air Force. His father arranged transportation for him to England on a vessel owned by a fellow merchant in St. John's, but James would have to work on the vessel to pay his keep. In July 1933, James set sail on the SS *Blue Peter*—en route from New-foundland to England.

One of the iconic photos from J. T. Swyers Co. Ltd., perhaps the most prominent wholesale and retail business in Bonavista during the 1900s. (Jim Swyers)

James kept a dairy, from which we have extracted pertinent sections. Note how those entries reveal an appreciation for everything from the sea and sky (and their inhabitants), wireless operations, pilots and their adventures, details of magnetic north, speeds, and directions. Though just a teenager, James already felt a passion for the world around him—a passion that would lead him through the years that followed. James had already been training himself for the RAF and would chase his dream.

July 21, 1933.
Left Cartwright (coastal Labrador) this morning at 8 o'clock. . . . Waters very calm. No work today owing to being up for two nights and I feel just about all in. This is my 22nd hour working without sleep. Guess I'll stand it.

This is my first time crossing the Atlantic.

Author's note: Although anyone might be inclined to note in a diary that this is the first time crossing the Atlantic, one can't help but wonder if James was thinking that this was going to be the first of many.

July 22.
About 300 miles out to sea, passed a steamer today. Weather warm, no wind. It it holds like this, I don't think I'll be seasick. Stopped last night owing to fog and fear of icebergs. Birds were in the thousands. . . . Painted the rails this afternoon.

July 23.
Beautiful day. No wind and the water is very calm. Lots of birds. Spent the afternoon with the wireless operator. Received news of Mollison flying over Halifax. Reading most of the day until about 2 o'clock.

Ship is now over six hundred miles out to sea. Averaging 11.5 knots. Expect to arrive in England on Saturday.

Author's note: Swyers was referring to Jim Mollison and Amy Johnson, a married couple, dubbed the Flying Sweethearts, who were attempting an around-the-world flight. The first stage was crossing the Atlantic from South Wales in Great Britain to New York. They departed around noon on July 22, 1933, but crashed in Connecticut. Both pilots were injured. Clearly, Swyers was aware of the event and was following its progress.

July 24.
Turned out at 5:30 o'clock this morning to go painting. We have almost all the rails around the ship painted. Water still a bit rougher than yesterday with the wind on the starboard side. Will be half-way tomorrow noon.

I feel mighty glad that I came on this trip now seeing how everything is turning out.

Author's note: Written across the page, Swyers writes:

Never give up. There are chances and changes. Helping the hopeful, a hundred to one and through the chaos, High Wisdom arranges every success, if you'll only hold on. Never give up, for the wisest is boldest knowing that Providence mingles the cup. And of all maxims, the best as the oldest is the stern watchwords of NEVER GIVE UP.

Ship now sailing S49E—the change in the compass direction is owing to variation of the magnetic attraction.

July 25.
Turned out at 6 o'clock this morning. Neptune did not come on board yet. The water is very smooth with a slight breeze on the starboard side. Saw some whales today and some sharks which followed the ship a long distance, waiting for food I guess. Painted the wheel today with grey paint. Saw another steamer—the wireless operator said it was the *Europa*.

July 26.
Turned out at 6:30 this morning. Got my breakfast and started to paint the deck. . . . The weather is very smooth. I haven't been seasick so far— "better not count my chickens yet" is the old saying.

July 27.
Turned out at 7 o'clock. Got my breakfast . . . and started to paint the anchors—finished them about 11 o'clock then painted some boards on deck. We are certainly working for our passage.

Just before dark we sighted Ireland. It wont be long now. We hope to see a lot of ships tomorrow.

James joined the Royal Air Force upon arriving in England. He also returned to Bonavista sporadically, as evidenced by the fact that he won a Bonavista three-mile road race in 1936. When Hitler invaded Poland in 1939 and England declared war on Germany, thousands of young men joined the war effort. James was already a seasoned pilot of the RAF. He was part of the first air raids into Germany in 1939 and supported Dunkirk in 1940. Later that year, he defended England in the Battle of Britain between the RAF and Nazi Germany's Luftwaffe—the first large-scale military campaign fought entirely in the air.

Bonavista 3-Mile Race trophy.
(Glenn Mitchell)

In 1941, James was sent to Picton, Ontario, among those leaders responsible for establishing the Royal Air Force's No. 31 Bombing and Gunnery School. The base officially opened in April 1941. Among his many responsibilities, James was a bombing instructor.

James Swyers (fifth from left, first row).
(*Wings*, the magazine of the RAF Picton. Vol. 2, No. 9. April 1943)

During his stay in Picton, James married a native of Picton, Elsa Maud Harrison. Their union was recorded in the local newspaper.

Marriage: Swyers–Harrison
At Picton United Church, Friday, August 20, 1943 by Rev. J. F. Raycraft and Squadron Leader R. Hooper, Elsa Maud Harrison to Flight Lieutenant James Swyers, R.A.F., Picton, son of Mr. and Mrs. J. T. Swyers, Bonavista, Newfoundland.

James and Elsa moved to England in late 1943 to again support the war effort. He rose quickly through the ranks to squadron leader but lost his life in the line of duty on June 7, 1944. James's brother, Ed, was, at that time, working in North Sydney, Nova Scotia. The *Sydney Post Record* wrote the following in the June 16 edition:

JAMES SWYERS OF ROYAL AIR FORCE KILLED IN ACTION

Word to the effect that his brother, Squadron Leader James Swyers of the Royal Air Force, 29-year-old native of Newfoundland, was killed on June 7th has been received by his brother here, Ed Swyers.

Squadron Leader Swyers, who was a son of Mr. and Mrs. J. T. Swyers, prominent Bonavista, NL residents and well known here, had been a member of the permanent RAF and had been in the service for the past seven years. Shortly after completing his high school education, he made application to get into the RAF while still in Newfoundland, and was accepted.

The late SL Swyers was a veteran of the Battle of Britain, of the historic air action over Dunkerque and had also taken part in the very first RAF air raids on Berlin after war had been declared.

After joining up and completing his training, he had been an instructor before the war started, and had served overseas in this capacity for several years. Later he came to Canada and was stationed in Picton, Ontario for two years, after which he again went overseas—returning to England last December.

SL Swyers had visited here a number of times, the last time being in October of last year, and he was well and popularly known by

Squadron Leader James Swyers.
(Jim Swyers)

many friends, all of whom will learn of his death with deep and sincere regret. He had made rapid advancement after joining the Royal Air Force and had much experience in actual aerial operations over enemy territory.

Squadron Leader James Swyers is buried at Lincoln (Newport) Cemetery, in Lincolnshire, England, not that far, as the crow flies, from Fordington—the home of his great-great-grandfather, Philip.

Notes

Details on the marriage of James Swyers and Elsa Maud Harrison were provided by the County of Prince Edward Public Library and Archives, Wellington,
Ontario. All additional information was provided via personal discussion and
private materials of Joan Grandy and Jim Swyers.

26 — CONFEDERATION

One of the well-known milestones in the history of Newfoundland is its inclusion as the tenth province of Canada in 1949. It is not as well-known that one of the key players, if not *the* most important individual with respect to that milestone, had ancestral roots with, and spent much of his life in, Bonavista.

John Bradley was born in Bonavista in 1825. When he was old enough to fish for himself, he, like many young men or young families in Bonavista at that time, needed to leave home. Tocque described conditions in Bonavista as he saw it during his visit:

> A great part of the poverty of Bonavista is owing to the want (or lack) of room to erect stages and flakes for the fishery. Half of the fishermen, in consequence of having no water-side premises, cannot "go on the plant" as it is called (all of the fishermen who keep a boat and employ men, or even keep a skiff and fish alone, are called "planters" in Newfoundland), they are therefore obliged to go as sharemen.

Tocque's description of a "planter" is quite different from the early use of that word in the 1700s, when a planter was someone who owned a plantation. His definition, however, is supported by Lovell's Directory, which makes frequent use of both fisherman and planter in denoting occupation.

Many in Bonavista in the mid-1800s left Bonavista and established communities along the "Straight Shore" between Bonavista and Notre Dame Bays. John's family moved to Musgrave Harbour. Their son, Noah Norman (1857–1924), moved to St. John's as a young man and, in 1881, began a five-year apprenticeship with a furniture company. He married Evangeline Trimm in 1886. Their son, Frederick Gordon Bradley (or F. Gordon, as he was generally known) was born in St. John's in 1888. As a young boy, he developed a severe attack of scarlet fever, with kidney problems and, according to Hiller, was advised by the family doctor to seek "fresh air and early nights" and, as a result, spent more time at the birthplace of his paternal grandfather in Bonavista.

After finishing schooling in 1906 at the Methodist College in St. John's, F.

Gordon Bradley returned to Bonavista as principal of the Methodist School. He spent three years there, then returned to St. John's, and eventually went to Dalhousie University to study law. He was called to the bar in 1915. He practised law until 1923, when he ran for a seat in Trinity Bay but was defeated. In 1924, he ran again and won a seat in Port de Grave by five votes. Within two years, he became disillusioned with the Monroe government, which, according to Hiller, "he persistently attacked for class bias, extravagance and failure to look after the interests of the fishery." In the 1928 election, under Squires, he was appointed to cabinet, was Solicitor General, and became a director of the Newfoundland Railway and a member of the Treasury Board. Hiller called Bradley "one of Squires's chief lieutenants."

F. Gordon Bradley. Taken in the 1930s. (Eric and Mary Searle via Ross Abbott)

Government collapsed in 1932, and (from Hiller) Bradley "resented deeply the pressures that were being placed on Newfoundland by its creditors, by the British Government and by large foreign corporations." "The state had a primary duty to serve the greatest good of the greatest number and to help those most in need." Bradley had come to believe that Newfoundland's future rested with Canada. Newfoundlanders needed to separate from England, as its future lay in North America. Plate tectonics had separated the island of Newfoundland from England millions of years ago. The people of Newfoundland now needed to do the same.

Bradley also believed that fishermen needed more control over their industry. "The profits of the industry should go to the producer (and) the producer in Newfoundland is the fisherman . . . he was given a bare crust of bread while the Water Street merchant pilfered the jam . . ."

Commission Government, in which Newfoundland was ruled from England, was installed in early 1934. Bradley spoke in the House of Assembly that "the voice of the people is stilled, muted, gagged and rendered inarticulate."

Bradley had little role to play in Commission Government because of his well-known hostility to it, but in 1935, he was appointed magistrate to Bonavista, which he gladly accepted. He and his family moved into the home in which his wife grew up, the home of Magistrate John Soper, originally the Mockbeggar Plantation (or Room) described in Chapter 11 and listed in Appendix 2.

The National Convention to determine Newfoundland's future began in 1945, and Bradley ran as a candidate. When the chairman of the Convention died in November 1946, Bradley became chairman, being supported by all sides. He also led the delegation to Ottawa. Hiller wrote that "the Canadians still viewed Bradley as the key figure if confederation was to be accomplished." Prime Minister Louis St. Laurent wrote that Bradley "is the individual on whom the movement (to join Canada) will rely." When Bradley returned to Newfoundland, however, he abruptly resigned as chairman, citing further attacks from which he could not defend himself. Health was publicly given as the reason for his departure.

The signing of the Terms of Union between Newfoundland and Canada. F. Gordon Bradley is standing, fourth from the left. (From: https://www. heritage.nf.ca/articles/politics/becoming-a-province.php)

In 1948, however, Bradley returned as president of the Confederate Association, making speeches, campaigning, and raising funds. After the second referendum decided in favour of joining Canada, Bradley was part of the delegation that signed the Terms of Union. He became Secretary of State in the federal cabinet and won the 1949 federal election representing Bonavista–Twillingate. In 1953, he moved to the Senate.

History had generally written that Joey Smallwood was the driving force in bringing Newfoundland into Confederation, a belief that Smallwood himself fostered in his writing. Smallwood wrote about his direction to Bradley while the latter was a member in the House of Assembly in the 1930s, and he gives Bradley a strict supporting role in the lead-up to the final referendum.

The historical facts, however, indicate otherwise. Hiller notes that the Smallwood assertions that he "virtually ran the opposition from the Colonial Building galleries seems improbable. Bradley was by this time an experienced politician, a good speaker, and a man who knew his own mind." Bradley himself wrote, in 1956, that Smallwood was "a truckling politician, with no ability except as a propagandist, ready to buy any and every influence to feed his own ego and betray everything he pretends to revere for the same purpose." Later, he called Smallwood "a man of no experience. He had . . . an ability to talk possessed by few individuals on earth. The inevitable result was that at the outset, he dominated the whole Government." Few contemporary Newfoundlanders would have disagreed.

F. Gordon Bradley (left) and Joey Smallwood. (Jennifer Bradley via Ross Abbott)

Bradley developed heart troubles in the 1960s, spent less time in Ottawa, and died in 1966.

Hiller, in his closing assessment of Bradley, wrote that Bradley had "a strong streak of the crusader, a compulsion to attempt to rectify injustices where he saw them, and a close identification with the needs of Newfoundland's workers." But "he had a caustic tongue which gave voice to strong principles, moral scrupulousness and firm opinions. He never suffered those whom he considered fools—and there were many of them."

George Sellars wrote to Bradley in 1949, saying "You had the ability and talent to envision just the trend things should take . . . you handled Smallwood, in coaching him and keeping him on the right track." Bradley, in 1964, wrote "I chose to follow a star and I failed to reach it. . . . The fact is that I failed." Perhaps Bradley failed according to his own assessment, but he was a key, though largely forgotten, figure in bringing Newfoundland and Labrador into Canada.

F. Gordon Bradley married Ethel Roper of Bonavista in 1923, daughter of the stipendiary magistrate for Bonavista, John Roper, Esq. They had two sons, John and Gordon, both of whom remained in Bonavista. Gordon was, for a time, the mayor of Bonavista. F. Gordon Bradley and his wife moved into the Mockbeggar Plantation (Mockbeggar Room, Appendix 2) in Bonavista in 1939, which, as we've noted, had been the home of John Roper while he had been magistrate. The Plantation was, at one time, the largest Fishing Room in Bonavista and is located in a prominent location at the northern entrance to Bonavista Harbour. We don't know its original owner, but in the 1700s, it was owned by Samuel White, one of the most successful early merchant families of Newfoundland. The Bradley family donated the Mockbeggar Plantation to the province in 1980. It has been restored to the early twentieth-century period and is now a Provincial Historic Site.

Notes

Quotes from Bradley's political career are taken from: Hiller, J. K., *The Career of F. Gordon Bradley*. Newfoundland Studies 4, 2 (1988).

Family milestones were retrieved from parish and census records.

27 — ADULT EDUCATION

Jessie Beaumont Mifflin was born in 1906 in Bonavista, the daughter of Heber and Elizabeth (Saint) Mifflin. Jessie had an older sister, Marion Amelia, and a younger brother, Thomas. They lived at Walkham's Hill, close to the courthouse overlooking Bonavista Harbour.

Jessie attended the Methodist School on Coster Street, just a few minutes' walk from her home. Upon completion, she attended the Methodist College and Memorial University College (MUC) in St. John's, taught for a brief period at MUC, then obtained a bachelor of arts degree from Mount Allison University in Sackville, New Brunswick. She later received a bachelor of library science from the University of Toronto.

Photo of seven members of the NAEA. Back row: Jessie Mifflin, Bertha Northover. Middle row: Kathleen Thompson, Elsie May Farrell, Ida Parsons. Front row: Laura Cantwell, Mary Maddock. (*Newfoundland Quarterly.* Volume 032. No. 3. 1932)

Beginning in the early 1930s, Mifflin spent considerable time in outport Newfoundland engaged in adult education, working for the Newfoundland Adult Education Association (NAEA), a newly formed organization funded by the Carnegie Corporation through coordination by local Newfoundland leaders in education. At its inception, the team was comprised entirely of women. Mrs. Elsie May Farrell led a contingent of six young ladies, one of whom was Jessie Mifflin, chosen specifically for their capacity to provide educational leadership to the adult community. An internal report from 1935 wrote that Mifflin was busy "with home groups three miles in one direction, four miles in another, and a mile and a half in a third." A later *Evening Telegram* article (May 10, 1947) noted that during those first years, "Mifflin travelled all over the island, covering the north coast down to the Straits of Belle Isle, and along the south coast, spending two months in one settlement, two months in another." Mifflin loved adult education. "It isn't work at all," she said. "It's a pleasure."

During World War II, Mifflin joined the Royal Canadian Air Force to support the war effort. She described it as "deadly dull—all I did was count nuts and bolts and airplane parts." In 1944, she took on the role of field secretary in Newfoundland for the NAEA. "It was an interesting and challenging [position]. . . . I remained in that job for some three to four years roaming around the outports preaching the gospel of education." Then, in 1949, she joined the Public Libraries Board, where she held a variety of positions, leading to chief regional librarian, deputy director, and acting director Public Library Services, through to her retirement in 1972.

During the Spring Convocation of 1975, Mifflin was awarded a Doctor of Laws from Memorial University of

Photo of Jessie B. Mifflin from *Newfoundland Who's Who*, Centennial Edition. 1967–68. Editor, James R. Thoms. E. C. Boone Advertising Ltd. St. John's, NL. 1968.

Newfoundland. The public orator, W. J. Blundon, on that occasion, spoke of the differences between St. John's and the rest of Newfoundland. He quoted a fisherman "some three decades ago on the dearth of public services. He said something like 'The trouble with this country (i.e., pre-provincial Newfoundland) is that everything is concentrated in St. John's except the people—they're scattered over every bay.' When we joined Canada, this complaint was given a wider context and dignified with the name of 'regional disparity.'" By way of highlighting Mifflin's role in addressing "regional disparity," Blundon noted that "Her longest and greatest contribution dates from 1949 when she joined the Public Libraries Board as Supervisor of Regional Services. From that time until her retirement, the number of regional libraries increased from 21 to 75." In closing, Blundon said that "her real travels are . . . within the confines of this province by which the joys of reading were brought to Newfoundlanders in every corner of every bay."

Mifflin was asked to give the convocation address at the graduating ceremony. Her speech was both wise and humorous. And it provided glimpses into her hometown. Some excerpts, with only minor edits, are repeated here:

It was with great reluctance that I accepted (the invitation to give the Convocation Address). I feel that "I have neither wit nor words nor worth" to do justice to the occasion. I feel somewhat in the same position as the Irishman who, meeting a friend whom he hadn't seen for quite some time, inquired after the health of his wife, to which the friend replied: "Oh, poor Mary's gone to Heaven." "Oh, I'm sorry," said that Irishman, which on reflection, seemed hardly the right response when she had achieved such a happy state, so he hastily changed it to "Oh, I'm glad," which sounded rather callous, so once again he changed it to "I mean, I'm surprised," which was, perhaps, the most inappropriate of all.

Women have come a long way since the first graduation at Memorial University College, where, incidentally, the first person to graduate was a woman—Dr. Helena Frecker, who gave the address at one of the Convocations last year.

Some years ago, I applied for a position. Within a few days, I was advised that . . . a recommendation for my appointment was to be made (but) they first wanted to be certain that I was aware that . . . I could not be given the salary advertised . . . since that was the amount allocated for a man. It was taken for granted that a man would be appointed; and indeed that no woman would be so brash as to consider herself capable of filling it. I ventured to intimate that it seemed somewhat unfair to assume automatically that a woman was less capable than a man. I expressed my disappointment to my friends, who encouraged me by saying "Pray to God and She will help you and the authorities will likely accede to your request." And I did, and She did, and they did. . . . I felt that I had struck a blow for Women's Lib long before the phrase had ever been coined.

Mr. Paton (former President of Memorial University College) tried to instill into each of us a realization that the privilege of obtaining higher education brought a corresponding responsibility—a responsibility to share its benefits with others less fortunate and to provide leadership in the community.

Most of us (i.e., students from outport Newfoundland attending Memorial University College) had never even seen a library before, much less used one, for there was no public library service in Newfoundland at that time, not even in St. John's. Apart from text books, there were few books in most outport schools, and in many homes, the entire library collection consisted of Eaton's Catalogue, Dr. Chase's Almanac and The Bible, and in many cases, the greatest of these was Eaton's Catalogue.

In Bonavista, the town in which I grew up, then one of the largest in Newfoundland, a small library was actually set up when I was in my last year of High School. It was sponsored by the local Church of England clergyman, a scholarly man who deplored the lack of reading material available to the people and undertook to try and remedy the situation. The books were mainly discards from the parish library of an English Vicar designed to improve the mind and uplift the soul. . . . It was considered broadminded of the clergyman to allow the Roman Catholic, Methodist and Salvation Army population to enter into the sacred precincts of The Library.

Not the least advantage of attending Memorial University College was the mingling of all types of people, to our mutual advantage, and the breaking down of barriers separating people of different classes and creeds. In the small communities from which many of us came, if there was any contact between the pupils of the different denominational schools, it was often in the nature of a less than friendly rivalry. If, for instance, it rained on the day our Sunday School Picnic was to be held, we knew exactly who to blame; it was not God but the children of the other major denominational school who had been killing spiders all week to ensure that it would rain on that day.

You will have influence in the community in which you serve. I urge you to use that influence to cultivate among the people you encounter a better public spirit, a finer concept of their duties as citizens, a realization that as members of the community, they are in a measure responsible for the welfare of that community, and that this responsibility applies to every one in the community, whether they labour in the fishing boat or the pulpit, in the forest or the office, in the factory or the school.

Dr. Jessie Mifflin served in a leadership capacity of the Atlantic Provinces Library Association, the Canadian Library Association, the St. John's Club of the Canadian Federation of University Women, and the Janeway Child Health Centre Auxiliary. In addition to receiving a Doctor of Laws from Memorial University and Mount Allison University, she was also awarded a Canada

Centennial Medal in 1967, an Outstanding Service Award from the Canadian Library Association, and honorary membership in the Newfoundland Teachers Association. She was the author of numerous articles and books—perhaps her best known publication is *Be You a Library Missionary, Miss?* She was appointed a member of the Order of Canada in 1973.

Notes

References:
Some of the details of Mifflin's life are taken from:
Adult Education on the Newfoundland Coast: Adventure and Opportunity for Women in the 1930s and 1940s. Leona M. English. Newfoundland and Labrador Studies, 26, 1 (2011).
More general information is found in:
Who's Who: Newfoundland Confederation Celebration 1949-1975 Silver Anniversary Edition. Editor James R. Thoms. Public Relations Consultants Ltd. St. John's. 1975.
The speeches at the 1975 Convocation are found in:
Memorial University of Newfoundland Gazette. Vol. 7. No. 18. 1975.

A note on family history:
Jessie Mifflin's second name, Beaumont, is worthy of note. Beaumond's Flake is recorded in the 1805–06 Register of Fishing Rooms (Appendix 2) as belonging to John Beaumond. John and Sarah Beaumond's daughter Thurza was baptized in 1805—in 1832 she married James Saint. Meanwhile, one of Jessie Beaumont Mifflin's aunts (on her mother's side) was baptized Therza Beaumont Saint in 1883 (spelling as recorded in the baptism records). Thurza Beaumond (daughter to the owner of Beaumond's Flake in 1805 and married in 1832 to James Saint) is almost certainly Jessie Beaumont Mifflin's great-grandmother. The name Beaumond/t has disappeared from Bonavista.

Photo of the seven members of the NAEA from *Newfoundland Quarterly.* Volume 032. No. 3. 1832. Page 11—*Newfoundland Quarterly*—Memorial University DAI (mun.ca)

28 — NORTHERN COD AND THE MORATORIUM

The Government of Canada closed the northern cod fishery in 1992. It was devastating not only to Newfoundland generally, but especially in Bonavista. Concern for the survival of the northern cod was expressed as early as the 1960s by a fisheries scientist with widespread respect not only in Newfoundland and Canada, but in fact throughout the globe. That scientist was born in Bonavista.

Wilfred Templeman was born on February 2, 1908, in Bonavista, the child of Charles and Sarah Templeman. His father was a fisherman, and his mother's maiden name was Fisher. These were good omens.

Wilfred went to the Methodist one-room school in Bayley's Cove, Bonavista. As a teenager, he perhaps learned his most important lesson.

Wilfred (as taken from *Wilfred Templeman: A Fisherman's Son*): "My father was a fisherman. I worked with him, fishing for awhile, and in one month, I earned four dollars. So I thought maybe it was time to move on from there!"

He applied himself to his studies in Bonavista, finished senior matriculation at Methodist College in St. John's, then attended Memorial University College. Following completion, he won a scholarship to attend Dalhousie University, where he obtained his bachelor of science degree, while playing on

Dr. Wilfred Templeman. (Photo taken from *Journal of the Northwest Atlantic Fishery Science*, Halliday and Pinhorn, Vol. 10, 1990)

the Dalhousie rugby team. He then won a Canada Fisheries Research Board scholarship to attend the University of Toronto. His completed his Ph.D. in 1933 working under Dr. A. G. Huntsman. He was twenty-five years old.

Huntsman was, himself, a pioneering oceanographer and nationally recognized fisheries biologist. The A. G. Huntsman Award for Excellence in the Marine Sciences is awarded, in his honour, by the Canadian marine science community to recognize excellence in research to marine sciences.

When Templeman graduated from U of T in 1933, he taught at McGill University, while working with the Fisheries Research Board of Canada and the Biological Research Station in New Brunswick. In 1936, he returned to Newfoundland as head of Memorial University College's Biology Department. Then, in 1944, he accepted the responsibility of Director of Fisheries Investigations at the Newfoundland Government Laboratory on Water Street in St. John's.

At that time, little research was being conducted, and a lot of data had been destroyed in a fire at the previous lab in Bay Bulls in 1937. A colleague, Allenby Pinhorn, said that Templeman put in eighteen-hour days. "He worked day and night on marine science. And of course he was director of the lab so he had a certain amount of administrative work to do but quite clearly his first love was marine biology. He just lived it . . . totally lived it."

But working in a laboratory was only part of the job of a marine scientist, at least in Dr. Templeman's view. He understood that Newfoundland needed to grasp a full understanding of the marine environment around Newfoundland. His Water Street laboratory needed to study not only the cod fishery but the large number of underutilized and even undiscovered species. Domestic refrigeration was to become a reality as well. The long-standing salt cod fishery needed to move aside for fresh-frozen products from a variety of species.

Gus Etchegary (from *Wilfred Templeman: A Fisherman's Son*): "The Newfoundland fishing industry would have to change its emphasis from being a solely inshore fishery to one that could compete."

In 1946, the Water Street lab was given the *Investigator II*, an eighty-two-foot vessel unsuitable in ice. Edward (Sandy) Sandeman: "She worked from April to December. It was an incredible little workboat. But it wasn't really the thing you wanted in the long-term."

While Templeman was gaining increased knowledge of the marine ecosystem around Newfoundland, lack of funds continued to plague the lab. Newfoundland was under Commission Government, of course, and World War II was over. There were staff shortages in the lab, lack of workspace, and insufficient funds for training programs for fishermen.

In 1949, Newfoundland joined Canada, and the Water Street lab became part of the Fisheries Research Board of Canada. In 1950, Templeman went to

Ottawa to help coordinate the transfer. Templeman went with a list of requirements necessary to ensure that the lab functioned effectively. His requests
were met, and management was passed to Dr. Templeman and his staff.

Dr. Templeman also established Fisheries Board scholarships to Newfoundland students who wanted to study the marine environment at Memorial University. According to Dr. Arthur May, he carefully interviewed and
selected them himself. It was a great success. Then, as these students entered
MUN, he conducted evening seminars and supervised their graduate degrees.

Meanwhile, a new research vessel was constructed: the *A. T. Cameron*,
a 177-foot research trawler, was launched in 1958. Dr. May called it the "Taj
Mahal" of research vessels compared to anything staff had used before. May:
"It was almost the equivalent of going from a small plane to a spaceship."

The *Cameron* was able to survey waters from the Davis Strait in the Arctic, through the Subarctic regions in the Labrador Sea, the Grand Banks, to
waters south of Newfoundland and into the Grand Banks. The volumes of data
collected through these surveys culminated in Dr. Templeman's landmark
work, *Marine Resources of Newfoundland*, in 1966.

Dr. May: Dr. Templeman "was very precise, very thorough, very pro-
fessional, very honest. The experimental method, hypothesis, and collecting
data. He knew how science was done and he was an exemplary practitioner
(of it)."

Throughout this period, and particularly following World War II, off-
shore waters around Newfoundland became increasingly exploited by foreign
fleets. To monitor and regulate this fishery to ensure stability, the Interna-
tional Commission for the North Atlantic Fisheries (ICNAF) was formed.
Newfoundland had joined this organization prior to Confederation (Dr.
Templeman had signed the convention which formed ICNAF on behalf of
Newfoundland), and he continued to play a role in ICNAF as a member of
Canada's delegation.

Pinhorn: "ICNAF was the only organization, the only opportunity where
Canada as a coastal state . . . could sit down at the table with these people and
hammer out an agreement and try to move forward enforcement regulations
(and) agreements."

Dr. May knew that Dr. Templeman "had a lot of foresight. He could look
ahead and guess at what was coming and his guesses were pretty accurate."

Dr. Templeman knew from his research that the cod stocks off the northeast coast of Newfoundland (known as northern cod) were different from
the Grand Banks. The northern cod matured at a much slower rate and were

therefore more susceptible to over-exploitation. Surveys conducted by the *Cameron*, under the supervision of Dr. May, confirmed these suspicions.

Dr. May: "I began that work in 1959. By 1966, that fishery had reached a level of something like 800,000 tons and in retrospect, the fishery was killed at that point, although it didn't die until about 25 years later."

Dr. Templeman related an incident in 1960, shortly after the arrival of the Soviet fishing fleet. The *Cameron* was researching stocks in the southern Grand Banks. They caught over thirteen tons of haddock in thirty minutes, and the skipper of the *Cameron*, as with most Newfoundland captains, spoke of it during radio chatter with other nearby vessels. The next morning, eight Soviet factory trawlers and four Spanish "pairs" were nearby. In 1961, Templeman reported to ICNAF that "the trend in the haddock fishery over the next four or five years is expected to be strongly downward." Within a decade, it was "virtually gone."

At that time, ICNAF had implemented a policy regarding mesh size to sustain the fishery by allowing smaller fish to escape the nets. Dr. Templeman and another scientist were asked to formulate new protocols. Templeman: "We recommended quotas and that's where quotas started." This meant that each country was allocated a quota for each species, with a hope that this would bring a measure of control to ICNAF.

But neither quotas nor ICNAF could stop the overfishing of the lucrative northern cod fishery. By 1970, hundreds of trawlers, and thousands of men were employed in the offshore fishing fleets.

Etchegary: "It was obvious, both within the ICNAF structure and the annual meetings that were held, and the scientific reports that were presented annually, that the resource from 1970, for example, onward, was in serious trouble. It was a downward trend, in practically every species."

On September 9, 1971, Dr. Templeman was invited as guest speaker at the weekly luncheon of the St. John's Rotary Club at Hotel Newfoundland. As quoted by the *Evening Telegram* on the following day, Templeman said that with respect to the cod fishery, there was little hope of reversing the long-term decline and that, under present conditions, Newfoundland fishermen would continue to be "only marginally engaged" in the fishery. With the increase in the participation in the offshore fishery, the result had been disastrous for both the inshore fishery of Labrador and for northern Newfoundland. Further, Templeman said, it was difficult to get other nations to agree to reduce their quota. "The problems in the Newfoundland fishery are not too difficult to see, but the solutions are not that easy to find."

On September 13, 1971, the *Evening Telegram* published its own commentary in the op-ed page. Entitled "A Word of Warning," the article commenced with "If someone with the authority and scientific background of Dr. Wilfred Templeman, Director of the St. John's Biological Station of the Fisheries Research Board of Canada, is pessimistic over the future of the fishing industry, it is time for provincial and federal governments to sit up and take notice.... In almost every area the story is the same. Heavy catches by offshore draggers and trawlers are cleaning out the great concentrations of fish on the spawning grounds." The editorial ends with a quote by Dr. Templeman: "If Canada is prepared to allow her continental shelf to be ruined by foreign fishing fleets there seems to be little future for our fishing industry. And waiting around for a law of the sea conference in 1973 is not going to do much good."

Dr. Templeman retired in 1972, after which he returned to his love of research. He took a position as the J. L. Paton Professor of Marine Biology and Fisheries. In addition to occasional teaching, he continued research, particularly on underutilized species. Ten years later, he moved to the Northwest-Atlantic Fisheries Centre, on the outskirts of St. John's, a complex for which he and Dr. May had laid the foundation in 1972.

On May 28, 1976, Templeman was awarded an Honorary Doctor of Science degree from Memorial University of Newfoundland. The "Deputy Public Orator," R. M. Mowbray, described Dr. Templeman as "a recognized world authority in his chosen fields and by his international reputation, he brings credit to Canada, to Newfoundland, and to our University." And, if this author might add . . . to Bonavista! Mowbray noted that Templeman was one of the founders of ICNAF, and that his conduct of meetings as a chairman earned him high praise and respect. Upon his retirement, "a collection of letters from ICNAF representatives in Scandinavia, Spain, Germany, Scotland, Portugal, England—even from the wilds of Ottawa—all attest to the high regard in which he is held outside Newfoundland, outside Canada." Mowbray closed his speech with the following: "We are to honour a Newfoundlander whose mastery of his field and devotion to his ideas have brought him acclaim in international scientific circles. He is, however, more than a detached scientist. Mr. Chancellor, as you clasp his hand in academic greeting, bear in mind that he has often been observed by his colleagues to be up to the elbows in fish gurry! I present to you for the degree of Doctor of Science, honoris causa, Wilfred Templeman."

Dr. George Rose was beginning his career just as Dr. Templeman was in his retirement. Rose based his Ph.D. thesis on Templeman's work and, in personal correspondence, noted that "I was lucky enough to have him for a short time in an adjacent office. He seldom, if ever, missed a day and he always read my papers. This was amazing as he was in his 80s! And yes, I remember hearing his slippers flip-flopping down the hall . . . I still refer to his work in my current research. He knew the fishery so well." In *Cod: The Ecological History of the North Atlantic Fisheries*, Rose further notes that Templeman's work "was marked by a combination of scientifically-derived knowledge and hard-won wisdom about the marine ecosystems and fisheries of Newfoundland and Labrador, and was rooted in boyhood observations from the wharfs of Bonavista. . . . He was the father of fisheries science in Newfoundland and Labrador. I shall remember him as 'Old Temp,' a brilliant and humble man, who possessed an unparalleled knowledge and interest in the fisheries of Newfoundland and Labrador."

In 1990, Templeman died of a heart attack. He was eighty-two. When he had been asked, in 1972, what motivated him, he answered, "What I did, I did for Newfoundland."

Dr. Templeman married Eileen McGrath in 1936, whom he had met while he was studying lobsters at the St. Andrews Biological Station in New Brunswick. They had three daughters. Sandeman: "He was a man who was absolutely dedicated to his work and to his family."

Dr. Templeman's awards:
i) 1948 — Order of the British Empire
ii) 1950 — Fellowship in the Royal Society of Canada
iii) 1976 — Honorary Doctor of Science Degree, Memorial University
iv) 1982 — The new research vessel, to replace the *A. T. Cameron*, was christened the *Wilfred Templeman*.

Dr. Templeman published over 250 papers in his career.

Two years after Templeman's death, on July 4, 1992, the federal Minister of Fisheries, John Crosbie, in the Radisson Hotel in St. John's, announced a moratorium on the catch of northern cod. It was an action, though necessary, of historical proportions to a region that had relied upon the fishery from initial settlement. Bonavista, at times described as Newfoundland's largest outport, and throughout its life dependent on the cod fishery, was, perhaps forever, changed.

Notes

The quotes by Templeman, May, Pinhorn, Etchegary, and Sandeman, as well as other information, are taken from the video *Wilfred Templeman: A Fisherman's Son*.

The incident of the *Cameron* on the southern Grand Banks and the decline of the haddock fishery is found in Rose, page 409.

Excerpts from the honorary degree presentation at MUN are found in the *MUN Gazette*, May 18, 1976. Vol. 08, No. 19. Retrieved from: http://collections.mun.ca/cdm/ref/collection/mun_gazette/id/2690

Biographical Information:
http://web.ncf.ca/an650/teach99/wrt/nfld/templeman.htm

The *Evening Telegram* articles (Sept. 10 & 13, 1971) on the St. John's Rotary Club Speech can be found on Microfilm at the A. C. Hunter Library, St. John's.

PART FIVE: TODAY
29 — POST-CONFEDERATION

The advent of the Bonavista Cold Storage Co. Ltd. to Bonavista in the early 1940s, led by New Brunswick native Hazen Russell, and including F. Gordon Bradley among its directors, radically changed the town. For centuries, fish was brought ashore, salted, and dried by the fishermen and their families before being sold to local merchants. This was not only labour-intensive, but also tied the fishing families to the coastline. With the introduction of the cold storage facility at the inner harbour of Bonavista, fishermen landed their catch directly from their boats to the facility itself. The plant, employing hundreds of men and women, processed the catch and distributed the frozen fillets to markets. Breakwaters were also constructed to protect boats and infrastructure. A few years later, in the early 1950s, larger vessels, known as longliners, fished in the ocean trenches several miles offshore. This radical departure from the small-boat traditional fishery was introduced under the guidance of Dr. Wilfred Templeman and the Newfoundland Fisheries Board laboratory and proved highly successful.

Other changes of the 1940s included the opening of the new Bonavista Cottage Hospital, in 1940, under the leadership of Chief Physician Dr. C. A. Forbes. But the end of World War II in 1945 and Newfoundland's entry into Confederation with Canada in 1949, which, as we've seen, to a significant degree was brought about by Bradley's efforts, were also consequential. As the people of Bonavista entered the 1950s, thanks to people like Forbes, Templeman, and Bradley, the old way of life had died.

Education in Bonavista at the turn of the nineteenth century relied on the persuasive efforts of a local magistrate (John Bland) to secure funds for a local teacher (George Bemister) from the Society for the Propagation of the Gospel in England (see Appendix 9). In the 1950s, a denominational school system, with teachers in most cases educated at Memorial University in St. John's, was well-established throughout the town. Well-trained young men and women from Bonavista became university graduates and returned home to teach, or came from elsewhere and made Bonavista their home.

Religious instruction in the 1700s and early 1800s relied upon occasional missionaries, ministers, and priests visiting sometimes from afar. Pastoral care in the those early years was sporadic. Church members, and perhaps their leaders, lacked trust in each other, and, as we saw in the flagstaff incident of 1814 (Chapter 12), it sometimes led to confrontation. In May 1950, an Anglican priest and United Church minister in Bonavista shared the same pulpit (Chapter 12) for the first time—similar gestures and ecumenical services occurred in following years.

Through the 1700s and 1800s, economic activity in and around Bonavista was governed to a large extent by merchant families in Trinity or even England. Through the initiative of young men of Bonavista such as James Ryan and J. T. Swyers in the late 1800s and into the 1900s, local businesses led the way in providing employment to the community. Meanwhile, the inshore and longliner fisheries, and the use of cold storage to supply new markets, provided greater stability to families.

The latter half of the twenty-first century was good to Bonavista. This changed in 1992 when the Government of Canada announced a moratorium on northern cod. The cod fishery was effectively shut down in Bonavista, and fishermen and plant workers were out of work. Although the moratorium was originally expected to last for two years, it remains in effect. And while government programs were implemented to support workers, the town of Bonavista would never be the same.

Notes

For further information of the Bonavista Cold Storage Co. Ltd., see:
http://www.ucs.mun.ca/~melbaker/coldstorage.htm
or Little's *Through My Grandfather's Eyes*.

For further information on the introduction of longliners, see Rose.

30 — TOURISM AND TOMORROW

The *Matthew* arrival in Bonavista on June 24, 1997, was the focal point of the larger Cabot 500 Celebrations, an effort on the part of the Government of Newfoundland and Labrador to improve tourism in the province in the aftermath of the cod moratorium of 1992. The province's own numbers proved that it was a success. Visitation to Newfoundland through the 1970s and 1980s averaged about 255,000, then increased to almost 300,000 in the first half of the 1990s, and then jumped to 370,00 for the Cabot Celebrations of 1997. Visitation continued to increase above 400,000 in the years that followed.

This was perhaps not surprising given the response to the 1997 celebrations. Well over ninety per cent of visitors in 1997 were happy with their visit, and for most of them, the *Matthew* arrival in Bonavista was the most popular event and even the highlight of their trip. Clearly, the Vista '97 Committee not only coordinated the four-day celebration of the *Matthew*'s arrival in Bonavista as the cornerstone of the Cabot 500 celebrations, in Newfoundland, but supported the emergence of tourism as a key component of Newfoundland's future.

Twenty years later, in 2017, local reporters took a second look at tourism since the Cabot 500 Celebrations and the arrival of the *Matthew* in Bonavista. Tourism leaders, in particular, noted that the "tens of thousands" of visitors to Bonavista and throughout Newfoundland in 1997 helped to change the tourism industry and, in fact, redefined tourism in Newfoundland. Joe O'Brien, a tour operator in Bay Bulls, noted that it changed how people viewed Newfoundland. "We're a unique destination that (tourists) hadn't seen. People travelled all over the world, but Newfoundland wasn't talked about as a travel destination. . . . Since (the arrival of the *Matthew*), we've adapted to many, many things. Everything has gone on the international stage and put us at the front of the international stage." Another tourism operator, Regina McCarthy, said that visitors came to Newfoundland for everything that Newfoundlanders take for granted: people, culture, history, fresh air, and scenery.

The fishery of today has evolved dramatically from a century ago, and tourism has taken hold during the past few decades. We don't know what the future holds for Bonavista. But its inhabitants have remained resilient through it all and will no doubt continue to thrive in the years ahead.

Notes

Krista Noseworthy (NL Department of Tourism, Culture, Industry and Innovation) and Brent Meade assisted in providing the following documents:

TCII Air and Auto Exit Surveys 1997: Cabot 500 Results.
TCII Non-resident visitors and spending estimates: 1973–2002.
Occupancy Report: Province, 1995–2000.
Occupancy Report: Economic Zone 15, 1995–2000.

Articles written in 2017 commemorating the Cabot 500 Celebrations:

CBC: https://www.cbc.ca/news/canada/newfoundland-labrador/since-cabot-500-adapted-20-years-look-book-1.4175466
Saltwire: https://www.saltwire.com/news/provincial/cabot-500-celebrated-20-years-ago-91345/?location=newfoundland-labrador
The *Telegram*: https://www.thetelegram.com/lifestyles/cabot-520-remembering-the-day-the-queen-came-to-town-28305/

CLOSING REMARKS

In the course of writing *Bonavista*, it became clear that the recorded word, in the early years of growth in the town, was dominated with reference to planters, merchants, agents, missionaries, teachers, magistrates, and other community leaders. The men and women, and their children, who caught and processed fish were generally relegated to secondary status. It was not until history documented the most recent past that the community as a whole was accurately recorded. Such is the case in this book. What Bland referred to as the "principal inhabitants" are noted in the early pages of this book—descendants of the long-term residents of Bonavista are followed more closely as we work through the centuries. But a community is more than the sum of the descendants of previous generations. George Clements reminds us that a young man, or woman, still in the midst of his teenaged years upon arrival to Bonavista, can make a lasting, perhaps even a historic, contribution. To some degree we are all newcomers.

Looking toward the east on Lance Cove Road leading to the Dungeon. The local farm animals are clearly unfazed by the force of the wind and the sea. (Eric Abbott via Ross Abbott)

But no literary work can do justice to the hard work, over the centuries, of the men and women of Bonavista necessary to provide support for a family and to build a foundation for a community. This author has only touched upon the successes and failures of some of the men of Bonavista and has hardly scratched the surface of the contributions of Bonavista's women. And we have done no service to those who walked on these lands before the first Europeans. Hopefully, however, these pages have at least given us all some appreciation for lives well-lived—on this small but gorgeous part of Newfoundland.

ACKNOWLEDGEMENTS

The author wishes to thank Ross Abbott, David Bradley, Grace Butler Difalco, Paul Cory, Michael Crummey, Catherine (Kay) Dusseault, Crystal Fudge, Carlos Garcia-Minguillan, Vina (Mifflin) Gould, Joan Grandy, Gertrude Karapita, Brent Meade, Glenn Mitchell, Bernice Mouland, Sharon Murza, John Norman, Krista Noseworthy, Lisa Ricketts, Dr. George Rose, Ken Stelmack, and Jim Swyers for their assistance. I also want to thank Dr. Gordon Handcock and Dr. Philip E. L. Smith for sharing their knowledge and guidance, and to Peter Hanes and Jerry Cranford of Flanker Press for their hard work on the manuscript.

Staff at the A. C. Hunter Library, Archives at The Rooms, Bonavista Archives, Ross King Library, United Church Archives at both St. John's, NL, and Sackville, NB, British Library, Poole Museum, County of Prince Edward Public Library and Archives and the Map Room, and the Centre for Newfoundland Studies at the Queen Elizabeth II Library of Memorial University were helpful and courteous at all times. Thank you.

Every effort has been made to assign ownership to photographs and images. Sincere apologies to anyone to whom credit has been omitted. All errors in this book are owned by the author.

APPENDIX 1

Letter from George Davis to Captain James Cook,
March 14, 1764,
Poole:

Sir,

When I last had the pleasure to see you, I promised at my arrival here to make enquiry and inform you when Twillingate and Fogo were settled by the English. I did not get here till the 10th, having taken a tour in my way home and made it my business to find Mr. Thos. Tizzard who was the first person that ever drove a nail at Twillingate, or settled here as a Englishman, which was in the year 1732. He tells me that Fogo was settled 3 or 4 years sooner and that he has known that part of Newfoundland for 40 years, and that he never knew a French boat or ship to the southward of Cape John—which is 14 leagues NNW from Twillingate, and the nearest place that he ever knew a French boat was at a harbour 2 leagues north of St. John called D'luce. Bonavista was settled as early as any part of the land and never any Frenchman yet fished there.

Mrs. Tizzard was born at Bonavista, whose uncle John Walcome was the first manchild born there, who was 80 years old when he died, and has been dead upwards of 30 years. In Queen Anne's War, when the French had Placentia, in the winter season, a party of French came overland, but was beaten off by the inhabitants of Bonavista. I think this is sufficient proof that the French have not occupied any part of the island from Cape Bonavista to Cape John for 40 years past. I wrote Mr. Arth. Merry to the same purpose of the above the 10th, and desired him to relate the whole to you, if you called, and if you have any further enquiry to make, relative to the Land or anything else, if you please to lay your commands, they shall intelligently be answered by one who has the good of his country at heart.

Your most humble servant,
Geo. Davis.

APPENDIX 2

Register of Fishing Rooms in Bonavista 1805–06:

Name by which the Room is usually known	Where situated	Name and residence of claimant	Nature of the claim	Name and resident of the occupant	In what manner held	Date of entry
John Abbott's Room	Bayley's Cove	John Abbott Bonvista	Originally built by the claimant's family	J. Abbott Bonavista	In right of inheritance	Aug. 9, 1805
Stephen Lander's Room	Bayley's Cove	Stephen Lander Bonavista	Built by the claimant's family	Stephen Lander Bonavista	In right of inheritance	Aug. 9, 1805
Pladwell's Room	Bayley's Cove	Hannah Pladwell Bonavista	Left by the claimant's husband	William Pladwell Bonavista	By permission from Hannah Pladwell	Aug. 9, 1805
Mesh's Room	Bayley's Cove	Rachel Mesh Bonavista	Left by the claimant's husband	Moses Keel and Richard Mesh Bonavista	Rented from the claimant	Aug. 9, 1805
Stephen Abbott's Room	Bayley's Cove	Sarah Abbott Bonavista	Left by the claimant's husband	Sarah Abbott Bonavista	In right of inheritance	Aug. 9, 1806
Kate's Room	Bayley's Cove	John Abbott Bonavista		William Hicks & Co., Bonavista	By lease	Aug. 9, 1806
Mockbeggar Room	Bonavista	Samuel Rolls Poole	Inherited by will from Samuel White	B. Lester & Co., Poole	By lease	Aug. 10, 1806

Name by which the Room is usually known	Where situated	Name and residence of claimant	Nature of the claim	Name and resident of the occupant	In what manner held	Date of entry
Beaumond's Flake	Mockbeggar	John Beaumond Bonavista	Built by claimant 1804	J. Beaumond	In right of building and possession	Aug. 10, 1805
Hooper's Room	Bonavista	Stephen Hooper Bonavista	Originally built by claimant	Richard &Thomas Ryder, Bonavista	By lease	Oct. 20, 1805
Mayne's Flake	Bonavista	John Mayne Bonavista	Built by claimant, 1805	John Mayne Bonavista	In right of building and possession	Oct. 20, 1805
Dewy's Store & Dwelling House	Bonavista	John Green Trinity	Built by a lessee	John Butler Bonavista	By lease	Oct. 20, 1805
Shambler's Room	Bonavista		Built by the claimant's family	B. Lester & Co., Poole	By lease	Oct. 20, 1805
Kean's Room	Bonavista	Captain Kean of the Navy	Built by the claimant's family	Thomas Street Poole	By lease	Oct. 20, 1805
White's Room	Bonavista	Charles Saint Bonavista	Purchased by claimant	Charles Saint Bonavista	In right of purchase	Oct. 20, 1805
Cole's Room	Bonavista	B. Lester & Co. Poole	Purchased by claimant	William Cole Bonavista		Oct. 20, 1805
Ford's Room	Bonavista	B. Lester & Co. Poole	Purchased by claimant	G. Ford Bonavista		Oct. 20, 1805
Old Room	Corneil, Bonavista	B. Lester & Co. Poole	Purchased by claimant	B. Lester & Co. Poole	In right of purchase	Oct. 20, 1805

Name by which the Room is usually known	Where situated	Name and residence of claimant	Nature of the claim	Name and resident of the occupant	In what manner held	Date of entry
Ryder's Room	Newman's Point	B. Lester & Co. Poole	Devolved to the claimant for a debt	Thomas Woodford Richard Dyke Bonavista	By lease	Aug. 10, 1805
Brown's Room	Bonavista	Jos. Brown & Co.& their bros. & sis.	Built by the claimant's family	John Bland Bonavista	By lease	Aug. 10, 1805
Burton's Room	Bonavista	Stephen Burton & his brothers	Built by the claimant's family	S. Burton & Humber Green	By right of inheritance	Aug. 10, 1805
Rolls' Room	Bonavista	John Bland Bonavista	Purchased from the former proprietor	J. Bland Bonavista	In right of purchase	Aug. 11, 1805
Walkam's Room	Bonavista	Solomon Mifflen Bonavista	Partly purchased & partly built by claimant's family	S. Mifflen Bonavista	In right partly of purchase & partly of inheritance	Aug. 11, 1805
Newell's Room	Bonavista	Thomas Newell & Giles Hosier Bonavista	Originally built by the claimant's family	G. Hosier Bonavista	In right of inheritance & by private arrangement	Aug. 12, 1805
Mayne's Store	Bonavista	John Mayne Bonavista	Built by the claimant in 1804	J. Mayne Bonavista	In right of building and possession	Aug. 12, 1805

Name by which the Room is usually known	Where situated	Name and residence of claimant	Nature of the claim	Name and resident of the occupant	In what manner held	Date of entry
Tovey's Room	Bonavista	James Tovey St. John's	Built by the claimant	John Mayne Bonavista	By lease	Aug. 12, 1805
Brown's Room	Corneil, Bonavista	Joseph Brown, his brothers & sisters	Built by the claimant's family	Joseph Brown & Co., Bonavista	In right of inheritance	Oct. 20, 1805
Cobb's Room	Corneil, Bonavista	Joseph Brown	Purchased at a public sale ordered by surrogate court	John Kelly Sons & Co., Bonavista	By lease	Oct. 26, 1805

Notes

Further details are contained in the original "Register of Fishing Rooms in Bonavista, 1805-06" in the Colonial Office 194 Series at The Rooms, St. John's.

APPENDIX 3

Petition of Bonavista Inhabitants to the SPG, June 10, 1742:

We the underwritten planters and other inhabitants of Bonavista in New-foundland humbly presume to address your Lordship upon the subject of our being lately deprived of a minister by the removal of the Reverend Mr. Henry Jones to another place.

As we never had warning or notice given of such a design, it was the more unexpected to us, especially as we are not conscious of ever giving our minister any just grounds of complaint, or in the least withheld what our abilities enabled us to contribute towards his support, there having, one year with another, generally been the sum of £50 raised for that purpose, by the voluntary subscriptions of masters and servants of this place. The latter, who are pretty numerous, have not indeed of late so readily contributed as usual, by reason of Mr. Jones officiating as a justice, by which many were disobliged and had an influence upon others. But as this caused no alteration in our dispositions towards him, it ought not to be laid at our charge. And as we can imagine no other reason for his desiring to be removed, and that we continue in the same dispositions as ever to contribute in the best manner we are able, towards the support and subsistence of a minister.

We therefore most humbly pray that your Lordship would please to take our case in consideration and as we are under a deep concern at our being thus suddenly deprived of the usual means of assembling together in the worship of God, you would also please to appoint us some other minister to supply the present vacancy. At the same time, we beg leave to offer to your Lordship's further consideration the sad state of the place in regard to the education of children, whereof there are not less than one hundred and fifty without the means of instruction or learning. Their parents, for the most part incapable, or otherwise by the nature of their calling, wanting the time to afford them any . . . if your Lordship shall please to grant our request, it would greatly add to our satisfaction.

Humbly crave your Lordship's pardon, for what may be deficient in this address, as being unacquainted of the methods of doing it in a more proper manner. We hope that for your Lordship's indulgence to our intent and meaning, and beg leave to subscribe ourselves with submission, My Lord.

Your most obedient and humble servants,

Bonavista in Newfoundland

the 10th of June, 1742.

Isaac Bonovrier
Sam D. Shamblear

John Blake
Richard M. Massey
Mary Walkam
Richard P. Philips
Richard Hodder
Jos. Hayward
William Clarke
Henry Wheeler
John King
Thomas Melles
William Parker

John Clarke
Joseph Randall
George Walkam
John Shepard
Mich R. Read
Thomas Hayward
George Brown

Stephen S. B. Barton
William
John Roe
Joseph Foquett
Mary
Martha M. N. Norton
William Amer
William Dull
Samuel Leigh

Notes

Name spelling is inferred from the original document. Names and letters are intentionally omitted on occasion.

Transcription by David Bradley.

APPENDIX 4

Petition of the Inhabitants of Bonavista
November 15, 1752:

The humble petition of the inhabitants of Bonavista in Newfoundland

That ever since the Reverend Mr. William Peasely left us to go to St. John's, we have been without a minister, why he left so soon we know not but we have not now any one to instruct us, which we want very much, for it's a miserable thing to see the people on the Lord's Day scattered abroad like sheep without a shepherd and many seems to live without God in the world, we hope you will take our miserable case into your consideration and help us to one as we are very desirous to have one to instruct us in our duty and keep us in the way we have been bred to that we may not be as castaways which God forbid but it's very miserable to be deprived of the benefit of the Gospel and to live in ignorance as most here does for want of a teacher.

And we will for our parts do whatever we can as far as we are able to maintain him and make his life here as comfortable as we can, there never was less than thirty pounds collected yearly and many times forty to fifty pounds which for our place is pretty well as the place is not so expensive as some others where they may collect more.

We humbly hope you take our sad case into your consideration, a᷉ⅎ let us be no longer without one but to furnish us with one . . . and your petitioners will be in duty bound to always pray.

Signed
  Joseph Randall
  George Walkam
  Sam Shamblear
  Walkam
  Wim Amer
  Thos. Bemister

Daniel Brown
Stephen Barton
John Clarke
John Sanders
John Foguette
John Shepard

There is a great many more which would gladly have signed that belongs to the place but are not at home but before went away. All Agreed.

Dated in Bonavista this 15th November, 1752.

Notes

First name has been intentionally omitted for "Walkam."

Transcription by David Bradley.

APPENDIX 5

1777,
To William Keen, Esq.:

The humble petition of the principal inhabitants and others of Bonavista, most humbly desirous that you'd please to represent to His Excellency the Governor, the many grievances that we laboured under by the illegal proceedings of Mr. George Rider before His Excellency was pleased to grant him a Commission of the Peace by taking that authority to himself of punishing many people severely and corporally without having any such power given him as there have been many instances of his following of people with divers (various) arms, especially when in liquor which he is very much addicted to, that His Majesty's subjects has been in great dread and fear of their lives both in the time of your father and yours holding a Commission of the Peace, and since the said Mr. George Rider has received a Commission of the Peace, he is daily threatening of us and putting us in bodily fear of what punishments and fines he will inflict on us has he has already began by exacting undue and unjust sums and had it not been for you, he would have given several severe punishments unjustly and undeservedly and, as you will know, the said Mr. George Rider has knowingly been guilty of premeditated and wilful murder for which he has never been acquitted by the laws of his country. We most humbly presume that His Excellency will be pleased to pardon the liberty we take in being obliged to say that it will be almost impossible for us, under the Government of such a man as Mr. George Rider, in the winter time, when there is Justice of the Peace to whom any of us may fly for mercy and justice, if he holds a Commission of the Peace, and that whereas you have taken the pains of punishing and bannishing of disorderly women from this district, he makes it his constant practice to give them all the encouragement he possibly can. We therefore, your petitioners, most humbly crave that you'll lay our grievances before His Excellency doubting not but that he will take the case into his wise consideration and relieve us from the hardships we now do and are likely to labour under, and Your Petitioners as duty bound forever pray . . .

Stephen Lander
Richard Mesh
Peter Parker
Elizabeth Walkham
James Lovis (?)
John Parker

Joseph Chipp
Stephen Abbott
William Abbott
John Rolles
Thomas Fitzgerald
Patrick Walsh

1777
To George Rider, Esq.

I have received the enclosed petition from Mr. Keen of Bonavista by which you'll see how reprehensible your conduct has been as Deputy Judge of the Court of Admiralty. And although I would wish to believe there is some malice in it, yet I cannot help supposing but a part is true.

I must therefore desire you will be very circumspect in your future conduct for be assured upon the first complaint which can be proved against you of further irregular and arbitrary proceedings now you are a Magistrate, I shall immediately recall my Commission.

I am, Sir, your humble servant,

J. Montagu.

APPENDIX 6

Pews in the First Methodist Church in Bonavista, 1823:

Body of the Church

Name	£	Shillings
Charles Saint	10	0
Alexander Strathie	6	0
Charles Saint and Mrs. Skiffington	5	0
Thomas Reader, Sr.	8	0
George Crewe	5	0
Mary House	5	0
James Mouland	10	0
Joseph Abbott, Sr.	11	0
Hugh Abbott/W. Abbott/ Richard Reader/G. Little	4	0
James Brown	9	0
Robert Brown	5	0

Gallery of the Church

Name	£	Shillings
Sarah Abbott	20	0
James Mouland	10	0
Samson Mifflin	7	10
John Mifflin	5	0
William Cooke	3	10
John and Thomas Hicks	8	0

Name	£	Shillings
Thomas Hicks, Sr.	6	5
Benjamin Cole	10	0
Gerald Ford, Esq., S.M.	8	5
Mrs. William Alexander	7	10
Messrs. Campbell	8	5
George Oldford	6	5
Stephen Sexton, Thomas Hampton	6	5
Richard Abbott	11	5

Notes

i) Lench states that "the purchasers of the pews had subscribed previously, during the ten years, to build and keep up the place of worship." He also indicates that the four men listed together in the first table were perhaps "four single men." The name "Gerald Ford" is noteworthy ("Gerald" as recorded should have been "Gerrard"), as this was the magistrate noted in the story of the flagstaff incident. "S.M." in this case is short for "Stipendiary Magistrate."

ii) James Mouland, with financial support to both the body and gallery of the church, was, according to Lench "an independent planter . . . always ready with his support." In those days, planter meant, in general terms, "owner of a plantation." Lench indicated that many Moulands of Mockbeggar are descended from James Mouland, a man of "stirling christian character."

APPENDIX 7

The Methodist Classes with their Leaders and Members, 1823 (from Lench):

Leader: Philip Swyers.
Members:

Joseph Abbott, Jr.	William Abbott, Sr.	Abigail Abbott
James Abbott	Thomas Hicks	John Hicks
Elizabeth Lander	Lydia May	William Abbott, Jr.
Charles Fisher	Elizabeth Bradley	Stephen Abbott
Martha Abbott, Jr.	Abraham Abbott	Hannah Abbott

Leader: Benjamin Cole.
Members:

Stephen Mouland	William Abbott	Henry Abbott
Catherine Mouland	Mary Jane Mouland	Mary Mouland of Hugh
Ann Mouland	Jane Mouland	Sarah Mouland
Elizabeth Mouland	Martha Mouland	Hugh Abbott
James Way	Martha Way	Emma Skiffington
Stephen Sexton	Honor Abbott	Mary Whiffen
Mary Lander	Thomas Reader	John Skiffington
Grace Hosier	Stephen Abbott	James Harrison
James Hampton		

Leader: Hannah Saint
Members:

Elizabeth Reader	Elizabeth Cool	Honor Little
Flora Oldford	Mary Harrison	Elizabeth Hampton
Ann Sexton	Elizabeth Campbell	Jane Little
Mary House	Mary Wells	Ann Romaine
Elizabeth Curtis	Dinah Cole	James Mouland, Sr.
Honor Ford	Mary Philpott	

Leader: Charles Saint
Members:

William Cole	James Mouland, Sr.	James Mouland, Jr.
William Cooke	George Oldford	Giles Little
George Philpott	John Romaine	

Leader: Joseph Abbott
Members:

Hannah Abbott	Roger Abbott	Richard Abbott
Elizabeth Hicks	Jane Hicks	Sarah Beaumont, Sr.
Sarah Beaumont, Jr.	William Brown	Jane Brown
Susan Campbell	John Abbott	Jane Hicks

APPENDIX 8

To His Excellency Sir Charles Hamilton Bart Vice Admiral of the White Governor and Commander in Chief in and over the Island of Newfoundland:

The Memorial of the Inhabitants of Bonavista,
Humbly Sheweth,

That two years ago, Joseph Brown, a native and planter of this place, died and left by will five hundred pounds towards building a place of worship for the benefit and accommodation of the members of the Episcopal Church of England, the old place of worship having fallen into decay.

The intended building since Mr. Brown's death has been in progress under proper directors and the sum of one hundred and sixty pounds in addition to Mr. Brown's legacy expended, there will yet require nevertheless a further sum of two hundred pounds or thereabouts to complete the building for its intended use, no part of which in the opinion of your memorialists can be expected from the inhabitants – they having already contributed to the extent of what their circumstances would permit.

Your Excellency must be sensible of the great importance of the object sought, and in a large and increasing community, of the advantage of public morals to have a place of worship to assemble in once a week. The entire population consists of about two thousand persons of all ages, of whom about twelve hundred profess to be of the Established religion and your Excellency's memorialists feel a conviction that their numbers would fail to increase, under the aids and incentives to piety which all communities more or less require.

Your Excellency's memorialists humbly solicit Your Excellency to represent to His Majesty's Government and to the Missionary Society for such aid to finish the building and otherwise further the interests of religion by law established, as their wisdom may see necessary, and your memorialists shall ever pray.

George Garland
George Robins
Sampson Mifflin
Robert Brown
Thomas Gaylor
Richard Dyke
Abraham Ackerman, Sr.
John Hillyard
John Hicks

Archibald Arnott
Gerrard Ford, J.P.
William Alexander
John Skelton
James Oakley
James Brown
William Wiseman
Thomas Drawbridge
Malcolm Campbell

Bonavista, Newfoundland
October 12, 1821

APPENDIX 9

To His Grace the Right Reverend Father in God, John (by divine permission) Lord Archbishop of Canterbury, Primate of all England, and President of the Society of Propagating the Gospel in Foreign Parts:

The humble petition of the inhabitants of Bonavista sheweth:

> That there are at this time in the harbour of Bonavista upwards of three hundred poor children. That the parents of these children have themselves been bred in the most gross ignorance and are not wholly incapable of conveying instruction to their offspring, but from their extreme poverty are destitute of the means of procuring for them so great a blessing.
>
> Thus yearly are multiplied numbers who have as little sense of the ends for which providence has place them in this world as the untutored savages of the woods. Deprived wholly of the assistance of a Missionary whose precepts and example might excite to piety and a moral life, the best cement of society, this poor people are also destitute of the most common means of attaining to that small degree of cultivation which the lowest orders profess in most civilized nations. To be able to read is among the first blessings since it furnishes the medium of improving the mind, and learning our duty to God and our neighbour. The end Your Grace's petitioners hope for in this application is to obtain a small salary for a schoolmaster, to enable him to instruct, gratis, poor children in reading and writing. There is at present here a person (George Bemister) who has been for some time past employed in that capacity; but those who are in a situation to pay him for his attendance are so few that the emoluments missing from his school will not furnish the most ordinary means of support.
>
> Your Grace's petitioners therefore humbly request that you will take into consideration the unhappy circumstances of the poor children of this place, and in charity grant a small annual gratuity to a schoolmaster;

for the purpose of instructing them in reading and writing gratis, and may the blessings and prayers of those who may happily benefit from Your Grace's benevolence add to that peace and serenity of mind, which can only result from doing good, and which Your Grace's petitioners wish you may to the latest period of life enjoy.

John Bland, J. Peace

Gerard Ford, J. Peace

William Brown, J. Peace

John Rolles

Giles Hosier

John Mayne

Joseph Prudham

William Ward Wright

John Cutler

Ed Pudner

Stephen Abbott

Richard Rider

Joseph Abbott

Stephen Lander

James Skiffington

J. Gethings

Samson Mifflen

Tim Phillips

Stephen Hooper

Thomas Coombs

Robert Dugale

John Collins

George Marsh

William Pledwell

Moses Keel

Henry Edmonds

Hugh Abbott

John Lander

William Hicks

James Lovey

William Baker

Bonavista, 11 November 1791

To Reverend Doctor Morice:

Sir,

The principal inhabitants of this place have requested me to transmit to you the accompanying petition, which is signed by all the proper in it of any consequence or property. I shall take the liberty to add that should it be judged proper to grant the charity they solicit, the end hoped for would be much forwarded by (?) a few necessary books on such whose circumstances can spare nothing from the common necessities of life.

The number of poor children stated in the petition I believe not to be exaggerated and, in truth, it reflects little honour on a great and en-lightened nation that population in Newfoundland should be making so rapid a progress without any system. It is a melancholy truth that the majority of the poor inhabitants of this place are in a very gross state of ignorance. An observer will find few examples among them of those relative duties and obligations which constitute moral rectitude. But how can we hope for the fruits of cultivation where the seeds have never been sown?

It were indeed much to be desired that a Missionary resided here, whose life and morals might then (set) an example worthy of imitation. It is true, the inhabitants who are circumstanced to contribute to his support are but few; but doubtless the donations of those yearly employed from home in the fishery, with other certain contingencies, in addition to his salary, would afford him a decent and comfortable maintenance; and I believe I may venture to assert that the respectable part of the residents here would be happy to see such a person established among them.

I am, with very great respect, Sir:

Your most obedient, humble servant,
John Bland.

Bonavista, Newfoundland,
November 12, 1791

APPENDIX 10

To the Right Reverend Father in God John (by Divine Permission) Lord Archbishop of Canterbury, Primate of all England and President of the Society for Propagating the Gospel in Foreign Parts:

The humble petition of the inhabitants of Bonavista sheweth that the town of Bonavista, the capital of this district, has been many years without a missionary, and that your Lordship's petitioners beheld with concern the declining state of the Protestant religion and the rapid increase of Popery for want of a person to instruct the ignorant and to instill into the minds of the unenlightened, a knowledge of true religion and the duties of Christianity until Mr. Abraham Akerman voluntarily and without any reward or emolument whatever, undertook to do the duty of the church, which he has constantly served these nine years, to the entire satisfaction of the inhabitants of this town and district – that our children may be brought up in the knowledge and fear of God, we your petitioners most humbly beg the sanction of your Lordship and the assistance of the society in granting to Mr. Abraham Akerman a small salary, to enable him the better to carry on his present laudable undertaking.

Your petitioners beg leave to inform your Lordship that Mr. Abraham Akerman has been married many years and has a wife and four children now living in Bonavista. In consideration of which of his zeal and attachment to the Protestant religion, we are induced to implore the aid of the society, humbly hoping that your Lordship and the Society will take his present situation into your consideration and your petitioners as in duty bound will ever pray.

Bonavista, Oct. 31, 1792

Gerrard Ford, J. Peace	Thomas Singleton	
William Brown,	J. Peace	John Collins
William Coles	Edward White	James Curdle
John Abbott, Sr.	John Hardy	John Abbott, Jr.
Stephen Lander, Sr.	Samuel Shearing	John Hayward

Stephen Lander, Jr.
Stephen Abbott
Solomon Mifflen
John Hillier
John Rolles
John Seaward
Thomas Bass
Charles Saint
Edward Pudner
Willilam Pladwell
Joseph Batt
George Oldford
Richard Dyke
William Burton (?)
Richard Rider
Richard Powell
George Crocker
Francis Bright
Will Hayward (?)
Martin Pottle
George Goff
Benjamin Hayward
James Hix
John Fling
John Pardy
George Brushet
John Selley
Edward Stag
Edward Gosling
John Peckham
Charles Miles
William Miles

John Hailey
Robert Cross
Thos. Fling
William Hix
William Paull
Luke Gould
Cornelius Mashfield
Richard Shearing
Stephen Shearing
Benjamin Davis
Thomas Hayward
Phillip Way
William Taylor
Robert Phevan (?)
William Lush
William Steeds
William Pardy
Moses Dorden (?)
John Philpot
Edward Lush
Henry Edmonds
Thomas Hix
Joseph Budden
James Moulam
John Street
Hugh Abbott
Stephen Hooper
John Bemister
James Hapgood
William Etsell
Richard Lancerstone
John Drodge

Stephen Burton
Henry Clouter
John Lander
John Burton
James Abbott
Thomas Heasey
John Cooney
Thos. Pollett
John Wheller
Samson Mifflen
Humber Green
George March
Richard Tilly
James Skeffington
James Lovey (?)
William Baker
John Fisher
Giles Little
Benjamin Ingram
William Oldford
George Gillinham
William Fielder Sr.
William Fielder Jr.
William Wheller
Robert Hobbs
John Sannons (?)
Isaac Short
John Gellett
George White
Robert Hix
William Porter

Notes

Name spelling is inferred as best from the original document.

APPENDIX 11

To the Editor of the Royal Gazette:

Sir,

The "Committee for the relief of the poor of Bonavista and Bird Island Cove" beg leave, through the medium of your Paper, to return their most grateful acknowledgements to His Excellency the Governor, for His kind attention to the prayer of the distressed Inhabitants whom they represent.

They beg also to state that His Excellency having given them permission to expend a part of the Provision sent for the relief of the Poor, in "such manner as they should consider most beneficial for their neighbourhood," they have cut a new line of Road to Catalina, and called the same "COCHRANE ROAD" of which His Excellency has been pleased to express his approbation.

The distance from Bonavista to Catalina, on the COCHRANE ROAD, is nine miles and a half.

The Committee beg still further to observe, that a Bridge has been built on the COCHRANE ROAD, over the large Brook running out of Little Catalina, which they have named "BRENTON BRIDGE" as a mark of respect for the handsome support and patronage afforded to their funds by the Honourable Judge Brenton.

I am, Sir,
Yours respectfully,
William Wilson, Chairman.

Bonavista, May 2, 1831.

APPENDIX 12

Carnegie Fund Commission Report:

<u>No. 677.</u>
J. Louis Little, aged thirty-seven, fisherman, helped to save four men, and as-sisted in an attempt to save two others from drowning at Bonavista, NF, Sept. 19, 1907. During a storm at night, a schooner was torn from her moorings in the harbour and wrecked on the rocks that bound it. She went ashore stern foremost and struck between two rocks at the shore line. The darkness was intense, the wind blowing sixty miles an hour, and the waves from twenty to thirty feet high, dashed up on the rocks for forty feet. Holding to a line in the hands of a fisherman upon a large rock, Little climbed down its steep and dangerous face and attempted to cast the line to the vessel, but failed. He hastily scrambled onward to escape an incoming wave, but it caught him and surged up around his knees. He coiled his rope again and as the water receded, scrambled rapidly down the rough surface until he was right under the stern of the schooner. He cast his line to the deck twelve feet above, where it was made fast. Little was caught by an incoming wave, and clinging desperately to the rope was washed into a gulch beside the rock, but was pulled back on it. The men left the wreck rapidly and Little approached close to it and assisted two of the men. He was awarded a Silver Medal and $1,500.00 for a worthy purpose as needed.

<u>No. 678.</u>
Robert Brown, aged fifty-five, sub-Collector of Customs, helped to save four men and assisted in an attempt to save two others from drowning (see award above). Brown descended far down the rock and attempted to cast a line on board the wreck before Little. He made another unsuccessful cast, and then remaining in a position of much danger, he helped get the seamen up the rock, several times narrowly escaping being washed away by the waves. Awarded a Bronze medal and $1,000.00 for a worthy object.

No. 679.

James C. Little, aged forty-five, fisherman, helped to save four men, etc., as above. Little descended to a point far down the rock and in a position of much danger helped the seamen up. He was swept off his feet once, but prevented himself from being washed away by clinging to the rope. Awarded Bronze Medal and $1,000.00 for a worthy purpose.

No. 670.

William Ford, aged thirty-five, fisherman. Ford descended on a rock to a point of much danger and assisted in the rescue work. When one of the seamen fell on the rocks, Ford grabbed him and helped him up on the rock. He saved himself from being swept away by clinging to the rope. Awarded Bronze Medal and $1,000.00 for a worthy purpose.

No. 681.

James Ford (particulars as above). Ford held to the rope with the other rescuers and assisted the seamen to get up the rock. His grasp on the rope alone prevented him from being swept away. Awarded Bronze Medal and $1,000.00 for a worthy purpose.

No. 682.

Eli Paul, aged forty-two, fisherman (same particulars). Paul assisted in the rescue work from a place of great danger, helping seamen up the rock. Awarded Bronze Medal and $1,000.00 for a worthy purpose.

REFERENCES

Books

Bannister, Jerry. *The Rule of the Admirals: Law, Custom, and Naval Government in Newfoundland, 1699-1832*. University of Toronto Press. 2003.

Beamish, Derek, John Hillier, H. F. V. Johnstone. *Mansions and Merchants of Poole and Dorset*. Poole Historical Trust, Poole, 1976.

Butt, Arthur S. *Telling It as It Was*. Glovertown Literary Creations. Printed by Economy Printing Limited. 1990.

Charlevoix, Rev. P. F. X. *History and General Description of New France*, translated by John G. Shea. Loyola University Press, Chicago, 1870.

Chubbs, Harold and Wade Kearley. *Facing the Sea: Lightkeepers and their Families*. Flanker Press Limited, St. John's, 2013.

Doyle, Marjorie. *Thirty-five who played a part in our History, The Book of Newfoundland, Vol. VI*, Smallwood, Joseph, R. (Editor). Newfoundland Book Publishers Ltd., St. John's, 1967.

Fay, C. R. *Life and Labour in Newfoundland*. University of Toronto Press, Toronto, 1956.

Handcock, W. Gordon. *Soe longe as there comes noe women: Origins of English Settlement in Newfoundland, Newfoundland History Series 6*. Breakwater Books, St. John's, 1989.

Head, C. Grant. *Eighteenth Century Newfoundland*. McClelland and Stewart Limited, Toronto, 1976.

Hild, Martha Hickman. *Geology of Newfoundland*. Boulder Publications, Portugal Cove–St. Phillip's, 2012.

Hollett, Calvin. *Shouting, Embracing, and Dancing with Ecstasy. The Growth of Methodism in Newfoundland 1774-1874.* McGill-Queen's University Press, Montreal, 2010.

Howley, James P. *The Beothucks or Red Indians: the aboriginal inhabitants of Newfoundland.* Cambridge, England, 1915.

Lench, Charles, *The Story of Methodism in Bonavista.* Harry Cuff Publications Limited, St. John's, 1985.

Little, Lewis C. *Through my Grandfather's Eyes.* XX Press. 2006.

Molloy, David. *The First Landfall. Historic Lighthouses of Newfoundland and Labrador.* Breakwater Books, St. John's, 1994.

Murray, Hilda Chaulk. *More than 50%.* Flanker Press Limited, St. John's, 2010.

Newfoundland Historical Society. *A Short History of Newfoundland and Labrador.* Boulder Publications. 2008.

Penhallow, Samuel. *The History of the Wars of New England with the Eastern Indians, Boston, 1726.* Reprinted by Edward Wheelock, Books for Libraries Press, Freeport, New York, 1971.

Prowse, D. W., Q.C. *A History of Newfoundland.* MacMillan and Co., London, 1895.

Rose, George A. *Cod: An Ecological History of the North Atlantic Fisheries.* Breakwater Books Ltd., St. John's, 2007.

Smith, Philip, E. L. *In Cod We Trust: Newfoundland's British Nomads. History Today.* December 2017. Vol 67. Issue 12.

Smith, T. W., *Methodism in Eastern British America, vol. II.* S. F. Huestis, Halifax, 1889.

Thomas, Aaron. *The Newfoundland Journal of Aaron Thomas 1794.* Editor: Jean Murray. Longmans. 1968.

Tocque, Philip. *Wandering Thoughts or Solitary Hours.* Thomas Richardson and Son, London, 1846.

Tocque, Philip. *Newfoundland, As it was and as it is in 1877.* John B. Magurn, Toronto, 1878.

Whiffen, Bruce. *Prime Berth.* Harry Cuff Publications Limited, St. John's, 1993.

Whitbourne, Richard. *A Discourse and Discovery of Newfoundland.* Felix Kingstorn, 1620.

Wilson, Rev. William. *Newfoundland and its Missionaries, in two parts.* Cambridge, Mass, 1866.

Winsor, Naboth. *Hearts Strangely Warmed: A History of Methodism in Newfoundland, 1765-1925.* B.S.C. Printers (1982) Limited, 1982.

Winsor, Naboth, *Building on a Firm Foundation: A History of Methodism in Newfoundland (1825-1855). vol. 2.* Economy Printing Ltd., 1987.

Websites and Articles

Hiller, J. K., *The Career of F. Gordon Bradley.* Newfoundland Studies 4, 2 (1988).

Rollman, Hans. "*Thy Real Friend George Skeffington: Quaker and Salmon Fishing Pioneer in Eighteenth Century Newfoundland.*" Memorial University of Newfoundland.
https://journals.sas.ac.uk/fhs/article/view/3508/3459 Retrieved March 24, 2020.

General References

Encyclopedia of Methodism in Canada. Rev. George H. Cornish. Methodist Book and Publishing House, Toronto, 1881.

Dictionary of Canadian Biography. www.biogaphi.ca.
The Wesleyan-Methodist Magazine:
https://catalog.hathitrust.org/Record/008421395

A. C. Hunter Library, St. John's, NL

Journal of the House of Assembly. 1841. Housed at the A. C. Hunter Library.
The *Evening Telegram*

The Rooms, St. John's, NL

Newfoundland Yearbook and Almanac.
Calendar of State Papers, Colonial Series, America and West Indies.
Letter Books of the Colonial Secretary.
Colonial Office Correspondence and Colonial Papers.
Thomas Gaylor's Diary. Occurrences at Bonavista.
Nimshi Crew Collection.
St. John's and Trinity Court Records.

Bonavista Archives, Town of Bonavista

Bonavista Historical Society Fonds.

Centre for Newfoundland Studies, Queen Elizabeth II Library,
Memorial University of Newfoundland

Society for the Propagation of the Gospel in Foreign Parts: Calendar of Letters
and Journals.
D'Alberti Transcripts of Governor's Office Correspondence, 1780-1830.
Newfoundland School Society.

Memorial University Digital Archive Initiative

William Sweetland's Diary
James Ryan Diary
Lester Diary
Slade and Kelson Diary
The *Royal Gazette*

The *Evening Telegram*
The MUN *Gazette*
Parish Records, Vital Statistics, Census Data, Cemetery Transcriptions.

Video

Wilfred Templeman: A Fisherman's Son:
https://www.youtube.com/watch?v=bd2lZdQbEts
Executive Producers: Bruce Atkinson, Joe Tillman.
Written and Directed by Rod Langley.
Produced by NAFC in co-operation with the First Fisheries Science Documentary Society
A Production of Rod Langley and Associates.

Bruce Whiffen was born and raised in Bonavista. He graduated from Memorial University (M.Sc., 1982) and worked for thirty-two years with Environment Canada. He lives with his wife, Joan, in Mount Pearl. They have two grown children.

INDEX

Versailles, France, 50, 59
Vickery, Joseph, 24
Vincent, A., 166
Vincent, John, 42-44
SS *Virginia Lake*, 151

W

Wakeham, John, 28, 30
Walcome, John, 25, 30, 222
Waldron, Thomas, 85
Wales, 7, 179, 192
Walkam, Elizabeth (Short), 25
Walkam, George, 42, 43, 45, 228, 229
Walkam, James, 25
Walkam, John, 156
Walkam's Bridge, 101, 106, 108, 179
Walkam's Brook, 42, 55
Walkam's Room, 42, 57, 225
Walker, James, 43
Walker, R. M., 169
Walkham's Bridge, 25, 36, 178, 180
Walkham's Hill, 25, 202
Wallis, Richard, 22-25
Walsh, John, 85, 179
Ward, William, 73, 74
Warminster, England, 112
Warrey, Thomas, 22-24
Washington, DC, 165
Water Street, 166, 181, 185, 198, 208
Watts, Robert, 28
Way, James, 79, 235
Way, Martha (Hicks), 79, 235
Weeks, Jane, 120
Wellington, ON, 196
Wesleyan Methodist Conference, 74
Wesleyan-Methodist Magazine, 87, 250

Wesleyan Methodist Missionary
  Committee, 123
Wesp, 37
West Country, 19, 24, 32
Western Charter (1634), 19, 22, 24, 32
West Indies, 31, 32, 36, 40, 60, 136, 250
Westville, NS, 173
Whiffen, Wilson, 55, 58, 107
Whitbourne, Richard, 15, 18, 249
White, Edmund, 182
White, Jeremiah, 149, 150, 152
White, Johanna, 149, 150, 152
White, Joseph, 43, 44, 112, 113
White, L., 138
Whiteley, William H., 60
White, Margaret (Ryan), 151
White, Mary, 155
White, Matthew, 150
White, Nicholas, 150
White, Philip, 173
White Rock, 110
White, Samuel, 34, 201, 223
White's Room, 44, 59, 224
White, Thomas, 151
White, Walter N., 182
Wilfred Templeman, 207, 208, 211-214, 251
William, 35, 36
William Hicks & Co., 56, 223
Wilson, Arabella Martha, 122
Wilson, Elizabeth, 122
Wilson, Matilda Faulkner, 122
Wilson, William, 73, 77, 78, 79, 83, 120-123, 127, 129, 131, 132, 135, 140, 156, 244
Wings, 194